SEARCHING FOR THE TRUTH ABOUT DRUGS

THE LIFE AND CALLING
OF
MARTY GRUBER

Written

By

Marty Gruber and Jack Donaldson

Inspiring Voices books may be ordered through booksellers or by contacting:

Inspiring Voices
1663 Liberty Drive
Bloomington, IN 47403
www.inspiringvoices.com
1-(866) 697-5313

ISBN: 978-1-4624-0106-2 (sc)
ISBN: 978-1-4624-0105-5 (e)

Library of Congress Control Number: 2012936205

Printed in the United States of America

Inspiring Voices rev. date: 06/25/2012

<u>TO MY WIFE, CHILDREN, AND GRANDSON</u>

This book is dedicated to my wife Golda, who for over fifty years stayed with me through my years of drug abuse and all that drug abuse brought into our lives. To our oldest son Gary: Your father and mother love you very much. We want to be a family again. Can you forgive me for all the pain and suffering I caused you? The door is always open. To our middle son Michael: Keep your life on track; we are very proud of you. To our youngest son Christopher: May you rest in peace. To our grandson Brandon: Thank you for breaking the chain of drug abuse in this family; we love you very much.

Marty Gruber

MARTY'S STORY, THE AUTHORS OF HIS STORY, THE PRESENTATION OF HIS STORY, AND THE USE OF THE MATERIAL IN THIS BOOK

Marty Gruber

Marty Gruber had about as rough a childhood as one can imagine. He went from being an abused child brought up in part by foster parents, to reform school, to abusing drugs for more than forty-five years, to attempted suicide, to finding meaning in life through his calling to tell teens about the horrors of chemical addictions. It was while attempting suicide that Marty discovered what he believes to be the source of truth and wisdom, and it was through this newfound wisdom that Marty discovered his calling in life. It was through finding his calling that Marty's life has taken on purpose and meaning.

Through this book, Marty openly shares what he learned about the living hell called chemical addiction, which he lived with for more than half a lifetime. The purpose of this book is to help the reader *avoid* the living hell of chemical abuse—or to assist a drug abuser in finding the help needed to *escape* the living hell of chemical abuse—and in the process find peace in living life with purpose in the belief that this world that extends beyond the here and now.

Chemical abuse is an unexpected living hell that traps a drug freak because of his or her bad choices in life. Marty's story demonstrates that there is hope for people who got a bad start in life and then compounded their problems through their own bad choices. Marty's story is fast moving and highly motivational, and it demonstrates that it is never too late to change. Good things happen to those who are willing to yield to wisdom greater than their own. The details of Marty's life are presented in the narrative of this book.

Jack Donaldson

In 2003, Jack Donaldson retired as the lead welding engineer at the Nevada Test Site. For the past forty years, Jack has been on a mission searching for truth, for wisdom, and for meaning in life; and he has expressed his thoughts in numerous manuscripts he hopes to publish in the future. As a retired person, Jack is devoting the final season of his life to writing about true wisdom and how he has learned to evaluate truth and wisdom in order to recognize purpose in life. This search has prepared Jack to help Marty get his story in print, to provide insights into Marty's early life, and to prepare commentary for portions of this book addressing Marty's search for meaning. Marty's search in many ways is similar to the quest to find meaning conducted by all people who seek to find meaning and purpose through illicit drugs. Illicit drug abuse is a dead end street.

About this Book

Marty's story provides a powerful demonstration that how the individual answers the basic questions *about* life helps him discern his personal mission *in* life. This story reveals that as we begin to understand this world and the people in it, from the perspective that there is more to life than we can see with our eyes and can touch with our hands, our idea of what is important changes, and how we make personal choices also changes. Our choices ultimately determine our path through life.

When we come to understand that there are more important things than personal peace and comfort, we may begin to experience the joy of looking beyond ourselves to find meaning in our personal life. The choices we make affect other people, and the choices other people make affect us. Everything in this world is interconnected by design; for this reason, we cannot escape the idea that we must support one another throughout life. The story of Marty Gruber is about how Marty, at fifty-three years of age, learned that his purpose in life was to serve the Designer of life, and Marty's purpose was to help teens avoid the destructive influence of drugs so that they could find their purpose. This changed Marty's understanding of what is important. This in turn changed his decision making process from being focused on himself to becoming focused on the well-being of other people.

Jack has been Marty's friend for more than ten years. Marty and Jack share a passion for finding truth, meaning, and purpose, and for making the decisions of life based on wisdom that is greater than their own. Jack has attended the presentations made by Marty in the schools of the Clark County School District of Las Vegas, Nevada, approximately twenty times, and he desires for Marty's story to be told after he is no longer able to go into the classroom and tell it himself. Marty's story is uplifting and generates hope for a better life for anyone who is willing to make the decisions of life under the influence of wisdom that comes from beyond the human mind.

Even though Marty celebrated his seventy-fifth birthday in May of 2011, younger people somehow realize that they need to learn what Marty has learned through the hard knocks of being born into a dysfunctional family and then building upon a bad start in life through bad choices. Marty tells his story so that those who listen to him may avoid the specific bad choices he made and that they may realize that a rocky beginning in life does not condemn one to a lifetime of heartache and failure. There is a wonderful world waiting for those who have eyes to see it.

Jack believes that Marty has been given a gift to communicate a specific message to teens. Clearly Marty has learned some things through life that teens may benefit from learning. To help this happen, Jack has volunteered his time and writing talent to get Marty's story in print so that others can learn: (1) How being raised in dysfunctional environments contributed to the bad choices Marty made in his youth. (2) How Marty built his life upon his shaky beginning and continued making bad choices for over forth-five years. (3) How Marty changed his understanding of life in ways that significantly have improved his decision making abilities. (4) Finally, it is our goal to present hope that will encourage the reader (young or old) to pursue a high quality of life based upon the expectation that life has meaning and that the despair and tumult many young people feel may yield to a beautiful pursuit of meaning and purpose by looking beyond self. Learning to pursue meaning beyond self works for older people as well. The key is to seek wisdom greater than man's wisdom by looking to eternity as a source of meaning rather than extracting meaning only from the here and now.

Day One and Day Two of Marty's drug awareness presentations were transcribed from DVD recordings of his classroom discussions. The details of Marty's personal life were transcribed from CD recordings made for this book. The events of Marty's young life were recalled from memory and exact dates cannot be established. Some commentary addressing the events of Marty's life were researched and prepared by Jack and edited by Marty. Details of specific events are accurate but their place in time is less accurate. Interpretation of some events has been made based on adult perceptions that have helped both Jack and Marty deal with the pain of living in the less-than-perfect world we all share. Section four was written by Jack with significant input from Marty. These paragraphs present the philosophical views that both men have come to adopt through the pain of living in a severely broken world.

This book is divided into five sections:

<u>Section One</u> presents Marty's personal story and the path that led him to become a drug awareness presenter.

<u>Section Two</u> consists of transcripts from two drug awareness presentations made by Marty in the classroom. These are followed by student written responses to Marty's presentations and the story of Marty's adopted grandson's struggle with drugs.

<u>Section Three</u> discusses how drug usage alters the body and brain of the addict, which explains why it is so difficult for an addict to turn away from drugs. This is followed by a report on the remarkable success of Teen Challenge, a program that uses a faith-based approach to dealing with the problem of addiction.

<u>Section Four</u> addresses several basic questions of life that we are all faced with and emphasizes the importance of personally answering these questions. How we answer, or fail to answer, the basic questions in life significantly affects our understanding of who we are and what is important in life. It is unavoidable that our lives become a living demonstration of what we believe truth to be. Thus, what we accept as truth affects our decisions. This section includes letters from students who have heard Marty's presentation over the years.

<u>Section Five</u> presents a letter to educators that explains Marty's approach to drug awareness training, which targets six groups of teenagers through two forty-five minute presentations. This is followed by the seven handouts Marty gives to students. Finally this is followed by fourteen attachments presenting the massive amounts of information on drug abuse published by the National Institute on Drug Abuse (NIDA). These attachments are freely available on the Internet (see Website http://www.nida.nih.gov/nidahome. html). Information on how to access this information is also included in the attachments. Marty also provides "Tips for Teens" (see http://store.samhsa.gov/pages/searchResult/ Tips+for+teens). These eleven tips are not included in this book but are available from the above website.

How To Wage War Against Drug Abuse

Do you wish to participate in the battle against drug abuse? If your answer to this question is yes, this book was written to help you. By the end of school year 2010–2011, Marty's presentations entitled "Searching for the Truth About Drugs" will have been presented to over 150,000 teens in the Clark County School District in Las Vegas, Nevada. This presentation is now available as a ninety-minute-long DVD presentation as an aid to those who want to present a message against illicit drug usage to individuals or to a group. This DVD includes the testimony of David, Marty's adopted grandson, who at 15 years of age was a recovering drug abuser. David's story is addressed in detail in Marty's presentation. This is followed by Marty's personal presentations made in class. This DVD is designed to help you prepare and present authoritative discussions about the horrors associated with drug abuse and will be an eye opener for someone experimenting with, or thinking of experimenting with, illicit drugs. To obtain this information, do the following:

1. Send for the DVD, which is available at a cost of $13 (this includes shipping and handling). Send payment to

   Searching for the Truth About Drugs
   P. O. Box 370610
   Las Vegas, Nevada 89137

2. Number of DVDs ordered:_____

   $13.00 payment for each DVD ordered = $_____
   Name:_____
   Mailing Address:_____
   State:_____Zip Code_____
   Country:_____

3. Judging from the approximately 80,000 letters I have received over the twelve years that I have done this program, it has helped many teens and their friends and families with drug-related problems. All proceeds from the sale of this book and the DVDs will go toward the operating costs of developing, presenting, and maintaining this program.

4. The seven handouts included in Section V, entitled "Marty's Handouts," may be copied and used at your discretion.

5. The fourteen attachments published by the National Institute on Drug Abuse (NIDA) are in the public domain; these publications may be freely used by the public. These attachments lead to volumes of information on drug abuse.

Copyright Statement

This book is copyrighted and is the specific property of Marty Gruber and John R. Donaldson Jr.. All photographs in this book are the property of Marty Gruber and John R. Donaldson Jr. Permission is herby granted to copy and distribute this information for those waging war against chemical addiction. This grant does not include permission to duplicate and sell *for profit* the copyrighted information owned by Marty Gruber and John R. Donaldson Jr.. In addition, this grant does not include information that is quoted and referenced in any section of this book that is not the copyrighted property of Marty Gruber and John R. Donaldson Jr..

Cover Photos: Cover photos are copyright Thinkstock.

TABLE OF CONTENTS

How To Search for Information in this Book

A section heading is at the top of each page. This section heading presents the primary topic in the section. Under the section headings are paragraph headings. The paragraph headings also carry a paragraph number (e.g., ¶#1). Thus, the most efficient way for a reader to search for information in this book is to (1) read the section heading; (2) read the paragraph headings and note the paragraph number; and (3) search for that paragraph by number through the text pages of the book by moving forward and backward through the text until the page where the paragraph searched for is found.

TABLE OF CONTENTS
SECTION ONE

SECTION TWO

SECTION THREE

SECTION FOUR

TABLE OF CONTENTS

SECTION FIVE

SECTION ONE
MEET MARTY GRUBER
VOLUNTEER DRUG AWARENESS PRESENTER

¶#1: A Progression from Chemical Freak to Drug Awareness Presenter

The world is filled with people who care about other people, but in general, they are not the one's who are most visible to someone seeking to answer the questions that come when the world begins to press them into its mold of uncaring hardness. A caring person may be defined as one who sees the reality of those around him and chooses to give his time and resources to make the experiences of those around him better out of concern for the person he wants to help (i.e., the person who is offering help is not selfishly motivated).

We all have caring people in our lives, such as Mom and Dad, Grandma and Grandpa, or special teachers, coaches, or friends who went out of their way to help us learn something important or to do something important. Sometimes we encounter people who care about us who do not even know us, but they are still willing to share their lives with us because they realize we need help in dealing with life, especially in making the decisions of life.

Perhaps the most caring people are those who help shape our lives by showing us answers to the pressing questions of life. It is ironic that those who care for others the most are not usually the ones teens will choose as the character model they seek to emulate as they grow into adulthood. However, caring people are the very people who enable young people to become who they are going to become as they travel through life. I do not mean to imply that young people are not caring. However, the caring people I have in mind have developed into who they are over several seasons of their personal lives. It takes time for a caring person to develop the characteristics that motivate and enable him to communicate what he desires to show others about life.

The caring people I have in mind are usually sensitive and have learned something that helps them function and relate to others in a very positive way. People we describe as caring want to enable others to grow the way they have grown or perhaps to avoid something that will damage their lives. The result is that caring people quietly go about doing what they can to enable others to learn what they have learned or to avoid some pitfall in life they have experienced

1

and know to be very dangerous. Their goal is to enable other people to make personal choices that will serve them well in the path they are progressively choosing through life.

It has been my observation that some people I believe are caring no longer realize how much they influence others, because whatever assistance they offer has become such a part of who they are that it is interwoven into their personalities. How they care has become who they are rather than simply what they do. I believe it is this way with Marty Gruber. His disdain for the abuse of mind-altering chemicals is so developed that what he teaches in his drug awareness presentations is simply part of who he has become and how he desires to use his time. Marty has made his life an open book for developing teenagers to read so they can understand the consequences of some choices open to them and choose a different path around a choice of life that can be majorly destructive.

People I would describe as caring have become living examples of what they want to communicate to someone else about life. Caring artists demonstrate something about their art with a strong feeling that is somehow transmitted to others through their art. This feeling is somehow communicated to another person who appreciates that art. Caring dancers imbue their dance with part of their personalities that communicates something others may feel as they watch them perform the intricate movements of their dance. Caring parents bring everything they are and have learned about life that will aid their children into their task of parenting. Their lives are ongoing demonstrations of the values they hope to communicate to their children through parenting. In a similar way, a caring drug awareness presenter demonstrates the pitfalls of drug abuse and what drug abuse will do for those who choose to become chemical freaks. Effective presentations on drug abuse communicate the destructive force of drug abuse in a way that teenagers can identify with. The result is that kids willingly listen to what is said and make their choice accordingly.

Marty Gruber is a caring drug awareness counselor. Marty explains his experiences as a forty-five-plus-year chemical freak, knowing that the life he lived as a junkie is similar to what other chemical freaks experience in the unwonderful world of drug addiction. Marty has concluded that the experiences of a chemical addict are far different from what most people actually desire as they begin their journey into drug usage. Marty has put much effort into developing a format for communicating what one will certainly encounter when traveling the road known as chemical addiction.

Marty has a passion developed out of the pain of life that has led him to dedicate the latter seasons of his life to teenagers as he tells them what lies down this very dark and foreboding road we call drug addiction. It is by knowing that some choices in life will produce great pain that we are enabled to make better choices. We are able to learn from other people's mistakes and from our own mistakes. Marty's personal life as a chemical freak and the lives of those he influenced to do drugs, and the lives of other chemical freaks he encountered traveling the same path, are his examples of what lies in the path of a drug addict.

The emphasis of Marty's presentations about the path of drug abuse he chose are (1) "Don't do it, and let me tell you why"; (2) "If you are hooked on drugs, you need help in becoming drug free"; (3) "Help is available to assist you in becoming drug free and choosing to remain drug free, but you personally must make the choice to remain drug free"; and (4) understanding that truth has great power to set you free from mistakes you have already made and then to keep you free from making additional mistakes that will destroy your life.

A teenager simply can't see as far down the road as a seventy-five-year-old man who has already been down that road to just short of its logical end—which is death. In Marty's case, this was attempted suicide. He has returned to warn others not to take that path.

If you have ever wondered what it would be like to travel the road that a drug addict has chosen to travel, sit back and read about the road into living hell—and back.

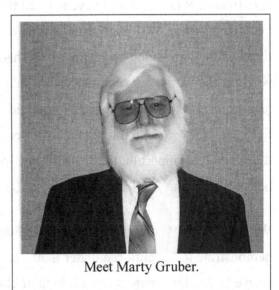

Meet Marty Gruber.

GETTING TO KNOW MARTY
BIRTH TO FIFTEEN YEARS OF AGE

¶#2: Marty the Boy

My name is Fred Martin Gruber, and I was born on May 20, 1936, in Cincinnati, Ohio.

I didn't find out what my real name was until I went into the navy when I was nineteen years old. Until then, I thought my name was Martin Frederick Gruber.

My father's name was Frank Joseph Gruber, and my mother's maiden name was Olive Julius Riggs. Mom was of Irish descent and was a very attractive young woman. Mary Elizabeth Gruber is my sister and is three years older than I, and Frank Joseph Gruber, my brother, is two years older than I am.

As I tell my story, there are many things I wish were different. However, let me be clear: I am not looking for sympathy for things that happened to me more than three-quarters of a lifetime ago. In fact, over the years I have learned that the childhood abuse I experienced actually has become a source of strength that is now enabling me to understand the crippling influence the dysfunctional adults who raised me had on me. This understanding also enables me to perform the work I was called to do in this season of my life. As I began to think about the larger questions on life, such as, "Where did I come from?" "What is life all about?" and "Does life have purpose?" the fact that I experienced an unhappy, painful childhood and survived it seemed less important than when I was young. I will discuss how my thinking about this has progressed as I tell my story.

What I do want to emphasize is that what dads, moms, and the guardians of children do and demonstrate to the children under their care has consequences. Through my journey in life, I have learned that parents owe it to their children to determine the best way to nurture their children and then provide that nurturing to them while they instill the values and skills their children will need in their personal lives. There is nothing more important to a mom or dad than the nurturing of their children in the home environment, and there is more to nurturing a child than providing them with food, shelter, and clothing. Nurturing begins with these things, but it requires much more—such as demonstrating how to love, how to give, how to receive, how to forgive one another in relationships, how to establish boundaries in relationships, how to provide for your family, and how to do all of this while demonstrating what you hope that child will grow into.

It is my observation that many families just seem to happen with very little forethought. Few people have lifetime goals in mind when they make decisions that ultimately prove to be life changing. For me the decision to flee the pain of life into the horror of chemical abuse was one such decision. The earlier decision that I had made to marry, and the decisions that my wife and I made to become parents, also meant that my decision to do drugs was a life changing decision for the people who were the most important in my life.

Marriage and parenthood just seem to happen to many, and the responsibilities of parenthood frequently catch both the husband and wife unprepared for the consequences of the decisions they mutually make. When this happens, their children may suffer the consequences of being raised in a family that does not work well (a dysfunctional home). When parents fail to assume responsibility for raising their children, the stage is set for the people to share the same dwelling, to live under the same roof, without developing intimate feelings and concern for each other, and then they grow to reproduce themselves in the world they have produced. This is the type of home that my brother, sister, and I experienced as we moved from dwelling to dwelling in our childhood.

¶#3: Life Principle #1

Regardless of how a child is raised, there comes a time when each person must rise to assume responsibility for who he or she is, and for whom he or she is to become in the progression of life. While the family my brother, sister, and I were born into has had consequences in our lives, we live in a free land that provides many opportunities, and we can choose to become something more than the lifestyle we were born into. Every one of us lives in a culture where we can work to become the person we desire to become, and regardless of birth circumstances, we have the capacity to set life goals and reach out for them. The first principle of life I desire for everyone reading this book to grasp is that **the individual is responsible for who they choose to become in the progression of their life**. The choices we make have consequences.

¶#4: Life Principle #2

The most efficient way to train children is <u>to be a demonstration of the person that you desire them to become</u>. As children watch their parents, they are being molded into the form of their parents, and as we progress in education, we are becoming demonstrations of the things we accept and practice as truth. Certainly most parents desire for their children to become healthy and happy adults, but many times in the ongoing struggles of life, parents fail to communicate that message to their children. What we demonstrate for them is many times what they will intentionally or subliminally become through the choices they make. Parents (knowingly or unknowingly) are the first to press their children into a mold for their personal lives.

I am a personal example that parents are the primary individuals that their children will pattern their understanding and approach to living after. I was a testimony to my children, and they patterned themselves after my example. All of my children have seriously damaged or destroyed their lives by following the example that I set for them. In addition, I am confident that this is what happened to my parents and stepparents. They passed their faulty parenting and marriage skills to me, and I passed them on to my children, and my children have passed them on to my grandchildren. Dysfunctional families have a way of reproducing themselves through their children, and I was raised and educated in multiple dysfunctional environments. But as each child grows and leaves home, he gains the freedom to choose what he is to become. There is an old proverb that states, "As a twig is bent, so grows the tree." There is an element of truth in this proverb, but as long as we have the capacity to choose, it is not too late to choose truth and in doing so to grow in a different direction. There is another proverb that says, "Truth caught in youth, serves for a lifetime."

¶#5: Life Principle #3: Chemical abuse will destroy your life

As you read my story, you will learn how I got into drugs, how I destroyed my life with drugs, and how I have turned from drugs to find a better way. Not everyone is as fortunate as I have been in that regard. My brother Frank died at the age of seventy-four as an alcoholic; both he and his wife would drink themselves to sleep at night, right up to the time Frank died. Frank also smoked unfiltered Camel cigarettes for most of his life. Even though Frank quit smoking eight years before he died, he still died of lung cancer. I am also an alcoholic, I am a drug addict, and I was a smoker for many years. My oldest son was an alcoholic and a drug addict.

My middle son has been a heavy drinker. My youngest son died in a motorcycle accident while high on alcohol and marijuana. Addictions run in our family. However, my biological grandson is currently twenty-eight years old and, to the best of my knowledge, does not smoke, drink alcoholic beverages, or do drugs. We hope and pray the cycle of addictions that has plagued our family for several lifetimes is finally broken.

¶#6: Life Principle #4: There is a path out of abuse and addictions

The purpose of this book is to inform individuals who are living dysfunctional lifestyles that there is a path open to them for change, but they must seek it. There is a path for all people to discern a fulfilling pattern for living if they are willing to seek truth and follow their seeking wherever it takes them. That path will become clear as I tell you what moved me from a meaningless, unfulfilling chemical dependence to find the purpose I have been called and trained to fulfill. In the process, I have become fully committed to my wife, and I have found a way to make a positive difference in this very dysfunctional world we live in. I have come to believe that the Designer of this world intends for mankind to realize that pain in life is the consequence of turning away from His intended pattern for living a fulfilling life and to develop a passion to find that fulfilling pattern for their personal lives.

¶#7: Children Are Arrows Shot from the Bow of Their Parents

I heard a teacher say that children are like arrows shot from their parents' bows. That seems to be an accurate description of me. My father was an alcoholic, and he must have been an alcoholic when my mother married him. My mom and dad divorced when I was very young, and I believe that alcohol played a part in leading to their breakup, although I never knew what actually caused it. Several years after their breakup, my mom and dad both remarried.

My stepfather's name was Tony, and he was a former boxer of Italian descent. My stepmother's name was Hazel, and she was of uneducated Tennessee hillbilly descent. I don't mean this in any insulting way, but as I remember Hazel, she was a very uncomplicated and straightforward woman who was more or less just there for my father. On the other hand, Tony was multidimensional and possessed the diverse Italian male personality. However, neither me nor my siblings bonded with our stepparents. Neither my dad nor mom had children by their second spouses. My dad was very uncomplicated and straightforward and almost seemed intimidated by life. My mother was a multidimensional personality who could be bubbly and happy one minute and a raging torrent the next; she used her personality to manipulate. Until I completely left home by being arrested at sixteen, both my mom and stepdad and my dad and stepmom lived just a few miles apart in the Cincinnati area, and I was frequently in both homes.

My dad had some very peculiar personal habits; for example, he never took a bath, and there was no shower where he and my stepmother lived; instead, he would take sponge baths in the kitchen sink. I do not know the reason that he did this, but it always seemed strange to me. In addition, he did not pursue personal friendships, and he only infrequently ventured outside of the family atmosphere. To the best of my knowledge, the only person other than my mother whom he actually cultivated a personal relationship with was Hazel, my stepmother. My dad and I had no interpersonal relationship whatsoever. I would describe his relationship with me as one based on my fear of him. I never really got to know him, neither did I develop a warm relationship with my stepmother; she was more or less just there with my dad.

My dad did have an interest in music and played the guitar reasonably well. Hazel came from a family of Tennessee hillbillies that played music in their free time, and this common interest caused us all to visit my stepmother's family from time to time. However, Hazel's family only tolerated my father and his music; there was no friendship between him and them. I remember during one visit to Hazel's family, as they were sitting around jamming on their musical instruments, my father became very drunk and just started to mechanically strum his guitar. One of them just reached over and unplugged the amplifier for his guitar, and he didn't even know the difference. I was about thirteen when this happened, and I remember the horror of embarrassment in realizing how these Tennessee hillbillies, seemingly very uncomplicated people, viewed my dad.

My brother Frank also played the guitar a little, and this allowed him and my dad to have something in common for a while. However, they did not have a friendly interpersonal relationship. Neither did my dad have a good relationship with my sister. I think that because my dad and mom were both very dysfunctional people, the family environments of both homes were dysfunctional. After my mom and dad divorced, we three kids went to live with our mom.

Alcohol abuse develops into a full-blown disease in time. It is also progressive in the sense that the longer and the more you drink, the worse it gets. At about the time of my dad's death, he would drink a water glass full of whiskey for breakfast and then go to work. Dad worked for Procter and Gamble from the time I was born until the time of his death. His health was so bad that just before he died, he worked as a security guard, where the only thing he had to do was wave trucks in and out of the plant. My dad died at the age of fifty-five as a confirmed alcoholic.

The day before Dad died, he fell at work and bumped his head on a railroad track. Someone brought him home, where he could lay down to rest. Later that night, he complained of losing feeling in his legs, and our family doctor was called. The doctor told Dad that he was okay and released him to go to work the next day. The following morning, when Hazel woke up, Dad was in a coma. He was rushed to the hospital, where he died that day. The same doctor who had released him to go back to work listed the cause of death on his death certificate as encephalitis, which is an acute inflammation of the brain. My stepmother dedicated Dad's brain to the University of Cincinnati, where they were studying alcoholism at that time. About three months later, she received a letter from the university, stating that Dad had not died of encephalitis, but of a blood clot on the brain.

Dad did not earn much money, but over the years, he and my stepmother were able to acquire many things, including stock in Procter and Gamble. Dad left me, my brother Frank, and my sister Mary Elizabeth each one dollar in his will. Hazel received the remainder of his estate. I believe this gesture was his final message that he had rejected each of his three children and did not wish to have any kind of relationship with them.

The most vivid memory that I have of the visits to my stepmother's family is how dirty their house was allowed to become. They didn't use sheets on their beds, and they slept on urine- and sweat-stained mattresses with pillows with no pillowcases. Their beds were never made. Some of the boys in her family were near my age, but they were all much bigger and stronger than I, and I felt insecure around them, but they didn't really pick on me. However, I dreaded visits to their house.

An interesting story about Hazel's father is that he had three or four wives over his lifetime, and when he was ninety-two years old, he fathered a baby through his much younger wife. When we went to visit them in Tennessee one time, I remember him sitting on the front porch of their country house playing his banjo and rocking his newborn baby's cradle with his foot.

After my parents divorced, we moved with Mom into a little apartment in Cincinnati. We did not have enough to eat, and my mom went on public assistance. We ate cereal for breakfast and potato soup for dinner. That was our daily ration because she couldn't afford anything else. One of my first childhood memories is that a bat flew into our apartment through an open window, and that terrified me. We all panicked and ran out of the house, and a neighborhood man come and removed the bat for us.

¶#8: Orphanage and Foster Care

When I was about two years old, someone called the welfare department in Cincinnati and told them of a woman with three kids in serious need, claiming that her kids were not being properly cared for. Next came a knock on the door, and when my mom opened the door, three people were standing there. A man shoved a paper into my mom's face and said that he was there to take her kids away, and a lady grabbed me from the arms of my mother and grabbed Elizabeth and Frank, and they took us down the walkway, crying. We were placed in a car and taken to an orphanage in Cincinnati. I don't remember much of this, and I suppose I have somehow blocked these memories from my mind because they are too painful to recall. Elizabeth, who is three years older than I, remembers this, and she relayed this information to me for the purpose of writing this book. All three of us lived in the orphanage for a couple of months before we were transferred to a foster home.

I remember very little about my early childhood, but I do have a few fragmented memories. My very first reconciliation is standing in an upstairs bedroom in semidarkness with all the shades pulled down, and people were downstairs talking and laughing. There was a little gate across the doorway to prevent me, Frank, or Elizabeth from leaving the upstairs room. We were in a foster home. I remember looking down the stairs, but we were separated from our foster family; we rarely mixed with them. My next memory about this same time is being kept in a darkened room, isolated from other people by our foster parents. I have never understood why they did not allow us to mix with other people or why they didn't care that we were not developing socially. I surmise that our foster parents kept me, Frank, and Elizabeth out of sight in a dark upstairs bedroom because we represented a dependable paycheck from the state of

Ohio. Our foster parents didn't wish to be bothered by the parenting responsibilities necessary to deal with three kids from another person's dysfunctional home.

Frank, Elizabeth, and I spent a great amount of time locked in that upstairs bedroom room in the dark. I really don't remember how long we were there, but we must have spent about two years in a dark bedroom. Most of my waking hours were spent in that upstairs darkened bedroom, but I don't remember much about this, or even that Frank and Elizabeth were with me; however, my sister recalls it vividly. I don't remember Frank and Elizabeth attending school during this time, but I suppose they did.

For those two years, I used to sit in the corner of the room by myself and rock on my knees and sing to myself; that is all I had to do. As you may perceive, in this environment we didn't have an opportunity to learn much or to develop socially. My mental and personality development were essentially on hold for these two years, as were Frank's and Elizabeth's. I don't remember how they passed the time when we were in this room together, but it is clear that all three of us were deprived of social development. I don't recall how we were returned to my mother, but we went to live with her and my stepfather Tony before I began kindergarten.

¶#9: Life with My Mother and Stepdad

Tony was in his mid-thirties; as noted, he was a former boxer, but he was also a victim of my mother. Basically Tony was a wuss, a pussycat who did whatever my mother told him to. Tony had zero parenting skills, because he had never been a father, and he gave no indication that he wanted to be a father. Tony was also on medications of some kind. He was from the old European school, which means he was taught to rule his home with an iron fist. Tony was an old school Italian man who said as long as you did it his way, we would be okay, but if we crossed him, he was going to kick our butt. As noted, Tony had never been a father, so he spent a lot of time kicking our butts.

At that time, men shaved with a straight razor, and Tony had a razor strop to hone his razor after sharpening it. This razor strop also served as a tool to whip me and Frank. Tony saw himself as an extension of my mother, and he did whatever she told him to do. This created problems with Tony, because whenever she told him we misbehaved, he would beat us. At times the beatings were severe; today, they would be classified as child abuse. However, in the late forties and early fifties, that was pretty much overlooked. Tony's attitude toward Frank

11

and me was, "I'll beat them to death or they will learn, whichever comes first"; it really didn't seem to matter to Tony. When we brought a failing report card home, no one thought to ask why this happened; the solution was to beat me and my brother with that razor strop. It was during adolescence that our addiction problems, which were to last nearly a lifetime and manifest themselves as multiple addictions in both Frank and me, began to surface.

¶#10: School and Early Social Development

As the result of not developing socially in early childhood, at the age of five, when I entered kindergarten, I was afraid of people. My contact with people had not been positive, and I feared the worst in new situations. In kindergarten, I did what I did in the dark bedroom in my foster parents' house: I sat alone and rocked and sang to myself. As I look back on this, I do not remember being openly rebellious; I now realize that I had a learning disorder that was undetected by my teachers.

Not knowing my past history, the teachers thought that I was somehow mentally challenged. I remember virtually nothing of kindergarten, first grade, or second grade. I do have some memories of the third grade, because I failed it. In the lower grades, in all probability I had been promoted to the next grade simply to make room for an upcoming student.

As a child, I had absolutely no interest in school, and I still do not enjoy studying or doing research. My experience with other humans did not lead me to desire social contact with anyone or to learn the things needed to advance through school. It is interesting to note that some of these attitudes are pretty much the same today as they were seventy years ago; I am still a loner. Knowing that being a loner may not be the best way to promote mental health does little to change how I actually feel on the inside. It is difficult to change attitudes that were developed from childhood right through adolescence and into the teenage years. However, experiences in Uncle Sam's Navy clearly taught me to understand the importance of being able to communicate with others in order to accomplish a specified task. This realization came late in my life, but it has served me well through the years.

¶#11: Passions in Life

As you read this book, you will realize that the one thing I passionately care about is communicating to other people that they do not have to live the life that they developed from being born into a dysfunctional family (or that they developed through making poor choices in life). It was both my dysfunctional family and the wrong choices that I personally made that led me into nearly forty five years of drug abuse and finally to the position of living only for drugs and attempting suicide, because I could not turn away from drugs. It is ironic that the very drugs that first promise escape and momentary comfort to a hurting person in the end only produce slavery to substance abuse. It is by reaching out to a Higher Power and expressing a desire to change that I gained the wisdom, the strength, and the stamina to make right choices that have produced sobriety and that are helping me maintain sobriety.[1] I have discovered meaning in life that only trust in a Higher Power can give.

Part of the dictionary definition of "grace" is "the condition or fact of being favored by someone." My definition of grace includes "allowing your Higher Power to do for you what you cannot do for yourself." It is my Higher Power that has led to my discovery of peace and forgiveness in this fallen world, even after making horrendous mistakes that have hurt both me and my family. I will address this in greater detail in the remainder of this book.

As a kid, my primary interest was anything with wheels or that spun around or that had lights. I now realize that I had a learning disability, and that learning disability seemed to direct me toward finding interest in spinning wheels or flashing lights. However, to this day I have no idea how that learning disability functions within me or why I have it. All I know is that as I began growing up, socially I was a destitute child who entered this world entangled in a host of problems, and those problems shaped my mental outlook on life in some very negative ways. Somehow I found interest in wheels and lights instead of relationships with people.

This learning disability was interpreted by my guardians as a detachment from people. My detachment from people meant that compliance with what people wanted from me was not important to me. This was interpreted as being willfully disobedient, and that may be partially

---

[1]   Higher Power refers to God, Allah, Jesus, Buddha, or any spiritual power that is defined as "good" by the addict and that is willing to help the addict deal with his or her addiction. It is helpful for addicts to realize that they are not facing their addiction alone, and there is more to life and the experiences of this world than we can see with our eye. I have come to believe that there is an invisible world beyond this visible world, but I can't conclusively prove that, nor can anyone else. Thus, I believe there is more to come in an afterlife. If addicts can see beyond this world to a place where they can find peace, it helps them find the strength to turn from the overpowering enslavement to their drug of choice. It also helps them to come to see that what they have experienced as pain in this world is part of a learning process that they will take with them into their life beyond this world. The Higher Power that I turned to is Jesus.

true, but in any case I did not see the need to be compliant. In fact, I now believe that as a very young child, I did not know what was expected of me or how to be compliant.

¶#12: Let the Beatings Begin

In my young life it seems that my guardians believed what I needed most of all was strong discipline, and discipline was administered accordingly. I was beaten in attempts to force compliance. However, compliance was something that I had no understanding of. I simply did not know what was required. Even today I don't know if I would have yielded in obedience to my guardians, if I had understood what they wanted from me. The truth is I had no idea how to submit to authority or how to willingly give obedience. What I remember is, "It was me against them." There were no boundaries handed down—only discipline when undefined boundaries, or boundaries I did not recognize, were crossed.

When hard discipline didn't work, the solution was to beat me longer and harder out of frustration. I have no recollection of anybody sitting me down and asking, "Why are you like this?" I don't remember anyone trying to determine if I had any mental abnormalities or developmental disorders. There were just many, many, many, many beatings. My recollections of early childhood and adolescence are filled with memories of beatings.

¶#13: Chemical Abuse Begins

I got drunk for the first time when I was eight years old, during the Christmas season. My stepdad and mom had friends over for a Christmas celebration, and I was able to steal wine from all the partially empty glasses. I went to the kitchen and sat cross-legged in the middle of the kitchen table and got drunk on the wine I had collected. That was my first exposure to chemical abuse, and I liked the way it made me feel; I could escape for a time into the world of "intoxicated make-believe," and I thought it was great. I believe that this incident at eight opened the door to forty-five-plus years of chemical abuse.

After getting drunk for the first time, the key was in the door; all I had to do was find an opportunity and the source of booze, and I would drink to get drunk if possible. In addition to that, I started smoking cigarettes when I was eleven years old. Alcohol was the gateway drug for me into other forms of chemical abuse, such as cigarettes, marijuana, and later cocaine, and then on to methamphetamines and opium. The fact that I smoked cigarettes made it easy for me to move up to smoking marijuana for the first time when I was about forty-one years old, and it was marijuana that allowed me to move up to cocaine about two years later.

Integrated memories of my childhood begin about the sixth grade when I was about thirteen. I remember going to school dirty and drunk. I would get drunk at home on my dad's whiskey and fill up my cough medicine bottle half full of whiskey, and in the sixth and seventh grades I would take whiskey to school just to get me through the day. In addition, after school I would go into the local bars and do a little dance, and they would throw change at me and I would leave with thirty or forty cents in my pocket. In addition, the bartender would usually take me into the back room and give me a couple of shots of whiskey. I would sometimes stand outside of the state-operated liquor store after school with the money I earned by performing at the bar, begging adults to buy me some whiskey, which they frequently did.

¶#14: Childhood Stories and a Developing Addiction

There are some interesting stories about that bar in Lockland, Ohio, and the game of shuffleboard. The bar owner's name was Mr. Ed Depraw. Mr. Depraw and several of his friends were very accomplished shuffleboard players (or so they thought). Shuffleboard was a very popular game in the late 1940s and early 1950s, and it was pretty easy to get a serious game going, and betting was common.

Around 1950, a couple of professional-quality shuffleboard players showed up in Lockland. Mr. Depraw and his friends begin to play very serious games with these guys, where thousands of dollars changed hands, which was a lot of money at that time. Mr. Depraw and his friends were soon in debt to these shuffleboard players to the tune of thousands of dollars. Finally it was decided that Mr. Depraw would bet the bar against all the debts that he and his friends owed. Mr. Depraw lost the bar in a shuffleboard game; at least it was his bar until the end of the game. This was big news in Lockland at that time.

There was also an alcoholic cat living in Mr. Depraw's bar. This cat had very little fur, and the patrons of the bar would feed this cat beer until he couldn't walk straight. Everyone had many laughs at the drunk cat. Looking back, this was funny when I was thirteen, but after my years of personal addiction, and the addictions of those in my family, it seems more pathetic than funny. Sometimes we get a warped sense of pleasure out of someone else's pain.

15

My brother and I had a friend named Barney. Barney was Frank's age; when they were fifteen or sixteen, Frank and I pulled Barney all around town in a wagon (he had sore and infected feet to the point that he couldn't walk very far). Even though Barney was just a kid like us, he was also an alcoholic. The old adage that "Birds of a feather flock together" seems appropriate. Barney would buy a half gallon of beer in Mr. Depraw's bar for about fifty cents. He would buy Frank and me all the beer we could afford. We would pull Barney to the bar, and he would buy us beer, and then we'd go someplace to drink it. It is at this time that I became a confirmed alcoholic.

One day after doing my little dance at the bar, I got so drunk that I couldn't make it home. I was sitting on the steps of the pool hall, which was very near the bar, and I looked up to see my dad coming to get me. Someone had called him and told him I was drunk and where to find me. When he came near, all he said was, "Let's go home." I was so drunk that I couldn't walk. Dad walked on in front of me, waiting for me to come along, and I stumbled along behind him, falling every few steps and getting my mouth full of dirt and who knows what else. The bar patrons who tossed me money for my dance were watching to see what was going to happen. They were disappointed, because Dad did nothing to me. When we got home, Frank helped me get to bed. When I awakened the following morning, I had the mother of all hangovers.

The next day, I went to the pool hall and Barney was there. When I walked up to Barney, for some unknown reason, he stood up and sucker punched me. The next thing I remember was waking up on a pool table with a bag of ice on my bruised face where Barney had hit me. About this time, Frank came into the pool hall and asked what had happened, and I told him. Frank just took me home without saying a word to Barney. When Dad asked what had happened to me, we made up a story about how we had tried to protect Barney from a stranger in the pool hall and the stranger hit me.

As usual, Dad was well on his way into drunken oblivion. Upon hearing our story, being filled with liquid courage, he grabbed a knife and off we went to find the imaginary stranger and take care of him. We searched several bars and the pool hall and couldn't find the stranger we had created out of thin air. In one bar, we encountered Barney, who asked us what was going on. We replied that we were looking for the man who had hit me. Barney replied, "I'll help you look." So we went from bar to bar, looking for the mythical man.

After that, Frank and I cooled our relationship with Barney because we thought he could be dangerous.

Years later, I got out of the navy and was visiting my dad and stepmom, who once again lived in Lockland. Frank had also returned to Lockland after getting out of the army. One evening, I asked Frank about Barney. Frank remembered Barney and knew where he lived. He said that Barney was a local drunk, that he lived alone, and that he was working as a helper in a local manufacturing plant. I said, "Let's go see him," so off we went.

Barney was in bed when we arrived at his apartment, but he let us in and then went back to bed. As we talked, Barney would jump up and run to the refrigerator every few minutes, but he never took anything out of it. I asked him why he did this. His reply is typical of an impoverished alcoholic. He said, "I have two quarts of beer in the refrigerator, and I want to make sure they're still there." I never saw Barney again, and I have no idea what became of him. I had no idea that Barney's fear of having his booze stolen was to be a mirror of me not too many years into my future, when I was living alone in poverty and in constant fear of having my cocaine stolen.

¶#15: Kicked Out at Ten

My mom kicked me and my brother out of her house when I was ten and Frank was twelve. We lived in Cincinnati on Jefferson Avenue; this was kind of the suburbs at that time. One day when Frank and I came home from a local playground, we found two small boxes on the front porch. When we looked in the boxes, we saw our clothes. There was a note and two dimes on my brother's box; the note said, "You two don't live here anymore … go live with your drunken dad." The two dimes were for us to ride the streetcar up to Lockland, which was just north of Cincinnati. Lockland was also at the end of the run for that streetcar. When we tried our keys in Mom's apartment door, they did not work; the locks had been changed. At ten and twelve years old, we were homeless, and the only money we had was a dime each for the streetcar to Lockland. So we went to live with my father and stepmother. In doing so, we had simply moved from one hell hole to another.

Lockland is an industrial town, and there was manufacturing all around us. My father and stepmother, Hazel, lived in an apartment above Golden's Bakery on Williams Street. Dad and Hazel lived in a two-story apartment with a large bedroom upstairs. The access to the apartment was via an inside staircase that was attached to the wall of the bakery. There were three dwellings and the bakery that used one common bathroom. As you may imagine, this posed some bathroom access problems from time to time (this may have been the reason that Dad never took a bath but took a sponge bath instead).

When we arrived at my dad's apartment, we told my dad and Hazel what had happened. I later discovered that the reason that my mother kicked us out was because she was having an affair with a streetcar conductor, and my brother found out about it. She was afraid that he would tell our stepfather, Tony. So she kicked us out, and we went to live with my dad and Hazel. Hazel seemed to resent us being there, but she tolerated us.

In the fifth or sixth grade, I was transferred to a new school that was more strict in discipline. Here I wouldn't (or couldn't) do the work. My teacher would give me a paddling in the hall outside the classroom, and then she would send me to the principal, where I would get another paddling; then the principal would call my dad, and I would get a beating again at home that night. The principal would tell me, "You're going to learn or I'm going to beat you to death." That was also the attitude of both my dad and stepdad.

In the sixth grade, in their attempts to encourage me to pay attention in class, I was subjected to a "pat-down search" every day. A woman staff member would meet me at a locker, where I had to dump everything in my pockets; it was locked up until I went home. The reason for this is that in class I would play with batteries, flashlight bulbs, or wheels during the class time instead of listening to the teacher and doing the lessons.

I can't remember if I actually did any of the school work they wanted me to do or not, but I can remember the beatings. My teacher would take me into the hall outside of the classroom and make me hold out my hands, and she would beat the back of my hands until they were swollen. As she beat me, she would say, "Cry, damn you, cry," but I wouldn't cry. I still remember that her eyes just gleamed, which indicated to me that beating me gave her some kind of pleasure. I believe that I was the whipping boy, where she dumped her frustrations because of her unhappy home life. Sometimes my hands were so swollen that I couldn't hold a pencil, and this meant a trip to the principal's office for another beating.

Whenever the principal would call my father and tell him how uncooperative I was, at home that evening I really got a beating. There were times that I went to bed with the belt-marks of three people on my body from the beating I had received that day. However, no one thought to look deeper into why I was so difficult to handle. Even today, I have no ready explanation for all the problems I had developed; all I know is I had plenty of problems.

I failed the seventh grade. For some reason, my teacher told me that if I would learn and recite three verses of "The Star Spangled Banner" in front of the seventh grade class, she would pass me to the eighth grade. I refused and so she failed me. The next year, about a month into the seventh grade for the second year, the school principal opened the class door and called me to him with his index finger. I thought to myself, *I'm not taking another beating from this man*, and so I went out of the classroom with my fists doubled up. As we were walking to his office, he placed his arm around my shoulders and said, in a fatherly tone, "Marty, school is not for everybody, and you are one of those people."

When we got to his office, he gave me some papers and told me to take them home to my parents. As I was leaving his office, he told me to never come back to that school again. As I left campus, I deposited the papers into a trash can.

By this time, I was spending more time on the street than at home, so my parents didn't know that I had been expelled until midterm grades, which came out more than a month later. When my dad and stepmom found out about me being expelled from the seventh grade, there was virtually no reaction. I guess they had just given up.

The effect of all this is that I was completely convinced that I was a bad person and that if God existed, I believed he hated me because I was such a bad person. Now I was all alone, with no one to watch me all day. It was 1951, and I was fifteen years old. To me, being beaten, rejected, and living in isolation was just the way things were in the world. I guess that's because I had never known anything different; I thought all my problems were my fault.

As a child, it never occurred to me that some of the adults in my life had problems themselves. As an adolescent, I thought everybody was treated this way; I just believed that "that's life." Of course, I now know that that is not true, but this didn't occur to me until after I joined the navy in 1955 at the age of nineteen.

As hard as it seems, I now realize that being kicked out of school at fifteen, may have been better than staying in school and fighting the system. I didn't participate in any sports, I didn't have any friends, and I sure didn't have a girlfriend. In my social life I was a pariah (someone with extremely low socially importance). In 1951, in Lockland, there were no social services to deal with dysfunctional families or psychological services to help wayward children from those families. But the state of Ohio was to deal with the issue of me being a vagrant child soon enough.

The only thing that brought stability into my life during this time was my brother Frank. This seems strange to me now because we fought like cats and dogs. In fact, we would frequently go out into the alley and duke it out. Fist fighting was just the way we settled our differences, but we both seemed to draw strength from one another. In reality, the only place of sanctuary that either of us had was a brother who was himself just a child in the same dysfunctional family, learning to live a dysfunctional life.

My dad and stepmother made it very clear that they despised both Frank and me. Hazel worked just across the street in a bar/restaurant called the King-Bee. We would frequently eat at the King-Bee, because this was the easiest way for my stepmother to handle meals. However, when we did this, she would let us know just how much she disapproved of us and how much trouble we were to her. Today, this home atmosphere would be described as dysfunctional, just as the home atmosphere of my biological mother and stepfather would be described as dysfunctional, and the atmosphere of my foster home was dysfunctional. By writing this, it is very apparent that the lives of my sister, my brother, and me were dysfunctional from birth on, but I don't believe that term had been invented at that time.

One other vivid memory comes to mind. My dad and step mom would make us go to bed at nine o'clock, even in the summertime. We would go up to our sweltering room while they would sit outside of our apartment in the cool of the evening and drink buckets of beer. I thought this was grossly unfair, and I also think that today. It seemed that we were in the way and that parenting was forced upon them, and that they provided the least amount of parenting that was possible. Looking back, I realize that they took care of us just because we had no place else to go. Frank and I were not wanted children, and we both knew it.

¶#16: A Kid's Solution

The question comes to mind that if a child's home-life is painful, or if children are not treated well by their parents, what can they to change it? In today's world, children are taught to go to their teachers and tell them what is happening at home, and the civil authorities will investigate. But in the early 1950s, children weren't taught to appeal to medical or state welfare authorities. Our method of changing our home environment was the same that almost all children think of at one time or another: we ran away from home. I was about fourteen and Frank was sixteen when we ran away. Frank had heard that the Army National Guard would hire young boys to be orderlies at Camp Perry in Sandusky. Of course, whatever Frank said, I believed. So we got our things together and started to hitchhike to Camp Perry.

Camp Perry is a National Guard training facility located on the shore of Lake Erie in northern Ohio, near Port Clinton. We had about five dollars each when we set out, and we thought that we could buy candy bars to eat along the way. Our strategy was to hitchhike during the day and sleep in barns along the way at night. This did not prove to be such a good idea because we were sleeping with rats, spiders, and other insects that scared us half to death.

It took two days to reach Camp Perry by hitchhiking. One driver took us right up to the front gate, but when we got there, the base was closed. All we could do was turn around and head home, and it took us two days to hitchhike home. By the time we got home, we hadn't eaten anything for about two days.

When we got to our apartment, Frank's guitar was on top of the trash can, smashed to pieces. In a burst of rage, our father had smashed Frank's guitar; it was a warning of what was to come next. Of course we knew we were in trouble, but we had little choice; we had to go upstairs and face the music. Up the stairs we went, to receive very substantial beatings from our dad. Our father's form of punishment hadn't changed since the day we came to live with him and our stepmom more than four years earlier.

When I was about fourteen and a half, Frank turned seventeen, and on his birthday, he went into the army. Frank never told me what he intended to do; he did this without my knowledge. This hurt my feelings severely.

¶#17: Arrested at Sixteen and Put into the Adult Jail

The day my brother went into the army, I came home from school and asked, "Where is Frank?" My dad replied curtly, "He went into the army." This reality hit me hard; I was instantly aware that I was alone in this world, without a friend. With Frank's leaving, my only friend was gone, and he was the only thing that brought any semblance of stability to my young life. Frank's leaving removed the last thing that prevented me from openly rebelling. The result was that I became a terror.

From the time that Frank went into the army, I began to get into trouble with the law; I began to spend nights on the street. When I came home, my dad would beat me until I begged him to stop. There was no bonding connection between him, my stepmother, or me; we hated each other. I was dirty and drunk most of the time. No one would have anything to do with me; I had no friends.

The result of all this was that I became a bully. My life had gone from bad to a life of horror, where brushes with the law landed me in juvenile hall on multiple occasions.

During this time, I used to sit in the stands of the high school football field at night and cry. I would try to pray, saying over and over, "Why do you hate me, God?" I can remember sleeping in the alley behind the apartment. I remember looking up one night and, with a street light at his back, seeing my father coming looking for me with the belt in his hand. I knew what this meant; he had drunk his fifth of wine and six pack of beer, and after a couple of shots of whiskey, he was looking for someone to beat—and that someone was me. This terrified me. Sadly, this was just another evening in the life of a confused child in the home of confused adults. I now realize that when people treat their children this way, they most likely have been treated this way by their parents or guardians. For a child, this was life in the jungle of adult humanity that did not know anything different, and they were raising children to be just like them.

Another time when I was on the street, I got caught stealing candy for food. I could only eat what I could steal. One time, when arrested by the Lockland police, instead of them taking me to juvenile hall, they took me to the adult jail. There was zero tolerance for delinquent teenagers in the Cincinnati penal system (I was still in my sixteenth year of life). Perhaps the reason that I was taken to the adult jail was that after a previous arrest and time in juvenile hall, the director of delinquent services wanted me to go home with him, but I refused. I was just a kid, but I knew what he must have intended. He said that he wanted me to go to his farm in Kentucky, live on his horse farm, and learn to take care of his horses. I suspected that he was up to no good, so I shot off my big mouth and told him what a no-good SOB he was. For this reason, I believe he was the person responsible for putting me into the men's jail.

¶#18: Mr. Blue

At sixteen, I was a tall skinny kid with sandy hair. I remember walking through the Cincinnati men's jail with the jailer, and prisoners on both sides were asking him to put me into the cell with them; they were making remarks and gestures that were repulsive, even to me, and it scared me. They made no bones about what they wanted, and it nearly made me sick. When we got to the last cell, the jailer opened the steel door and pushed me in, as he said to the very large, mean-looking black man sitting on the bottom bunk with his shirt off, "Here Blue, here's some new meat for you."

When you get into an adult jail as a teenager, that is exactly what you are—a new piece of meat for the dogs to fight over.

As I stood there with my back to the bars, with tears in my eyes and my fists doubled up and the other prisoners shouting inappropriate remarks, the large black man in that cell got up and came toward me, shouting, "Shut up!" Instantly, the cell block was quiet. Immediately, I knew Blue was the boss in that cell block; this was the prisoner that no one crossed. He then looked at me with my fists doubled up and asked, "Are you going to hurt me with that?" He continued, "What I need is for you to come over here and sit down and talk with me. I'm not going to hurt you, I have sons your age."

When he got up from that bunk, I saw his many scars that he had earned on the streets of Cincinnati from knife fights and razor fights. He had just been convicted of killing two men in a razor fight, and he was awaiting sentencing. This was my cell mate. I sat down on that bottom bunk with Mr. Blue, and he told me that if I would stick with him, no one would bother me while we were together. He also told me, "You better hope that you leave here before I do, because if I leave before you do, you are going to be in trouble." I was the only sixteen-year-old in the adult jail.

I did stick with Mr. Blue; I carried his money in one pocket and his tobacco and cigarette rolling paper in the other pocket. I was his "bag man." Mr. Blue was my protector, and while I was with him, I was safe.

The only social pastime that we had in that jail was gambling. There was a ping-pong table set up in the middle of the cell block, and the prisoners would gamble on the games. One day I was standing there watching, when another prisoner came up behind me and touched me inappropriately. Mr. Blue saw this and reacted by knocking this guy completely over the ping-pong table, knocking the prisoner out cold. Mr. Blue turned to the other prisoners and told them, "If any of you touch this boy, you will answer to me." The other prisoners were afraid of Mr. Blue; they knew that he could handle himself in a fight and that he would enforce his words with whatever violence it took.

After that, I pretty much had the run of the cell block; no one bothered me. One day a prisoner walked right up to me and leaned into my face, and then extending his arms out to his sides, he said, "See, I didn't touch him." He then turned to me and said, "You better hope that you leave here before Blue, because if he leaves first, you're going to be mine."

Well, I did leave there before Mr. Blue. I was sent to the Ohio Boys' Industrial School to serve an undetermined sentence in the youth reform prison in Lancaster; time spent in the Boys' Industrial School was determined by behavior. One day, after I had been in Lancaster for about eight months, a guard walked up to me with a rolled-up newspaper in his hand. He showed me a small article at the bottom of a page that he had circled and asked, "Is this your hero, Mr. Blue?" This article said that Mr. Blue had been executed for the murders of the two men he had killed in Cincinnati. In my many conversations with Mr. Blue, he told me that he had killed the two men in self-defense; he was defending himself from their attack on him. I believed him then, and I believe him now.

I took that newspaper into the furnace room and cried for Mr. Blue. Here was one of the few men I had ever met that I could respect, and he had been executed for defending himself. I cried for Mr. Blue, and I cried for myself and the way my life was going. To this day, I still love this black man who took me under his wing and protected me from the sexual predators in jail. I wondered what had been Mr. Blue's personal experiences in life up to the time he found himself in jail accused of murder. If it hadn't been for Mr. Blue, I still wonder how things would be different in my life. Students often ask me if he sexually molested me; the answer is no, he did not.

¶#19: We Do What We Have Learned To Do Through Watching Our Parents

Later on in life, as I made a home for my wife and children, that home was also dysfunctional because that is all I knew; the things that I had learned prior to leaving home at about fifteen were to become the pattern I followed for a good part of my life. I treated my wife the way I had seen my dad and stepdad treat their wives, and I treated my children the way I had been treated. Children learn how to manage their lives by watching how their parents manage themselves, and especially how they manage their problems. When parents do not know how to handle life, their kids do not learn how to handle life. Almost everything I had learned from birth until well into my seventeenth year was dysfunctional, including my experiences at school. It seemed as if there was no guidance, no love, no nurturing atmosphere for me anywhere. I believe that Mr. Blue had a greater positive effect on me than any adult I had known from birth to finding myself in the adult jail, and he was executed for murder.

¶#20: Life Had Prepared Me To Be a Candidate for Chemical Abuse

To sum my young life, I was an excellent candidate for becoming a drug addict at some point in life. In my case, it didn't take long; that is what I did at eight years of age when I began to drink and at eleven when I began to smoke. In the absence of loving parental guidance, early life had not prepared me to deal with life head on, and the pattern that I had accepted was extremely dysfunctional. Anything that would bring even temporary relief from the continual emotional turmoil of self-rejection, guilt, hate, self-pity, and whatever other negative emotional mind-set one can muster at first became a welcomed friend. Then add the pressures of being newly married, earning a living, paying bills, expecting your first baby, the pressures of life squeeze out what's inside, and you look for an escape. When you drink as I did, or abuse drugs, your inhibitions are lowered, and what is inside comes spilling out in an unvarnished form. Then you have to live with the consequences. In addition, there are physical and mental changes that chemical abuse brings to your body; I will address these in a later section.

The emotional pain inside of an abused child is not very pretty. When my first son, Gary, was born, it was as if he provided an outlet for all my pent-up emotions. Gary took the brunt of my inability to handle the emotions of my undisciplined lifestyle, and I responded according to the pattern that I had learned in my home from those who took their frustrations out on me.

Like many children today, I followed the pattern that I had learned from birth. I verbally and physically abused my defenseless son. I treated him the way my father and stepfather had treated me; that's all I knew, and that is what I did.

My wife, Golda, also took abuse. She was forced to choose between leaving me or enduring the pain of living with someone that didn't know who he was supposed to be as a husband or father. To her credit, even after losing our house she did not divorce me, and we were reunited after a year of separation. In September of 2011, Golda and I celebrated our fiftieth wedding anniversary.

Golda is, and always has been, a committed lady, but it was impossible for her to nurture a family in the environment that I provided. Before stepping up to cocaine, I drank a lot of booze and smoked a boatload of cigarettes. I made Golda and my kids victims, like I was a victim. Because Golda and I had different home environments growing up, we saw life from different perspectives. Golda was from a big family with strong family ties; she was raised as a country girl, and she was very shy. After we were married, if we went to a party, she was very ill at ease. To this day, she is not very outgoing. She prefers to spend time with family and enjoys having a small gathering of friends come over occasionally. She is also an avid bowler.

Marty and Golda Gruber after fifty years of marriage in September of 2011.

When Golda and I married, I was one year out of the navy. I was very introverted, I hated myself, and I was convinced that God hated me. I was an absolute emotional mess but didn't realize how emotionally damaged I was. This internal emotional stress was a formula for the drug abuse and self-destruction that was to come.

¶#21: Marijuana

When a person has nothing to tell him what he should do, he is left only with what he can do. I did what many abused people do: I looked for a way to escape the pain of life, and this is what alcohol began to do for me at eight. Alcohol is a step drug, and in my case, it took years to move up to the next level, but move up I did. When I was introduced to marijuana at about forty-one, Golda and I had been married for about 16 years years. I cannot fully explain how drugs sometimes release the ugliness that is within the human heart, but that is what seemed to have happened to me. When we are under the influence of drugs, our inhibitions are lowered, and we do things we wouldn't do when sober. Drugs unleashed the full potential of self-hatred, with a bent toward self-destruction, that had been pent up within me from years of abuse in my youth. In Part 2 of my life's story, we will begin when I was about fifteen after Frank had joined the army.

SECTION ONE
GETTING TO KNOW MARTY
FROM AGE FIFTEEN TO FINDING LIFE'S CALLING

¶#22: The Raging River of Life

One night as I sat in the football stadium, crying and sadly reviewing the pain in my life, I realized that I did not know how to combat the evil that I saw all around me. I was just a little fish in a big pond, and I couldn't see how the direction of my life was going to change. It seemed as if I was being swept along by the raging river of life, and I believed that what ever Power lay beyond our senses was angry with me, but I did not understand why He was angry or what to do about it if He was angry. I had no explanation for why life was so painful, and my future looked hopeless to me; I wished I had never been born.

Since that time, I have observed that some people who do significant things in this world realize that they have a calling to accomplish something special. They somehow discern a Providential upward call to use them some way, even though they do not recognize the source of that call. Looking back, I now realize how that was true of my life, although I did not realize it when I was fifteen. I was to experience this call in a motel room at the age of fifty-three, after being a drug abuser for more than forty-five years.

It is not necessary to explain that life can be unfair to some people; they have learned about the pain of life the hard way: they have experienced it. This is how I felt. I had no idea that the things I was experiencing would uniquely prepare to me to communicate truth later in life. I felt that if God was real, He didn't like me; that He was punishing me for being a bad person. I believed I was a misfit and that no one wanted me—not even God.

I had no understanding that the seemingly random act of kindness extended to me by Mr. Blue had happened before, and that it was going to happen several more times in the course of life.

As a boy of fifteen, I knew nothing of the religious stories of paradise lost; I knew nothing of what some describe as a wonderful divine presence that reaches for us through the pain of this world, or of a Providential call to teach drug awareness that I was to receive thirty-eight years in the future. Through my pain as a fifteen-year-old, I wondered if there was a Higher

Power capable of caring. I had no thought that an intelligence beyond this world was aware of my pain. However, as explained below, I have come to believe that some form of Providence was protecting me in ways that I could not recognize. In fact, I did not recognize this for another thirty-eight years, and even then it took time for me to grasp a little bit of what it all means. The fact that I was under the protective hand of divine Providence has only become visible to me in hindsight.

It also seems that at times, the world of evil may even have an awareness of someone whom Providence has chosen for performing good works—individuals that Providence is grooming to perform significant works in the lives of other people in a later time. The good works they have been prepared to do, many times, are the testimonies of how a Higher Power has made a difference in their personal life, even as they endured the pain of this world. This was happening to me through the events disclosed below, but I did not realize what was happening as I endured the pain of child abuse and substance abuse related in this book. However, this Providential care has extended right into the present time, as will be evident as I share what has happened, even in recent years. I believe that most of us have such stories, but not everyone recognizes the hand of Providence as it is working in our lives.

While sitting in the football stadium at fifteen, the time when I would make a covenant with Providence to spend the remainder of my life performing the good works that I was called to perform was still thirty-eight years in the future. I was going to endure a lot of pain from drug abuse during those thirty-eight years, as were those around me whom I loved. At fifteen years old, I believed that I was the source of all my problems, and the adolescent mind of a fifteen-year-old boy, deceived by the evil in this world, had concluded that "God," if He exists, was mad at him. However, later but still as a teenage boy, I pondered that if God was mad at me, why would Mr. Blue protect me at the risk of his own life, when seemingly there was no benefit in it for him? Why did this man do what he did? I pondered this for many years with no clear answer.

However, it is from Mr. Blue and the following events addressed below that years later I would understand that we sometimes endure great pain so that we can effectively steer others around a major reef in life they can choose to avoid—if they will. It was as if divine Providence was grooming me to warn young people of a big reef that they seem not to see as they are being lured into throwing their lives away for the very temporary and self-destroying experience of getting high on drugs. It has become my purpose in life to tell young and unsuspecting teenagers of the drug predator who desires to use them for his personal financial gain and for whatever else he can draw them into for his personal benefit, without regard for the pain his snare will cause them in their lives. I've heard it said that we have a guardian angel to protect us; I don't know if that is true, but I believe that I have experienced that protection.

¶#23: Nearly Electrocuted

While growing up, there were times that I thought that my next breath was going to be the my last. Over and over, it seemed as if Providence would intervene in the nick of time to save me from a horrible wound, or even death. The first such time came when I was about twelve, while my brother and I were living with our dad and stepmom in the apartment above Golden's Bakery on Williams Street.

My brother and I shared a room facing Williams Street, where the neon lights of the city would shine into our room at night. We had no air conditioning, and in the summertime, this room was hot and humid at night, making it difficult to sleep, so we slept with the windows open.

Even though we lived on the edge of a city, our local community of Lockland still retained a small town atmosphere. Around our apartment was an array of stores. Mr. Lawrence owned a small mom and pop grocery story across from our apartment. Mr. Lawrence used to help me collect paper and metal so that I could sell them for recycling. In this way, I made a little extra money. One day, Mr. Lawrence said he needed someone to mow his lawn; he was willing to pay me fifty cents to mow both the front and back lawns at his home. At that time you could get a candy bar for a nickel and a Coke for six cents, a pint of whiskey for forty-five cents, and a half gallon of beer for fifty cents. I thought I needed all of these things, so I took him up on his offer.

When I arrived at his house, I discovered that the grass was quite high; the mower was a cast iron reel push mower with a wooden handle that was quite heavy and difficult for a twelve-year-old boy to handle, especially in high grass. In addition, the grass was wet from the dew and mist of the overcast early Cincinnati summer. But the fifty cents was beckoning to me, so I started to cut the grass. I did not always focus all of my attention on the work that I was performing; I had the understanding and attention span of a twelve-year-old boy. This may have contributed to what happened next.

In Mr. Lawrence's backyard, there was a grape trellis supported by steel poles, and some of these poles also supported wires that went back to his garage. I knew Mr. Lawrence expected me to do a good job, and this meant cutting the grass in hard-to-reach places. The layout of the backyard required that I had to move the steel poles so I could mow right up to the edge of the walkway through his backyard. So I began removing them one at a time.

When I grabbed the third steel pole to remove it, I instantly felt like I had been kicked in the chest by a mule, and I slumped to the ground. I could not let go of the steel pole. I was receiving an electric shock, and I remember hearing the sound of the alternating current sizzle as it burned my left hand and left foot. I slumped down in extreme pain from the burn, and I was traumatized from the continuing shock. As I lay slumped down, I remember calling out for help. It seemed that I cried out for a very long time, and the pain in my hand and foot just got worse and worse. It seems weird, but as this experience was progressing, I saw a very bright, beautiful white light that at first seemed to be a great distance away. As I looked, this light came closer and closer.

It so happened that Mr. Lawrence's neighbor, Mr. Copsey, was looking out of his back window and saw me slumped down on the ground. As he opened his back door, he could hear me screaming in a broken, distressed voice. Upon hearing the call for help, Mr. Copsey ran from his house and leaped over the low fence, coming to render whatever assistance he could. As all this was progressing, the light I saw was getting brighter and larger and coming ever closer.

Mr. Copsey recognized immediately that I was being electrocuted; he grabbed the mower by the wooden handle and flung it away. This action broke the ground to my left foot, and the electrical circuit through my body was broken. The next thing I remember was lying on the ground, fading in and out of consciousness. Next I remember hearing a fire truck's siren, and then I remember hearing the voice of a police officer, saying, "There is no help for this boy, because he's dead." I don't know how long all of this took, but it must have taken anywhere from fifteen to thirty minutes.

The next thing I remember was hearing a lot of voices, and something clamped over my face, suffocating me. The firemen had placed an oxygen mask on my face, but they did not realize that nothing was coming out of it. It was at this point that I began to struggle, but the harder I struggled, the harder they pushed the mask on. I realized that if I stopped struggling, I could breathe through a small gap where the mask did not cover all of my mouth. In a small span of time, they realized I was conscious, and the police and firemen took me home, which was just a short walk from Mr. Lawrence's house. They carried me up the stairs and put me in my bed, and I finally got that mask off of my face so I could breathe.

My dad and stepmom were home, and of course they thanked everyone for saving my life; they even called our family doctor, who came to our apartment and checked me over. I had burns on my left hand and left foot, and my muscles were extremely sore and everything in my body ached. Somehow, this event got into the local paper, and I was the center of attention in the neighborhood for a day or so.

Two days after this accident, I went to visit Mr. Copsey, who was an older retired man. His wife had made chocolate chip cookies, and after she filled me up with cookies and milk, we began to discuss what had happened. We went into Mr. Lawrence's yard, and there was the lawn mower, right where Mr. Copsey had flung it two days earlier. He struggled to pick it up, but it was too heavy for him; we laughed about the fact that he had flung it away with ease just two days earlier. It is amazing what adrenaline will do to alter one's strength. In addition, the fuse box that was the overload protection for the electric circuit was open; Mr. Copsey had removed the fuse as a safety precaution. The poles that supported the electric line were also lying on the ground. I later found out that Mr. Lawrence was cited by the police for having an unsafe condition in his yard.

As I learned about electric circuits later in my professional life, I realized that if there had been a good electrical connection between my hand and that pole, I probably would have died. I never told anyone about the fire department nearly suffocating me or about the bright light that I saw, because I didn't think anyone would believe me. As I have learned about near death experiences and people seeing bright lights during that kind of experience, I realize that an angel must have come near and somehow rescued me from the jaws of death, and he used Mr. Copsey to do it. This was the second time that a divine Providence rescued me from a very dangerous experience that could have ended my life.

¶#24: Mr. Goldstein

Another incident of providential protection, which was not so dramatic on the surface, occurred in Lockland. On the corner where my brother sold papers after school, there was a blacksmith's shop that had been there since the late 1800s. We had never gone into it, because it was no longer open for business. One day there was a lot of activity in this shop, and we looked inside to see what was happening. A young man and his wife were in the garage, and there were children playing around the shop. They were there with a work crew cleaning up this large building. The young man was Mr. Goldstein, the building's new owner. Mr. Goldstein intended to open a blacksmith and welding shop.

As it turned out, I got a job with Mr. Goldstein. He couldn't afford to pay me much, but he was willing to teach me how to weld and pay me a little to help him. He needed a helper and I needed extra money, so I began working after school and on weekends for him. I really thought Mr. Goldstein was a very nice man, and he was someone I could look up to.

As things worked out, our milkman needed an assistant for the coming Saturday, and he offered me more money than Mr. Goldstein was paying. About nine o'clock, as we were delivering milk, we heard an explosion and saw billows of black smoke coming from the blacksmith's shop. Of course, we had to see what had happened, and so we immediately drove to that area.

Laying in the street with coats over him and people attending him was Mr. Goldstein, badly burned. His burns were so bad that his clothes had been burned off; he was burned over a large percentage of his body. When we asked what happened, we were told that he was working under the dashboard of his truck, attempting to fix the fuel gauge, and he had taken the cap off of the gas tank. He decided to have a smoke so he just stretched out while under the dashboard, and lit up. The old Dodge truck he was working on had a gasoline tank behind the front seat, and apparently fumes had somehow collected under the dashboard. When he lit up, these fumes exploded, and he had been blown from under the dashboard through the wall of the shop into the street, where we saw him. He was so badly burned that he died en route to the hospital. If I had been working for Mr. Goldstein that Saturday, I probably would have been under the dashboard with him and would have been killed too. Was a Higher Power looking out for me? I believe so.

In addition to losing my employer, Mr. Goldstein, the only adult in my life that I looked up to had been killed. I was alone again in the world.

¶#25: The Ohio Boys' Industrial School

Another near death experience occurred while I was in the Boys' Industrial School in Lancaster, Ohio. This "school" consisted of three-story dorm buildings with the sleeping dorms on the third floor, a day room on the second floor, and a basement where we spent most of our time when we were not in our work area. I was supposed to be learning the welding trade, but this was a joke. We did nothing but sit; there was no training.[2] These buildings were called "cottages" in an attempt to make them sound less intimidating, but that was also a misnomer. They were more like very clean prisons for boys. They were not prisons because the buildings were bad, they were prisons because the administration did nothing to help the boys sent there for rehabilitation and education, and we were not free to leave, and at least in my case, they tolerated physical abuse. Calling this facility an "industrial school" was a mischaracterization.

---

[2]   The following description of the Ohio "Boys' Industrial School" was taken from website http://www.ohiohistorycentral.org/entry.php?rec=2113 on February 25, 2011. The experience recounted herein by Marty Gruber and the Ohio History Central website are not consistent with each other. That discrepancy hardly renders the description of Marty's experience there inaccurate or unreliable. There have always been stories of brutal abuse of inmates in prison, and especially in youth prisons, where the children frequently are abandoned by guardians. In modern times these abuses have been substantially reduced, but despite the best intentions of government, they still occur. It is not the intention of this story to discredit any person or institution, it is merely the goal to present Marty's experiences.

In 1857, the Ohio government established the Ohio Reform School, the predecessor to the Ohio Boys' Industrial School. The Ohio Reform School was a reformatory for boys between eight and eighteen years of age. It was located approximately five miles south of Lancaster, in Fairfield County, Ohio, and the institution accepted its first inmate in 1858.

Before the creation of this institution, the state of Ohio imprisoned male juvenile offenders in the Ohio Penitentiary with adult criminals. The Ohio Reform School was not like a traditional prison. Walls and fencing did not surround the inmates. Rather, the Ohio Reform School utilized the "open system." The boys could traverse the grounds freely. They lived in cottages, not prison cells, with forty boys to a cottage. The cottages were named after rivers in Ohio. Guards, cottage matrons, and other workers supervised the boys, but the intent was to create an institution that would educate and instill good and productive values in the boys. Because of the Ohio Reform School's success, by 1901, twenty-eight states adopted the "open system" for their juvenile prisons.

Each boy arrived at the Ohio Reform School with a certain number of demerits, which were based on the severity of their crime. For good behavior, students lost demerits. Once they reached zero demerits, the boys were freed and returned to their families. Students could also have demerits added for bad behavior, and in extreme circumstances, corporal punishment was permitted.

The boys spent one half of the day in school and the other half either working on the Ohio Reform School's farm or learning a trade in one of the vocational education buildings. In 1901, the school offered training in blacksmithing, tailoring, baking, carpentry, stenography, brick making, shoemaking, horticulture, and cattle-raising, among numerous other professions. This same year the institution also boasted a forty-two-member band, and the children received military training as well.

In 1884, the Ohio Reform School became known as the Boys' Industrial School. Comedian Bob Hope spent some time at the Boys' Industrial School as a child. As an adult, Hope donated sizable sums of money to the institution.

The Ohio Department of Mental Hygiene and Correction began overseeing the Boys' Industrial School in 1954. In July 1980, the institution ceased to operate as a juvenile reformatory, and the campus was converted to a medium security prison. (This paragraph was taken from website http://www.myqualitytime.net/2009/09/boys-industrial-school-rd-to-revenge.html)

In 1964, the institution became known as the Fairfield School for Boys, and in 1980, the school became the Southeastern Correctional Facility for adult offenders. In 2004, juvenile inmates were held in eight juvenile detention centers across Ohio.

Behind the cottage was a fairly level grassy area, where we were allowed to play flag football. In 1953, this whole compound was fenced in with a high chain-link fence topped with barbed wire. Unknown to me, there was an area in the back of the compound, down a small hill, where it was hard to see the fence. Two of the boys had found this location and were digging an escape tunnel under the chain-link fence. Our "home parents" (supervisors of our dorm) were watching the football game, and older boys were patrolling the grounds. When the two boys finally finished digging the tunnel that afternoon, they made their great escape. I was sitting on the grass with my back to the boys who were digging their way out, watching the football game, with no knowledge of what the two boys were doing.

All the inmates wore blue denim pants with white pinstriped shirts and sailor hats, and we marched in formation everywhere we went; everyone had their assigned spot in the regimental formation. I suppose this was designed to make it easy to spot missing boys. As we fell into formation to march to dinner, the two open spots in the formation were spotted, and this set off the warning sirens. Two boys had run away, and prison management didn't like that very much.

Mr. Richardson, one of the home parents, came to me and asked, "Where are the two missing boys?" I told him I didn't know, and he seemed to accept this. I thought this was the end of it.

Dinner came and went, and afterward the boys went to the basement, where we spent most of our time sitting and doing nothing. Then at eight o'clock, we were required to prepare for bed, which meant removing all of our clothes and hanging them on a rack behind our assigned chair and then putting on a nightgown over our otherwise completely nude bodies.

In the evening, after we had prepared for bed, communications from the home parents to any boy in that cottage was passed from one hall monitor to another until the individual boy received the message intended for him. That night, a message came: "Gruber, to the day room." I got up and proceeded to walk up the stairs to the day room as ordered. As I went up the stairs, the two hall monitors in the basement fell in behind me. When I reached the day room, all the furniture had been removed, and there was one dim light in the middle of the room. When I saw this, I hesitated and was immediately kicked from behind, knocking me to the floor. It was then that I heard Mr. Richardson say very coldly, "Get under the light."

I got up and stood under the light. Then Mr. Richardson said, "I'm going to ask you one more time where those boys went, and if you don't tell me, we are going to beat you to death." I started to cry and said, "I don't know." Immediately my nightgown was ripped from my body, and I was standing there naked. Then fists and boots came from every direction; the beating had begun. Mr. Richardson repeated over and over, "Where did those boys go? I want to know where those boys went." The punches, kicks, and stomps come from all directions and didn't stop. I was kicked in the left ear, and my eardrum was broken; all I could hear were the thuds of punches and kicks and stomps. This went on until I didn't feel the blows to my body any longer. As the beating progressed beyond this point, there was no more pain. It was at this time that we heard the voice of an angel as she entered the room.

Mrs. Richardson walked into that room and screamed, "My God, what are you doing to that boy? You stop that right now!" It was then that I passed out, but she had saved my life. When I regained consciousness, I was in a dark room on a bed, but I couldn't open my eyes or raise my head, and my left ear was buzzing, and every part of my body felt as if it was on fire. I was sobbing. I couldn't raise my head because it was stuck to the pillowcase with my own dried blood.

I panicked and ripped the pillowcase from my head. I then stood up and began looking for the door. I found a light switch. It wasn't until I turned the light on that I realized that my eyes were swollen shut. I took my index finger and thumb of each hand and opened my eyes, and then I realized that I was in an isolation ward. The isolation ward was for those who got sick; this is where they were taken so that the whole ward didn't catch whatever they had. I was the only person in this ward. Somebody had put my underwear on me, but I didn't have a nightgown on. I had no idea how long I had been there.

It was soon after I regained consciousness that I heard the voice of the school's alcoholic doctor, talking to Mr. Richardson. When I heard Mr. Richardson's voice, I wet myself. I heard the doctor say, "My God, Rich, this boy should be in the hospital."

Mr. Richardson replied, "Shut up, you damn drunk, and treat him. Do you know what would happen if we put this boy in the hospital, the questions that would be asked?"

The doctor repeated, "This boy should be in the hospital; I will not be responsible for him."

The room in the isolation ward consisted of a light in the center, a sink, a chair, and a bed. No one cleaned me up or attended to my wounds; that was up to me. When my eyes began to open, I saw what a mess I really was. I was black, yellow, green, blue, and purple; my sides were yellow and ached; and my ears still were ringing (and after fifty-eight years, they are still ringing, and I am still partially deaf in my left ear). Fortunately I had no broken bones. I was in the isolation ward for two weeks before I was healed enough to leave. The doctor visited me two other times while I was in the ward.

The only other visitor that I had during those two weeks was a night watchman, who was an outside contractor. He brought me some reading material, which I appreciated. I was served cold food from the cafeteria after dinner was over. In addition, the large windows were covered with yellow paper, and Mr. Richardson warned me not to remove the paper. I was afraid to touch it. After two weeks, my body had healed up pretty well. The isolation ward was essentially solitary confinement, where no one could see the evidence of the beating I had received.

One day the door opened, and in walked Mr. Richardson, holding a new set of clothes: new pants, new shirt, new underwear, new socks, new shoes, the works. He was also holding a blue badge. In the Boys' Industrial School, new clothes were the most important status symbol that any inmate could have; anybody that had new clothes, or clothes that were not worn out, was not to be fooled with. The other status symbol was a blue badge. The inmate monitors wore blue badges, and the people who were serving the last six months of their sentence also had blue badges.

Mr. Richardson walked in and ordered me to sit down on my bed, and then he sat down. He told me that the boys who had run away had been caught, and he now knew that I had nothing to do with their escape. He thought that I was their lookout. He did not apologize but said, "If you ever tell anyone about this, I will kill you." As he said this, he stared intently into my eyes, and I had no doubt that he meant what he said.

He informed me that he had arranged for me to become a night telephone operator. He said that I would sleep during the day in a small separate dorm and that I could come and go as I pleased to the dining hall. He said that I was to report for my new position at five o'clock that evening for training. After Mr. Richardson left, the door was left unlocked, and I was free to leave in time to fill my new position.

When I got dressed in my new clothes and put on my blue badge, I felt like a king. I walked out of the isolation ward to my new position of night operator, just like I owned the world. The inmate monitors who had beaten me up came to me and told me that if I ever had a problem, I was to let them know and they would take care of it for me. I was never beaten again or had a significant problem with anyone in that prison.

Later, the prison buzz said that the boys who had escaped had been beaten nearly to death after they were caught. I never saw them again or heard from them after that. I have no idea what happened to either of them.

The night operator position turned out to be just as Mr. Richardson had said. It was a responsible position, and for the first time in my life, I was treated with an element of respect. This was a great job for me, because I worked nights, Monday through Friday, slept during the day, and I had the weekends off. I was alone except for the weekends, and I liked it that way.

One of my responsibilities as the night operator was to awaken staff members that lived on the campus at five o'clock in the morning. One of these staff members was a chronic drinker, and many times he wouldn't come in until after the bars closed at two o'clock. After I had awakened him, this man would go back to sleep, and I had to awaken him several times before he finally got up. One morning, I got a little testy with him, and he made a formal written complaint to Mr. Kemper, the Boys' School disciplinarian. His complaint was that I had been disobedient to his order.

Soon after the complaint was filed, I was awakened and told to report to Mr. Kemper's office. The path to Mr. Kemper's office took me by the Boys' School hospital. As I was passing by the first-story rooms, there was a boy about my age sitting in one of the open windows. He taunted me, "You're going to see Mr. Kemper. You're going to see Mr. Kemper." When I looked at him, he asked, "What did you do?" So I briefly told him.

He responded, "You're in trouble." He said, "Look." He stood up and pulled up his nightgown, and his backsides from the buttocks down to just above his knees were black, blue, purple, red, and yellow, and they were still swollen; he had received a substantial beating with a paddle. This brought back an instant memory of my encounter with Mr. Richardson. He said, "Mr.

Kemper put me in the hospital." I walked on to Mr. Kemper's office, trembling, believing that I was going to receive the same treatment.

When I came to Mr. Kemper's office, I had to wait a short time before he came to summon me. He was a tall, mean-looking man with blond hair. When I went into his office, I stood at attention in front of his desk. He said, "Before I do anything, I want to hear your side of the story." So I told him just what had happened. He said, "I ought to beat you half to death and put you in the hospital; you don't get smart with any staff member. I've got a couple of letters here from staff members who have gone to bat for you, so I'm going to give you a warning. But if you ever come back here,"—he pointed to a line of paddles of various shapes and sizes hanging on hooks lining his wall—"I'll beat you to a pulp." He pointed to two footprints painted on the floor and said, "I'll beat you with your pants down and with you holding your ankles." He then pointed to the door and said, "Now get out of here and never come back." I speedily complied.

Over the year and one-half that I was in the Boys' Industrial School, I had exactly one visitor. My sister Mary Elizabeth came to visit me one time. Neither my parents nor stepparents came to visit. However, I survived it. I now realize that it was the grace of divine Providence that saw me through this very trying time in life. I got out of the Boys' Industrial School when I was seventeen. By Ohio law, I was required to continue my education until I was eighteen.

¶#26: The Shooting Range

The following events took place about fifty years after I left the Ohio Boys' Industrial School. As with the events described above, what happened on the shooting range could be entirely coincidental. On the other hand, the protection of Providence could have been working its wonders.

The story of David, my adopted grandson, is presented under Section Heading #2, under "David and Me." The incident on the shooting range took place while David was recovering from a near fatal drug overdose.

David and I enjoyed going to an indoor pistol range and shooting the two pistols I owned; shooting was actually physical therapy for David, as he was working to regain hand-eye coordination from brain damage he had received from his drug overdose. One of the pistols we were shooting was a Davis .380 semiautomatic; the other was a Smith and Wesson .38 Police Special. We enjoyed going to an indoor range at a gun store in Henderson, Nevada.

This range was typical of indoor firing ranges. It was in the back of the store, separated from the gun store in the front. Each shooter had his own stall with a target on a cable trolley system; each shooter could set his target and then retrieve it without interfering with other shooters. The target was held in place on the trolley with a heavy metal clip.

David was in the stall on my left, and I clipped his target onto the trolley carriage and reeled it out, ready for him to shoot. I reeled David's target to about forty feet—a good distance for a pistol shooter. He was becoming an accomplished marksman with that pistol. I clipped a target on my carriage and reeled it out, also about forty feet.

David was shooting the semiautomatic and I was shooting the .38 revolver. His gun jammed, so I gave him the .38 and took the .380 from him. I cleared the jam, reloaded it with a full clip, cocked it, and took aim. A shot rang out from David's stall, and my target floated to the floor.

This infuriated me; I asked David, "Did you shoot my target?"

He said, "Yes, but I aimed low."

So I asked him, "Why did you do that?"

He said, "I don't know. I aimed low; I didn't even aim up there."

In a huff I told him, "Finish shooting the shells in the revolver; I'll clean up and we'll leave." I walked back to where I had laid the .380 and saw what appeared to be a crack in the right side of the slide mechanism. This crack was less than a half-inch long. I turned the pistol over, and there was another crack just like it on the other side. I showed the cracks to David. I removed the clip, removed the shell from the firing chamber, and took the pistol into the store to show it to the salesman behind the counter.

He looked at the cracks and said, "Yep."

I looked at him and asked, "Yep what?"

He said, "Yep, if you would have fired this gun one more time, it would have blown apart in your hand and probably seriously harmed or killed you." This gun expert took my .380 semiautomatic and tossed it into a pile of scrap metal. He said that pistol had to be destroyed because it would never be safe to shoot again.

David and I went back into the shooting range and looked at the target that David had shot with the .38 revolver. It had been cleanly cut just below the point where it was attached to the cable trolley. We couldn't figure out how the shot had cut the paper so cleanly; it looked to be a nearly impossible shot. We concluded that the bullet had severed the paper as cleanly as if it had been cut with a sharp knife. Did this occur entirely by accident at the very moment it was needed to save me from serious injury or death?

Looking back on my life, there have been six significant events when I was miraculously spared from harm that would have killed me or caused my life to be drastically altered:

1. My near electrocution in Mr. Lawrence's yard while mowing his lawn. The vision of the bright light moving closer to me also appeared to me in a dream after I got off of drugs and Golda and I had gotten back together, about thirty-six years later. This is addressed under Section Heading #1, "An Invitation to Change My Life."

2. Being asked to perform work one Saturday by our milkman and escaping the accident in Mr. Goldsmith's shop, when he was burned to death in the gasoline explosion.

3. The protection given to me by Mr. Blue in the men's jail in Cincinnati when I was about sixteen.

4. Being nearly beaten to death by Mr. Richardson in the Ohio Boys' Industrial School, only to be saved by Mrs. Richardson.

5. Hearing a voice speak to me when I was attempting suicide while high on cocaine when I was fifty-three. Soon after, this same voice visited me in a dream, telling me I was called to speak to kids about the horrors of drug abuse—but I had to get off of

drugs myself. It was this communication that gave me hope that rehabilitation could really happen.

6. Escaping serious injury in Henderson, Nevada, while shooting pistols with David.

The probability of my life being saved six times as described above is exceedingly small.[3]

¶#27: The Move to El Sereno, California

While I was in the Ohio Boys' Industrial School, they had a list of my family members, and on several occasions they had contacted them to see if any of them was willing to take me as my legal guardian. For approximately one and one half years, none of them were willing to take me. When I was nearing eighteen, they wrote to my mother and told her that they were prevented from releasing me under my own recognizance until I was twenty-one years old. If no one took me, when I turned eighteen, they were required to place me in the Ohio Men's Reformatory or the Ohio Men's Prison. It was only then that my mother and stepdad agreed to take me as my legal guardians. In addition, by becoming my legal guardians, they were agreeing that I was to live with them until I was twenty-one.

My mother and Tony had moved to the East Los Angeles town of El Sereno while I was in the Ohio Boys' Industrial School, so it was necessary for Ohio to reach an agreement with the state of California before I left. The letter given to me when I departed the Boy's School was on letterhead of the Ohio penal institutions. This letter essentially said that I was given the liberty to travel to California to my mother's and stepdad's home, and if I got into trouble en route to California, or in California before I turned twenty-one, I would be returned to the Ohio penal system.

My mom and stepdad sent money to the Ohio Boys' School for my bus ticket to California and $5.00 for meals for the four-day bus trip. Things are just a blur after that. I was immediately outfitted with a new set of clothes, given verbal instructions on how to act en route, and given the letter I mentioned above. Off I went with an escort to the Greyhound bus station in

---

[3] If the probability of my life being saved by each one of the above events is 1 in 100 (i.e., 1/100; the probability is undoubtedly much lower than that), then the probability of my life being saved six times is calculated to be one chance in 100^6, which is a probability of one chance in a trillion ($1/10^{12}$; i.e. = 1/1,000,000,000,000). The probability is actually much lower than this. The probability of my life being spared six times as described above is so small as to be almost zero.

Lancaster. Fortunately I was to ride the same bus all the way to Los Angles. I had no intention of ever going back into the Ohio penal system.

At the time I left the Ohio Boys' Industrial School, I had been incarcerated for about one and one half years. Between the ages of about sixteen to seventeen and seven months, somebody had made all my decisions for me; I was poorly equipped to be on my own in the world of competitive people, where I had never developed social skills and where I had never learned to make the decisions that I now had to make. I left the school with a letter explaining my situation and with telephone numbers to call if I got into trouble or if something went wrong. My bus ticket was paid, and I had $5.00 in my pocket to feed me for four days en route. I did not know the working of the world, and to say that I was a frightened child of nearly eighteen on his own for the first time is an understatement. I was afraid to get off of the bus for fear that I would somehow get confused and get lost or get into some kind of trouble and be sent back to Ohio.

¶#28: Another Black Angel

The bus route went through every small town along a less than direct route to Los Angeles. At every stop, passengers and luggage would deboard and board. There were no rest stops along the way. We went from terminal to terminal and exchanged drivers as needed. Of course there was a bathroom on the bus, but there was no food. By the time we reached Saint Louis, Missouri, a day later, I hadn't been off the bus for more than a day and I was very hungry. It was at this stop that a very large black lady boarded the bus. There was only one seat open, and that was next to me. I prayed, "Lord, please seat her next to someone else." But there was no place else to sit. She asked me if the seat next to me was open, and of course I said yes. So she sat down, taking her seat and half of mine. I thought, *Oh Lord, why me?*

The woman had a small picnic basket in her lap. We began traveling, and after about two hours passed, we hadn't spoken at all. Finally she asked, "Are you hongry?" I said, "I'm starving." She said, "Chil', I've got some fried chicken in here and some home-made biscuits with jam and honey; would you like to share some fried chicken with me?" She opened that basket and gave me the best home fried chicken and biscuits that I have ever tasted. After that, we talked for a long time, sharing stories about out lives. We rode together all the way to Albuquerque,

New Mexico, where she got off the bus and met her brother. This lady bought me a couple of meals on the trip, because she knew that I didn't have a lot of money.

When we got to the LA area, I saw what seemed to be smoke everywhere. I later learned this was smog (smoke and fog). LA was my first exposure to smog. In the LA basin, residents had to learn to live with it.

¶#29: Free

When we got to the bus terminal in downtown LA, my mom and my stepdad were waiting for me. When I got off the bus, it suddenly hit me that I was free; I didn't have to go back to that place anymore. This hit me so hard that I cried. Mom hugged me and Tony showed the little emotion that he was capable of displaying in public.

I got along good with Mom and Tony. I had matured a little in the Ohio Boys' Industrial School, and I was beginning to understand that I had to work with others to get along. In California, I saw my probation officer just one time, about two weeks after I arrived in Los Angeles. After he spoke privately with Mom, he told me that if she had any trouble with me, I would be sent back to Ohio. He also insisted that I go to school until I was eighteen. The last thing I wanted was to be sent back to Ohio. I made up my mind that I was not going back, so I attended a school managed by the California Youth Authority for misfits. The school seemed to be specifically designed for gang members. When I was eighteen, I quit school and set out to seek my fortune in life. Needless to say, I was poorly equipped for the conquest of life with a seventh grade education.

¶#30: Butch

Several of Tony's family members lived in an apartment building nearby. Tony's sister had a son named Butch, who was about one year younger than I. She also had a daughter named Mary Francis, a little younger than Butch. Mary Francis and I got along very well, but Butch and I were kind of like a dog and cat; Butch was very mouthy and I didn't like that. Butch seemed to think it was fun to insult me; he would call me foul names whenever we met. Butch seemed to have a really sour attitude toward life, and I didn't need that kind of influence. I just didn't take Butch seriously; I just tried to ignore him.

One evening, Mary Francis was sitting in her living room and I was sitting on the front porch, talking to her, when Butch and one of his friends walked by. Butch took the opportunity to call me a few of his favorite adjectives. Butch's friend looked "buff," like a weightlifter; they were both juniors in high school. Butch also wore his shirt open to show his muscles. Butch's mom and dad were downstairs playing cards with Mom and Tony, and Butch was showing off for his friend by insulting me.

I got tired of the insults, so I left the apartment and went outside. I was walking through the parking lot, still feeling the sting of Butch's insults, when Butch and his friend came up behind me, still insulting me. I turned to Butch and asked, "Why can't we just be friends?" and put out my hand to shake hands. Butch continued to insult me as he reached his hand out. When our hands met, I grabbed his hand and pulled him into me as hard as I could while hitting his nose with my left fist as hard as I could. He hit the deck with his nose spread all over his face and bleeding rather profusely. He jumped up with his head down and arms swinging wildly, and I grabbed him by the back of the head and slammed his head into my upcoming knee—and that was the end of the fight.

Butch and his friend ran into the apartment, where our parents were still playing cards, and began to emotionally scream and cry, trying to tell them what I had done. Of course all parents came running and they had to put on their scene. Tony grabbed me and took me home, and that broke up the card game. Mom tried to smooth things over with Butch's parents. I was the bad boy of the family after that event.

For as long as I lived with Mom and Tony, I tried to be friends with Butch. However, he never spoke to me again. True to my promise to my probation officer, that was the only trouble I got into after arriving in Los Angeles.

¶#31: The Navy

I continued to look for a job, even though I had no skills and few people would hire someone without a high school diploma. I just kicked around the Los Angeles area, doing odd jobs until I landed a job in a machine shop, where I worked as a helper. I did not care much for that job but I kept it until I was nineteen and joined the National Guard. At nineteen I went through army boot camp at Fort Ord near Monterey Bay, California. In 1955, I graduated from army boot camp.

Boot camp at Fort Ord was tough, but I made it through. It didn't take me long to realize that the National Guard was not for me. Upon graduation, the world was between Korea and Vietnam. At that time, National Guard boots could transfer into the navy if approved. However, those who did so had to go through navy boot camp. I applied for this transfer and was accepted into the Navy. I went through navy boot camp at San Diego. This was a piece of cake after the more rigorous army boot camp. After boot camp, I volunteered for naval air service and was assigned to the anti-submarine squadron VS-37 based out of San Diego. I was in the Navy for four years. Because America was between wars, I never saw any combat action.

My job at San Diego Naval Air Base was duty driver, which meant that I was to drive pilots around, pick up and deliver mail, and shuffle both navy brass and civilians around the base. This kept me pretty busy, and it was interesting. One day, a young legal officer asked me, "Gruber, what are you going to do with your life?" I really didn't have an answer. He continued, "I have made arrangements for you to start in the electric shop tomorrow; you're going to learn how to work on airplanes and be an electrician." So I started in the electric shop.

My first job was very challenging: I had to keep the coffee hot and available. However, this assignment allowed me plenty of spare time, so I began to learn about airplanes just by being around them and observing and asking questions. I would help whomever I could and learned a great deal about the airplanes without ever being formally trained. Because I had no education, I couldn't take naval training courses. So I began to take correspondence courses. After eighteen months, I was deployed aboard the USS *Philippine Sea*, which was a straight decked aircraft carrier, a rust bucket from World War II. The anti-submarine squadron flew Grumman S2F airplanes with two piston-driven engines. Aboard the aircraft carrier, I somehow became flight deck electrician, and I worked very hard twelve hours per day; I learned a lot about that airplane.

When we got Stateside, I was transferred to Alameda Naval Air Base, where damaged jet airplanes from the Korean War were being restored. It was my job to evaluate these airplanes to determine if they were sound enough to undergo restoration. During this time, I continued to pursue correspondence courses. Eventually, I was allowed to take the test to become Electrician 3rd class, and I passed it. One year later, I took the test to become Electrician 2nd class; I also passed it. Because of navy rules, I had to wait two years before I could take the test to become Electrician 1st Class. Thirty days before being discharged, the captain called me in and gave me the obligatory sales pitch to reenlist, but I declined. I was burned out working on airplanes. When I left the Navy, I never intended to work on another airplane.

I got out of the Navy in August of 1959, when I was twenty-three years old. I learned two very important things in the Navy: (1) if you are going to be considered for a job, you have to have a skill that someone is willing to pay you to perform, and (2) hard work pays off.

¶#32: Learning About Work

My mom and stepdad still lived in El Sereno, in the East Los Angeles area. I kicked around LA for a while, doing odd jobs. Even with navy credentials, no one wanted to hire someone without a high school diploma. At my mother's suggestion, I went to the airport and applied for a job as an airplane mechanic. I applied at Western Airlines for work as an aircraft electrician.

Western Airlines was in desperate need of people with jet aircraft experience. They had just begun using the Lockheed Electra L-188 turboprop aircraft for hauling passengers. Because of my jet experience, I was fortunate enough to get an interview. It so happened that the person who interviewed me had a starter from a Lockheed Electra laying on his desk. This starter had become a problem for Western Air. I told the interviewer about the problems we had with the starter's centrifugal control switch. I also mentioned how we addressed the issue at Alameda Naval Air Station. Because of this, I got the job. After three months of probation, I worked for Western Air for the next eleven and a half years.

At Western Airlines, I learned what it meant to work hard; I also learned what hard work would do for a dedicated workman who was a valuable asset to his company. It was at Western Airlines that I developed the work ethic that was to allow me to share in the American dream. After eleven and a half years, I moved from being willing to work to knowing how to organize and perform work, and I was learning how to manage people to get work done through them. In 1971, I quit Western Air and moved on to better opportunities with the McCullough Oil Corporation, managing electrical maintenance on the Lockheed Electra L-188 turboprop aircraft.

At McCullough, I used my skills as an airplane mechanic and my skills in organizing airplane maintenance activities. Over the next five and one half years, I rose to manage six departments simultaneously, and my income reflected the ever increasing levels of responsibility. This went on until I got into a disagreement with McCullough's vice president, which led to me being fired. Six months later, this same vice president called me and asked me to come back and supervise the maintenance operations on swing shift, and I was glad to do so.

¶#33: From Marijuana to Cocaine to Pain to Telling Others What Not To Do

After I left the Ohio Industrial School for Boys, I continued drinking and smoking cigarettes. This continued through the Navy and through my time with Western Airlines and my first tour of duty with McCullough. It was after I came back to McCullough that I met and hired a young man who lived near me in Fountain Valley, California. This young man showed promise, and I wanted to help him if I could. Because he was short on money, he would drive to my house to ride with me to and from work. One morning as we were coming home, he reached into his shirt pocket and pulled out a funny-looking cigarette, asking me if I knew what it was. I told him that I had never seen a cigarette that looked like that. He told me it was a joint and asked me if I wanted to smoke it. I said, "Sure, why not?"

This was my introduction to smoking marijuana, which was one of the biggest mistakes that I have ever made; I was about forty-one or forty two when I smoked my first joint. I liked the feeling that it gave me. It helped me relax after a hard day under the pressures of work; it calmed and slowed me down; I thought I needed that. For this reason, I started smoking marijuana regularly. About two years later, I moved up to cocaine and became a coke addict.

It has been known for many years that marijuana is the so-called "gateway drug" to the white powdered drugs such as cocaine, methamphetamine, and heroin. Marijuana was the beginning of a downward tailspin for me. In just a few years, I went from being a smoker and alcoholic to also being a full-blown drug addict.

In preparing this book, I have thoroughly reviewed many of the above details of my life for the first time in many years. I didn't realize it as I progressed through life, but it seems as if Providence has always been preparing me for what is to come next and protecting me as needed. Looking back, I truly am convinced that a Higher Power has directed my steps through all the pain I have experienced in life. Divine Providence not only protected me from death on the several occasions listed above, but it also provided food for me when I was very hungry on the bus—and it protected my employment.

While I became very good in my profession, few employers would tolerate the things I pulled as a substance abuser. However, Providence has used the things that I experienced as a substance abuser to thoroughly prepare me for the work I was destined to perform later in life. Through my experience as a substance abuser for almost forty-five years, and my study of drugs after coming into sobriety, I believe divine Providence has prepared me to present the horrors of substance abuse to young people in a way they will listen to. I have had the experience of sitting in class and looking at teenage substance abusers in the audience, knowing that they were high and also knowing the substance some of them were using. Most people who teach about substance abuse do not have this comprehensive background, and the kids somehow pick up on that.

It is nothing short of miraculous that Providence seems to open the doors of opportunity and provide the understanding needed to effectively communicate or perform a specific feat at the time it is needed. I have come to see that the things I have related here didn't just happen by chance, but that the unifying foundation of truth that lies beyond this world is somehow involved in the events of this world. I have no explanation for why I was never busted by the police while high on drugs; it most certainly wasn't because this was an infrequent occurrence or because I was very clever in the way I did drugs.

Two of the great truths that I have come to grips with are that I have no purpose in and of myself, and that because Providence has led me this far it, will lead me to the end of my life in this world if I will remain willing to be led. The pain in my life has etched this idea deeply within my mind, where I believe I will retain it for eternity. As we experience pain, we frequently fail to see how it will change who we are. Certainly we fail to see that what we are experiencing today may be preparation for what is to come tomorrow. At the time we are in extreme discomfort, it may well be that we are in training, and while we may be uncomfortable with what is happening in our life today, we probably do not desire to hear that Providence may be preparing us for what will come later. But my experience is that whoever or whatever Providence is, it can pile pain higher and higher, until it finally gets our full attention.

The fifteen-year-old boy in the football stadium that night in 1952 knew none of this. However, by looking back over the years I see that divine Providence has given me understanding that has allowed me to put some of the puzzle pieces of life together. I now understand that one reason we are allowed to experience pain in this life is so we can be equipped to help others avoid the pitfalls of life that we fell into. Looking back, I have thought that if I could go back to being fifteen again, I would willingly devote my life to learning how to help others avoid the pitfalls of life. However, if I did that without going through the training process that life has brought me through, I would not have the very experience that allows me to share personal experiences about child abuse, about drug abuse, and about being part of a dysfunctional family. These experiences assist me in connecting with kids. I realize that I certainly would not have developed the ability to communicate the horrors of drug abuse, and the path out of drug abuse, to young people as effectively as I can through those personal experiences.

Before being addicted to illegal drugs, I became successful in managing the electrical disciplines needed to keep a fleet of planes flying safely. When working for McCullough Oil, I managed six departments at one time. Because of my thorough understanding of an airplane's electrical wiring, I was never without a good job. This was true even through my periods of extreme drug abuse. My business success allowed me to buy a nice a home on a cul-de-sac. I was to meet a wonderful girl, get married, have children, and reproduce a dysfunctional home similar to the one that produced me. **Then I was to lose it all because I became a drug addict. A drug addict is someone to whom drugs have become more important than anything else in life.**

¶#34: My Mother

I have described the dysfunctional character of my dad and his later life. My mother's life was equally dysfunctional. She suffered from multiple personality disorder (MPD), and her personalities would appear when she needed them to help her get what she wanted. My mother was very manipulative, and she used her various personalities to get what she wanted when she wanted it. I do not know how many personalities she manifested through her life, but I am aware of at least three.

First, there was the nice person who could make you believe that she was the sweetest person in the world, and in fact, this is how she generally presented herself. I believe the sweet person was the dominant personality. I used to call this the "mommy personality." I am not aware if the dominant personality knew about the other personalities, but in reading about MPD, it seems that this was probably the case. Next, there was the personality who would have almost anyone believing that the world was against her; this was her "pity me personality." When Mom wanted to control someone, this was the personality she frequently resorted to. Then there was the "vicious personality." When Mom was unhappy with you and was prepared to fight to win, this personality appeared.

An example of all three personalities appeared once when I visited Mom in her later years. She was living in the Boatman Retirement Home, a combination assisted living and full care rest home in Cincinnati, with a hospital and an Alzheimer's ward attached to it. Mom was in the hospital attached to this facility. While I was visiting her, a nurse's aide came into the room with a pair of support hose for varicose veins. She asked Mom to put these stockings on, as the doctor had prescribed them to treat her legs. She replied sweetly, "I'll put them on later; I'm visiting with my son right now."

A little later, the same aide came back into the room and said, "The doctor wants you to put these stockings on." Then the pitiful personality appeared, and the poor aide left, believing she had somehow hurt Mom's feelings.

After a little while, the same aide came back and said with a little more force, "The doctor wants you to put these on now."

Mom's eyes narrowed, and she said in a very deep voice, booming and resonating, "I said, I don't *want* to put them on!"

The startled nurse looked up and asked me, "Did you hear that?" I simply responded, "Yes." She left and didn't come back. I had heard that voice more than once in the past.

When Mom was done with you, it was usually a "once for all time" decision. When Tony got older, Mom decided she was done with him. She convinced the facility staff that Tony had Alzheimer's disease and had him put into the Alzheimer's ward. When Golda and I went to visit him, he asked pitifully, "Why are they keeping me here?" We spoke to the staff and they put him back into a regular room, away from Mom. She never visited Tony again after that, and she wouldn't allow Tony to come back to live with her. They lived separately in the same rest home from that time until Tony died.

¶#35: Seek Wisdom Where It May Be Found

It is not my desire to alienate anyone, but Providence has shown me that my life in the here and now may have meaning through the work that I have been called to perform. If preparation for becoming a drug abuse counselor required me to endure a little pain to enable me to help others avoid this specific pitfall in life, then so be it. I have concluded that the pain of training in the vacant halls of drug abuse for more than forty-five years has enabled me to speak with the authority that comes from doing what is right in my own eyes and suffering the consequences. If eternity lies beyond this world, as I believe, and if eternity is in the hands of Providence, the pain of my life has taught me that real wisdom and righteousness lie within Providence itself rather than within the essence of fragile humans who are helpless to look beyond their very limited understanding of what is immediately before them.

If this be true, then certainly I am willing to lay down my life for the benefit of others as I traverse this very dysfunctional society. I am willing to share what I have learned so that others may avoid the specific mistakes I made. Providence may introduce us to ultimate reality; I am looking for the city on the hill in which wisdom and righteousness dwell. I believe that Providence has led me into a life that finally makes sense out of all the pain I endured.

The message that I have been given to share is that the horrors of neglect and physical abuse, which I have already partially addressed, need not be the final chapter in any life. It certainly was not necessary for me to allow the abuse of my youth and my personal and willful ignorance in early adulthood to continually dictate my future. There is a path around much of the suffering I experienced, and I could have avoided many pitfalls in life if I simply had opened my eyes and learned by observing why I was having pain in life and why others around me were having pain in their lives. I have learned that our view of life and of ultimate reality is much too small. If I had been willing to hear the words spoken to me, or observe the message of consequences following my actions and the actions of those all around me, I could have avoided many pitfalls in life. But I was focused on *my* pain; I felt sorry for myself and blamed myself for my problems, and I sought escape from them, rather than dealing with them and proactively changing who I was, and who I was becoming.

Apart from being raised in a dysfunctional family, I persisted in doing what is right in my own eyes for many years, after I was old enough to see the pain of life and figure out how to avoid it. Thus, I persisted in my self-centered approach to life way past the time I should have, and could have, turned to a better way. That being said, the pain I have experienced has enabled me to understand the larger message that substance abuse is certainly self-inflicted pain that is completely avoidable in our very prosperous society.

The message of physical abuse and drug substance abuse are only the preparation that now allows me to present another message, which is to search for wisdom through life and follow the golden nuggets of wisdom to the mother lode of Providential wisdom. I have come to understand that there may be a message in physical abuse and substance abuse that may open the eyes of some to see the sheer folly of human wisdom apart from Providence and eternity. The message then is, "Seek the wisdom and guidance of the primary people around you, and look for meaning that transcends this world." The things that I have experienced along my path through life have become tools that enable me to point out specific snares in life to young and old people alike. It is my hope that my story may somehow enable them to make better decisions in their future. It is also my desire to help them find inner peace through the wisdom of discerning there is a world of wisdom and comfort beyond the world we see with our eyes, hear with our ears, feel with our hands, and taste and smell.

It is ironic that so many people seem to believe they can do things that have clearly destroyed the lives of other people, without getting hurt themselves. The testimonies of those who have willfully gone their own way while they pursue what is right in their own eyes and then stumble in the darkness of self-inflicted blindness is beyond my comprehension. However, I did exactly that for more than forty-five years—right up the point of attempted suicide. It is the provision of Providence pointing to eternity that has enabled me to discern a path through life that does not include wallowing in the pitiful gutter of self-inflicted pain that is the product of willful ignorance and rebellion that some of us refuse to outgrow.

SECTION ONE
GETTING TO KNOW MARTY
THE RECOVERING DRUG ADDICT

¶#36: From Marijuana to Cocaine, to Crash and Burn, to the Discernment of Wisdom and Recovery

The term "gateway drugs" has been developed from the idea that the use of less damaging chemical compounds may lead a person to using more dangerous drugs. This progression is associated with the use of hard drugs, which is also believed to lead to criminal behavior. Hard drug use is often attributed to the use of several gateway drugs, including tobacco (nicotine), alcohol, coffee (caffeine), and cannabis (marijuana).

Certain drugs are known as gateway drugs, because they are the drugs where chemical abuse begins for many people. The progression into chemical addiction usually moves from cigarettes to marijuana, and on to the white powdered drugs. My progression was a little different; my introduction to the unwonderful world of chemical addiction was alcohol at the age of eight. I then went to cigarettes at the age of eleven, to marijuana at about forty-one, and on to cocaine at about forty-three. Cocaine was to become my white powdered hard drug of choice. I was hooked on cocaine for ten years; I smoked marijuana for over twelve years; I smoked cigarettes for forty-two years; and I got drunk for the first time when I was eight years old. I was to abuse alcohol, cigarettes, marijuana, and cocaine until I turned from chemical addiction to sobriety at the age of fifty-three. The term gateway drug simply means that the addict has to begin someplace, and there is usually a progression from the gateway drugs into chemical addictions involving harder drugs.

As you read about my progression to white powder drugs in this section, realize that most hard core addicts undergo a progression from one drug to a harder drug (or a combination of drugs) until something stops this progression. This was how I progressed, but my progression was slower than most addicts today. When I began the unwonderful world of drugs, the distribution of drugs had not progressed to be as organized is it is today, and the progression of addiction from first time user into full blown addiction is generally far more rapid today than it was when I began drinking in 1944. In addition I did drugs mostly alone rather than with a group of drug buddies.

¶#37: Cocaine

The first time I saw cocaine was when I went to my drug dealer's house to get marijuana. Looking toward a coffee table, I noticed a mirror with lines of white powder laid out on it with a cut-off straw laying next to it. My dealer saw me looking at it and asked, "Have you ever tried cocaine before?" I answered, "No. I've heard about it, and I'm curious about it." He walked over and picked up the mirror and straw and asked, "Would you like to try it? Your first line is free."

Before I had finished sucking that line of cocaine up into my nose, I was so addicted to cocaine that it was to control my life for the next ten years. I was about forty-three at the time.

This addiction was going to cost me everything that is dear to me in life—*everything*. I was to lose my family, my home, my career, my decency, my self-respect, my bank account, my retirement, my future; it all went up my nose as cocaine. For the next ten years, cocaine was to become like a god to me because it was what I served in life. Cocaine is what I organized my life around and thought about during all my waking hours.

What cocaine gave me was an escape. It allowed me for a brief time to escape from the pressures that we may think of as the down side of life. The down side of life is the things that we all have to deal with that we find dull, boring, unpleasant, painful, demanding: things that we hate and wish to avoid, things that force us to act responsibly and focus our attention on someone or something other than what brings pleasure to "self."

When I was high on cocaine, it was as if I was all alone with myself and all I needed was myself. Other people or things were no longer important to me. "I" was all I needed, and "I" was there. When high on cocaine, "I" was euphoric; when high, "I" was free. Pain, responsibility, hate, worry, anxiety, fear, other people's expectations for me were simply gone. I felt good, I was hyped up; cocaine produced in me a sense of euphoria, it gave me a place to go where the down side of life simply did not exist—while I was high.

There are times when I sat in my vehicle after the cocaine high had dropped me back into reality, and I thought, *Life is not worth living without cocaine*. Cocaine and other drugs that produce a euphoric high seem to cause us to turn inward to self and live for the high that we experience within ourselves to the extent that cocaine is all we can think about. Cocaine causes

55

us to be completely selfish; the white powder drugs cause us to do whatever is necessary to avoid the down side of life, no matter what the cost; the ultimate down side of life to an addict is life without his drug of choice, which in my case was cocaine.

Soon after my first line of "free" cocaine I was spending more money on drugs than on my family, our utilities, our home mortgage, our food, our transportation, or our health needs. I lived for cocaine; I was an addict. The only way I could support this addiction was to sell drugs myself, because I could not earn enough to support my addiction without selling them. Addicts are not concerned about what drugs do to them or anyone else; their only concern is getting enough drugs for their personal needs; they'll do what is needed to support their addiction. It is my belief that drug addiction reveals nearly total self-centeredness.

Most of my supply of drugs came from teenagers who were addicts turned suppliers themselves. I had three sons, and I started doing drugs with them. I certainly am not proud of this fact, but it is reality. If this story is to help others, I must be truthful about the depths to which drug abuse will lower you. I was probably the worst father and the worst husband that can be imagined—only this was my reality and my family's reality; it was not imaginary. I was not there for my family when they needed me. Cocaine was my highest priority.

The simple truth is that I didn't know how to be a husband or father or how to give instead of take. So, I gave up trying. I had not learned to give and take growing up. When I should have been learning values and how to shoulder the responsibilities of being a husband and father and of how to implement workable values that would give me and my family guidance in making life's decisions, I was learning how to be self-centered. I'm not saying this gives me an excuse for becoming a drug abuser, it's just what was, and what I was.

After using cocaine for the first time, my only concern immediately became my personal need for cocaine and the escape into my self-centered world that cocaine provided for me. At this time what was happening to my mind and body was not a concern, and what was happening to my family was not a concern; **my only concern became filling my immediate and overpowering passion for cocaine. This is the life of a drug addict. The importance of other things simply vanishes, and your drug of choice becomes your only reason for living.**

56

In my drug abuse awareness presentations to teens, I tell them, "One time is forever." The truth is that for most teens and adults, one time is forever. After my first free experience, I used cocaine for ten years and I still am addicted to it, although I don't do it any longer. At this writing, I am seventy-five, and I have been sober for twenty-three years—and I still crave cocaine. You do not outgrow drug addiction.

For the past twenty three years, it has been my desire to never again do cocaine again as long as I live. However, I now am living with the continual urge to escape from the realities of life, into the world of make-believe, where "I" gets what "I" wants—uninterrupted during the high. Drug addiction for addicts is a lifelong noncurable disease. This self-centered and self-inflicted disease will *never* go away while we are alive in this world and live in a body that is addicted to a mind-altering drug.

When we are young and physically and mentally healthy, our body and brain have the ability to recover from the trauma we force on them in drug abuse. However, over time, the body and brain are weakened, and when the rapidly aging addict attempts to do drugs with a body and brain weakened by age and past abuse, what they used to tolerate may now kill them. Their bodies and brains in the weakened condition can no longer take this kind of abuse. In fact, even young and otherwise healthy teens may try to push further, or they simply miscalculate the amount of drugs they are taking. The result frequently is an overdose. This is especially true of the first time drug abuser. The result may be a stroke, a heart attack, or some more grueling form of dying. Or if they don't die, they become a physical wreck or a traumatized soul living in an incapacitated body for someone else to care for.

It is ironic that when the substance abuser reaches the point where they need care, the caretaker will not supply them with the drug that they so passionately desire. What they live for, and what they gave up their mental and physical well-being for, is now denied them. They are left with the pain they have created for themselves and for others without the very escape that destroyed them, and they live in greater pain than the pain they tried to escape through drugs.

The drug abuser will generally settle upon a drug of choice, and this is what I did. I first used alcohol but in time moved up to marijuana, and then I tried methamphetamines a few times, and I tried opium once. Then I moved up to cocaine. I didn't like marijuana or methamphetamines or opium as well as cocaine. Marijuana no longer could deliver the punch

I needed, and the methamphetamines made me paranoid; I would hallucinate so bad that I couldn't recover in time to function on my job. I could not recover fast enough from opium to remain employed, so I stuck with cocaine.

A friend that I attended night trade school with suggested that we try opium one night after school—and so we did. After a night class one evening, we drove my truck to a remote parking lot and smoked opium. When it was my turn to smoke the opium pipe, he told me take one hit (inhale one puff). Instead, I took two. I have never been so high, before or since. I have no idea how long we were in that parking lot, but at some point I realized that we had to go home. After I drove him back to his parked vehicle, I tried to drive home. When I got to within two blocks of my house, I was so high that it took me an hour to find my way home—from two blocks away. I never smoked opium again.

Cocaine became my drug of choice because it produced what I believed I needed to get by in life.

The one thing junkies must have to support their addiction is money to buy drugs. This is what lands many junkies in jail. The junkie will do whatever is needed to get the necessary money. I used to devise some really unique schemes to get money out of anyone who had it. Once when refinancing our house, I tried to talk the refinancing company into giving me the money directly, telling them I wanted to write checks to pay off our bills, but they weren't that stupid. They had me give them a list of creditors, and they sent checks directly to our creditors.

I owed my company credit union about $3,000, and the refinancing company paid them off directly. Two weeks later, I went to the credit union and tried to take $400 from my account. The cashier called up my account and said, "You don't have $400 in your account." I got angry and said, "What do you mean? I just put $3,000 into that account." The manager came over to see what all the fuss was about. I told him, "I put $3,000 into my savings account two weeks ago, and now she's saying I don't have any money. She says it was used to pay off my loan, but it was supposed to go into my savings account."

The manager checked the records and then apologized. He said he would reinstate that loan immediately, which meant he would transfer the $3,000 loan payment into my savings account, saying it must have been a banking error. In a few key strokes of their computer, it was done and I walked out of there with $400 in my pocket.

Before I went to the credit union, I had planned on going to work that afternoon. But with $400 in my pocket and a drug dealer close by, that idea didn't last long. I had enough money for a three-day coke binge, and that is just the way it was; I was an addict. Every vestige of how a decent and honorable person should treat another was gone. No matter how I tried to resist drugs, my addiction was stronger than my resolve, and my addiction was robbing me of everything I was working for; the attraction to drugs was too powerful; I simply did not have the inner resolve to resist for long. **Drugs had a grip on me that I did not *WANT* to break**. This is just an example of how my life began to crumble, piece by piece. My wife's life was crumbling, my kids' lives were crumbling, and I was like poison to everybody I came into contact with.

In 1982, we lost our house. I had refinanced the house so many times that the payments were more than we could afford. I was spending $1,100 a month on drugs because drugs were my priority.[4] In the mind of a junkie, the only honorable thing to do is whatever is needed to get money for drugs. This meant my family was out on the street; I had to sell the house so that all my money could be used to buy drugs. This is what I did, and the Gruber family became homeless. At this time Golda was forced to leave me. She took our two younger boys and moved to Lake Tahoe to live near her brother. She was able to find work in a casino on the Nevada side of the Lake.

I remember taking my last $50 out of the bank and buying cocaine with it and then trying to float another loan at the company credit union. When I finally did turn from cocaine in 1989, I hadn't paid a bill in three years, and I owed the state of California and the federal government thousands of dollars in back taxes. The only valuable item I owned was my worn out pickup.

The addict is generally in denial about what is happening to him, even as his life unravels before his very eyes. Drugs take such a hold on the junkie's life that he simply cannot see

---

[4]   According the inflation calculator on website http://www.westegg.com/inflation/infl.cgi, it would take $2,452 in 2010 dollars to buy what $1,100 would buy in 1982 dollars. This gives a more accurate understanding of how much money I was spending on drugs.

the evil thing he is yielding his total life to. This evil of drug addiction has its hands around the junkie's throat, and the drug addict will do whatever is needed to support his addiction. And that is exactly what I did. I spent all of my money on drugs; I refinanced our house to take what equity I could get so I could buy more drugs. Finally the payments became so high that I could not meet them, and my wife and my kids and I were kicked out on the street. As noted, Golda took our two younger boys and went to live near her brother in the Lake Tahoe area.

Golda knew she had to do whatever it took to support our family, because her husband was completely dedicated to drugs. Like most addicts, I had reasons that I used drugs. Most people recognize them as excuses, but to me they were valid reasons, and I became very adept at using them to justify my need for drugs. To me, my reasons totally justified my use of drugs.

By this time, my oldest son, Gary, was very, very bitter toward life and his father—and rightfully so. When we lost out house I left Gary who was 20, in despair in Fountain Valley, California; Gary did not wish to leave the LA area, but he couldn't live with me because I was homeless. Gary was able to temporarily live with one of his old high school friends until other arrangements could be made.

At first I lived in my truck. Eventually one of my unmarried coworkers allowed me to stay with him. He rented me a room in his condo with the firm understanding that while I lived with him, I would use *no* drugs. I promised, but of course I did not honor my promise; I even did drugs in his condo when he was not home.

About this time, I broke my nose in a swimming accident, and for a time I was unable to snort cocaine because I had gauze up my nose. So I improvised. While waiting for my nose to heal from the operations needed to straighten it out, I would soak the gauze with cocaine mixed with water, using an eyedropper. A broken nose was not going to come between me and cocaine.

Golda and I were separated for about a year. Sometime in 1983 I drove to Tahoe to get Golda and the kids. I told her I had quit doing drugs. The truth is, I intended to quit drugs, but the reality was I couldn't make good on that commitment.

When I went to get Golda and the boys I didn't have the money to rent a truck to move our furniture back to LA. Golda's brother loaned me his credit card to pay our moving expenses.

We moved into a cheap, roach-infested apartment in Tustin, California. About a year later we moved to an apartment in Westminster, which was a little better. I was constantly struggling and promising to quit drugs; my addiction had not gone away. I was to continue on drugs for another six years. I even went through traditional drug rehabilitation in 1983 or 1984, after Golda and our younger boys came back LA to live with me. I was desperately trying to become drug free but I just couldn't do it.

¶#38: The Unwonderful World of Drugs

One day, I walked into a drug dealer's house to buy some cocaine, right after he had finished shooting up one of his other clients. The guy before me, who had just been shot up by the drug dealer, had taken a seat on the couch. He was wearing only a pair of shorts and a pair of thongs. I noticed that he had numerous bruises all over his arms, legs, back, and neck, each about the size of a dime. These were spots where somebody had slammed him with a needle, trying to find a vein to inject cocaine.

As the drug dealer was getting ready to shoot himself up, his previous buyer fell to the floor and went into convulsions; he had overdosed.

I said to the drug dealer, "Hey, you better do something, this guy has overdosed." He simply looked at me and said, "To hell with him, he can die right here as far as I care." The drug dealer had already filled his syringe with his fix. He had to slam his arm four times before he found a vein. He injected himself and sat back with his eyes closed, waiting for the cocaine to take him into ozone land; he just left the needle in his arm (he was what we call a needle freak).

After about twenty minutes, the guy on the floor stopped convulsing and got very quiet. Then he jumped to his feet. He had urinated all over himself, and just stood there, weaving, with his pants dripping urine and with blood running out of several places on his body where the drug dealer had tried to inject him. He said, "Wow! That was great; let's do it again."

The drug dealer was a seventeen-year-old boy, and his client was a fifteen-year-old boy. Neither one of them made it to the age of twenty; they both died of a drug overdose. This is the wild, violent, uncaring, unwonderful world of drugs.

Prior to cocaine, there was a time when I was active in the lives of my children and their friends, especially with Little League baseball. I remember both of these young men as children. I remember their bicycles, the Cub Scouts, the skateboards, and Little League baseball. However, they made the wrong choices in life, and their wrong choices killed them. I also made the wrong choices in life, and I should have died over and over again. I am absolutely sure that Providence kept me here to fulfill a purpose that I was being groomed to fulfill. That purpose is threefold: (1) To tell kids what their choice to do drugs will bring into their experiences of life, if they choose to go down that road; (2) to tell them there are better choices to be made and that there is a power greater than drugs that is willing to help them find their way into a fulfilling life, if they will call out for help; and (3) to tell them that a superior power brought me from a badly drug damaged life to find fulfillment away from drugs through seeking wisdom greater than the wisdom of mankind. As I will address soon, this Higher Power assisted me in building a restored life based on wisdom much greater than my own.

¶#39: Janice

I once knew a young lady by the name of Janice. Janice was nineteen, with long blonde hair down her back; she was pretty enough to have been a model. She also had the brains to go along with her looks, being an "A" student in high school. Janice had family and many friends who cared a great deal for her.

Janice made the mistake of falling for a drug dealer. Her friends told her, "If you continue to hang around with your bimbo drug dealer, we're going to disown you." Of course, Janice didn't listen, but her friends meant what they said and quit hanging out with her. Five months passed.

One day, this drug dealer called and asked if I would help him with an electrical problem on his boat. I said okay and met him in his garage at 8:00 a.m. as requested. He told me there was coffee in the kitchen. When I went to get coffee, I was greeted by an individual I didn't immediately recognize.

In front of me sat a young woman, making an unsuccessful attempt to eat a bowl of cereal—it was Janice. Her cheeks were sunken in, big patches of her blonde hair had fallen out, her skin had a grey pallor about it, and her arms were so skinny that she looked to be in the final phases of starvation. She had large sores all over her body about the size of a quarter that were weeping pus and blood. When she saw me, she walked toward me, and when she was in front of me, we made eye contact; I was looking death in the face. The smell of rot and decay was overwhelming. This was that beautiful and intelligent young woman, five months after moving in with her drug dealer boyfriend.

Janice walked past me and into the bedroom and locked the door. I went into the garage and got into a heated argument with the drug dealer and left, without looking at his boat.

I finally made contact with one of Janice's good friends and told her about Janice. At first she would not believe me; she didn't believe that anyone could go downhill that fast. I finally convinced her that if she had any feelings for her friend, she'd better act fast. Janice was in bad shape.

Janice's girlfriend and her girlfriend's boyfriend who was a football player, went to the drug dealer's house and confronted him. He wouldn't allow them in the house, but the football player just brushed him aside and went and kicked in the locked bedroom door. There stood Janice, coke pipe in hand.

They wrapped Janice in a blanket and rushed her to the hospital. Janice died there five days later. The death certificate said that she died of acute malnutrition. She starved herself to death in her quest to pump drugs into her body. She couldn't put the coke pipe down long enough to eat. When Janice died, she weighed seventy-five pounds and was nineteen years old; chalk up another victory for white powder drugs.

The human body is no match for white powder drugs. They will take over your body and your life, and in the process they will turn you into an empty shell before taking your physical life.

¶#40: Company-Sponsored Rehabilitation

Even though I tried, I could not hide my drug abuse from Golda. By mid-year 1984, it was obvious that I had to do something to change; my family was falling apart and I was not functioning well at work. AirCal had a program for their employees who were experiencing drug abuse problems. At risk to my job, I informed my supervisor of my drug abuse problem, and he arranged for me to attend a company-sponsored program at Raleigh Hills Rehabilitation Center in the LA area. This program involved voluntary confinement, but the patients could leave at any time they chose. However, leaving meant termination of the rehab program, but more importantly it also meant termination from employment with AirCal. I was committed to rehabilitation.

The procedure for checking into Raleigh Hills involved a physical examination and a psychological interview. During this interview, I was required to tell the doctors why I chose to do cocaine. From there we went into group therapy sessions and individual counseling. Discussing drug abuse in the absence of the drug-induced security (under the intoxication of cocaine), was very difficult for me. I was very reluctant to become involved in honest and open discussions of why I did drugs and why it was so hard for me to quit.

In addition, shy Golda was very reluctant to become involved in group therapy sessions. During therapy, I called a lot of people and apologized for trying to manipulate them into supporting my drug abuse. After thirty days in rehabilitation, I was informed that I had advanced to the point that I could continue recovery outside of voluntary confinement, and I was released to return to work. I was scheduled to continue outpatient treatment of two therapy sessions per week.

When I left rehab, I was terrified. I had been in a safe environment for thirty days, and now the return to driving on the LA freeway system and busy surface streets was frightening, and the competition in the experiences of life was intimidating. The thought of being on my own again was threatening.

The following week, I was scheduled for my first outpatient rehab therapy. The very first night that I returned to the treatment clinic for outpatient follow-up, the building was closed and locked with a chain. There was a letter taped to the door, stating that the clinic was closed; there was no explanation of why or if therapy was to continue elsewhere. I sat down and cried like a baby.

The way I received this was, "Marty has been rejected again." I thought, *Even God hates me. Nothing ever goes right for me.* I knew that I couldn't stay off of drugs alone. The experience in the motel room described under "The Road to Freedom" was years in the future.

It is my belief that if traditional rehab had continued, it would have been helpful. The way it actually turned out, I was physically rehabilitated, so that I could return to drug abuse physically stronger than when I left drugs. I also understood something of why I had made so many bad decisions in life. However, at this point, I had no knowledgeable support group and therefore no hope beyond myself, and I was not strong enough to stay off of drugs by myself. I believed I had messed up so bad that I did not deserve forgiveness, and I could not forgive myself. Perhaps because I believed I did not deserve forgiveness, I did not understand how anyone else could forgive me. Drugs provided a place of escape from the pain of this world that was simply unavailable elsewhere, and I soon returned to that place of temporary escape.

¶#41: Crash and Burn

I did not do drugs at home. Some very cheap motels can be rented by the hour, and I eventually found that the safest place for me to do drugs was the cheapest motel room that I could find. They usually don't ask questions—they just want their room rent up front.

Use your imagination—what else are cheap motel rooms used for besides drug abuse? I've heard it all and seen it all.

The police frequently made busts in adjoining rooms, but I was never busted. Because I was alone and was quiet, I didn't attract attention.

A second reason for renting a cheap motel room was that I didn't want to share my drugs with anybody, and in a party atmosphere, people having drugs frequently lose those drugs to their drug-abusing "friends."

Sometimes I would do too much coke, and I would see imaginary bugs crawling on me and on the walls and floor and ceiling. Addicts usually refer to these imaginary bugs as "coke bugs."

For the Addict these imaginary bugs are visually indistinguishable from real bugs; the only difference is that coke bugs can't be brushed off and real bugs can.

Sometimes while doing multiple lines of coke, I would crash and burn (i.e., I would become so exhausted from drug abuse that my body would force me into sleep, until I rested enough to get up and do coke again).[5] Frequently I would be in and out of sleep for who knows how long.

---

[5] Street cocaine is about 10 to 15 percent pure cocaine. Not knowing the purity of the cocaine one is using poses a dangerous problem to the addict. Depending how many times the cocaine has been cut will also determine its purity and strength, and when one buys cocaine off the street, one can never be sure of just how pure it is, no matter what the dealer says. Dealers will cut cocaine as much as possible to maximize their profits. In 1980, I came into possession of cocaine that was of a higher purity than I was used to, and this almost cost me my life through a cocaine overdose. I snorted four lines and ended up overdosing. If it had not been for some addicts who knew the symptoms of cocaine overdose, I would have died. They fed me bananas and milk to raise the level of potassium in my body, and in doing so saved my life.

A number of people die from heart attacks or strokes when they are high on cocaine; it is a very dangerous drug, especially when smoked as crack. First-time users are at greater risk when using the high-powered white powder drug because in general they release a large amount of dopamine from the pituitary gland into the bloodstream. The pituitary gland is the master gland that triggers the other glands in the endocrine system of the body. As such the pituitary gland is the master control for the pleasure center of the brain. Once a large amount of dopamine is in the blood, it tricks the other glands into releasing large amounts of their hormones, including adrenalin. Cocaine puts the user into a condition similar to a panic mode. This is similar to looking up while driving and seeing an eighteen-wheeler in the oncoming lane racing directly at you; it is a panic mode. This is the level to which cocaine hypes the body. It also floods the body with sexually stimulating hormones. People getting high on cocaine have joined the "feel good" society.

The use of cocaine changes the person into someone hungry to experience pleasure, and this is what the addict lives for. Without going into greater detail, this is especially damaging to young women; cocaine will lead them to do things sexually that they would never consider doing apart from cocaine, sometimes turning them into what is called "coke-whores." On the other hand, cocaine may render some men impotent.

Parents dream that their children are going to mature and become well educated, well rounded, and physically and intellectually attractive people. But the white powder drugs in time will produce a dangerous and unstable personality that is paranoid, unpredictable, and volatile, someone that hallucinates and that can turn on anyone at any time without provocation; and who will do anything to support the addiction to feeling good. Drugs will rob you of everything that is decent in life, *everything*. They rob you of your family, your sports career, your education, and your hopes and dreams for your future. Addicts will trade their family and friends for drug buddies, and they will lie and steal or do anything to get money to buy drugs. Drugs will turn kids who had great promise into street bums, and in time will lead them to the "big house." Drugs, alcohol, and sex become the focus of kids on drugs. There has never been a greater battle for the minds and hearts of kids that is literally a war being waged in the schools all across America.

The drug cycle is sometimes called a merry-go-round, taking about three days to go around. This merry-go-round goes something like this: (1) The addict looks for money to buy drugs; (2) he looks for drugs to buy; (3) he buys the drugs and goes to his favorite place to do the drugs; (4) he does drugs; (5) he comes down from the drug-induced high and waits for his body to recuperate so he can do it all again. The stress from being on hyper-alert tears the entire body down, and the addict may sleep twenty or more consecutive hours while his body recuperates. White powder drugs completely drain your endocrine glands of the hormones needed to function and maintain smooth moods, and it takes time for your body to heal after a drug binge. (6) The addict's pituitary gland becomes drained of dopamine, and the other endocrine glands are also drained of their hormones. These glands serve to keep the body balanced and to maintain good moods and a healthy outlook on life. The result is that the addict goes around shuffling his feet with his head down, in a very depressed mood. The depletion of hormones from the endocrine glands very quickly prohibits the drug of choice from producing the desired effect. In addition, the addict when not high must deal with all the issues his lifestyle has created for him, and this makes

cont. on page 67

Once, after I had slobbered into my long, bushy beard in my drug-induced sleep, I awakened to see a cockroach crawling up my beard; I just watched to see what he was going to do. He took a big drink from the saliva in my beard—then he just rolled over on his back and died.

There were times I was so out of it that I had to call the motel switchboard operator to find out what day it was. Many times after doing excessive cocaine, I hallucinated. I would stand and watch the door with a loaded and cocked .38 revolver in my hand, expecting someone to burst into my room to harm me. At times I would go to sleep cuddled up to a loaded and chambered 12 gauge pump shotgun, hallucinating and believing that someone was trying to harm me or that the cops were coming to get me and take my drugs away.

¶#42: My Cry for Help

When you first begin doing drugs, you think, "Wow, this is the greatest experience of my life. I have found what I've been looking for; my life is now complete."

Later, when your life is falling apart right before your eyes, it is not a just a simple choice to stop. Your desire for drugs is so overpowering that *you can't just choose to stop; **it is my opinion that you CAN'T stop without help**.*

As your life falls into shambles, you will have made many enemies. People who used to look to you for guidance now hate you and wish they had never known you. Golda and our kids must have felt that way about me. In fact, while all of this was going on, Golda went into a state of silence. She was watching everything that she had ever wanted in life go up my nose as cocaine. At the beginning, in her ignorance of drugs, she helplessly watched her husband and all three of her sons turn into drug addicts. No matter what she or anyone else said, none

---

life immensely more difficult. As a consequence, many addicts become severely depressed; suicide is a frequent cause of death because they can no longer live outside of the fantasy land they have created for themselves.

Cocaine robs your body of potassium. There are three main electrolytes in the human body: sodium, potassium, and calcium. Potassium helps in the functioning of kidneys, pancreas, and heart; smooth functioning of muscles; nerve transmission; and conversion of glucose into glycogen, which gives energy to the body. Low potassium electrolyte levels may cause a heart attack or a stroke, or the kidneys may shut down, leading to death. This is what happens in a cocaine overdose.

Cocaine overdose symptoms are intense and generally short in nature. Depending on weight, metabolism, physical heath, and other factors, different doses of cocaine can cause an overdose. Too much cocaine leads to a serious increase in blood pressure. Cocaine overdose can lead to seizures, heart attack, brain hemorrhage, kidney failure, and other complications that may lead to physical incapacitation or death.

of us were going to stop. To make her pain even worse, I was never there for her in any way—my higher priority was doing my own drugs. I simply ignored my family.

In time drug abuse was to take the life of our youngest son Christopher, in a drug related accident. It is painful to remember that this accident took place after I turned from drugs in 1989. In addition my oldest son Gary was to lose a prosperous plumbing business to prescription pain relievers and to spend time in prison. Only our middle son Michael, was to escape the trap of drug abuse. Drug abuse is living hell.

Drugs lead you to lie and cheat and beg and connive and do whatever is needed to get drugs. I once had a beautiful, forty-gallon combination fish tank and bookshelf that a friend made for me—I gave that away for a gram of cocaine. I had an industrial-style air compressor that I traded for a gram and a half of cocaine. Before we lost our house, I sold all of my tools out of my garage to get drugs, and later I sold my home to get drugs. By the time the addict gets to this point, there just doesn't seem to be any light at the end of the tunnel. As noted, I even went through 30 days of drug rehabilitation only to return to drugs soon after rehab was complete.

This is Gary (right), our oldest son, and Michael, our middle son.

One day in April of 1989, I went to my dirty and dingy motel room, full of roaches, and did cocaine. All I did was crash and burn. I was sitting on the floor, cross legged, with the fleas and roaches crawling all over me and with pus and blood running out of my nose and ears, because I had totally destroyed my sinuses with cocaine. I decided to end my life. I knew that I couldn't become drug free, and everything in my life was gone. ***EVERYTHING!*** The only possession of value that I had left at that time was a worn-out Toyota pickup sitting in the motel parking lot and a pile of drugs sitting in front of me. This was not much to show for nearly fifty-three years of life.

I took my loaded .38 revolver and cocked it. I put the barrel into my mouth and closed my eyes. I started to shake so violently that I couldn't pull the trigger. I changed hands and still couldn't pull the trigger. I put the pistol down and started to cry. There in the dingy, dirty, roach-filled motel room, sitting cross legged and nude, I called out to Providence, just as I had done while sitting in the football stadium in Lockland, thirty-eight years earlier. I said, "God, I need your help; I can't do this alone." I said, "I need your help to get off of drugs." I said, "Father, if you help me get off of drugs, **I will devote the remainder of my life to helping kids stay off of drugs.**"

Immediately a **Higher Power came into my life—***IMMEDIATELY!*** I had one foot in hell, being dragged in by the forces of evil, and a power greater than cocaine heard my cry and rescued me from the fires of hell—plain and simple, there is no other explanation. Whatever this Higher Power was, it gave me hope that I could quit drugs.

¶#43: The Healing Process Begins

In 1989 I was a broken man who had reached the bottom of the drug scene, with nothing left in life. I was crying out to an undefined presence that I had never before known to be real. I inwardly knew this was my last chance to change. Prior to this, I didn't know if a Higher Power[6] even existed, but I knew that I couldn't get off of drugs by myself. I needed help. The only thing I knew about what I will call a Higher Power was what I had heard about Him in general conversations and what I knew about Him from His communications with me in drug-induced delirium and in dreams. I had been to church a few times in my youth, but church seemed to be just another activity to me. I had a vague idea that that this world is not self-existing, but beyond that, I knew nothing about a Higher Power.

My life was a total failure; I owed a tremendous debt of bills and taxes. Earlier my family had been forced to leave me and even though my drug usage slowed a bit, that did not turn me from drugs. I had no friends left, my kids were drug abusers just like their father and we had no ongoing relationship. Even though Golda was still with me, I felt alone in the world I had made for myself. It was a miracle that I still had a job and that we had not been kicked

---

[6]   "Higher Power" is a term used in Alcoholics Anonymous and other twelve-step programs. It is also sometimes referred to as a power greater than ourselves and is frequently abbreviated "HP." (This definition was taken from website http://en.wikipedia.org/wiki/Higher_Power)

out onto the street by my landlord (which was what he should have done). But somehow I was still employed as an airplane mechanic and I still had a faithful wife who wanted to help me and I had a place to live. As I look back on that moment, it stills seems impossible that Golda had stayed with me. I had no understanding of the painful path that Providence would lead us through in the coming months. Entering into the world of functioning people was to be painful because there are consequences associated with the choices we make in life.

I now realize why very few people can beat their drug addiction. Most drug addicts die in their addiction because becoming drug free requires help, and many never find that help. It is my opinion that it is impossible to beat drugs alone.

I flushed my drugs down the toilet, and then I tried to talk to my new found higher power. I knew that a power bigger than me had heard my cry and entered my life at my request, but I had no idea what lay ahead of me. I could not see how I could possibly fulfill my pledge about teaching teenagers about the horrors of drugs. In addition, I could not see how I was going to fulfill any normal responsibility to family or friends; it was beyond my hope that any acquaintance would ever again look to me for help. I certainly could not visualize being elevated to a position where I could help kids—the very people I had promised to help. How could a man on the bottom of the drug culture, having my problems, rise up to do anything for anybody? I could not envision that one day I was to speak in lecture centers in large middle schools and high schools to overflowing crowds of kids.

For me, actually speaking to kids was an impossible dream, but it was not impossible for this Higher Power. As I look back, I can imagine that if Providence actually called the complexity of this world and all living things into being, that nothing would be impossible. However, at that time I had no concept of how any of this could come to pass. I had much to learn. Even with the help from Providence, climbing out of the pit I had dug for myself was going to be a tough road. But on this first day of the rest of my life the afterglow of encountering a personality greater than a cocaine high was causing me to ponder if change could be possible after all.

Years earlier, I had read in *Reader's Digest* about how a lady who was an addict cried out to God, and she was instantly delivered from her drug addiction. I am glad for her, but this certainly wasn't to be my experience.

Perhaps such Cinderella stories are real, but my experiences in drug abuse tell me that that kind of immediate deliverance is not a common experience. However, every person is an individual, and every story will be different. My story was to be one of upward struggle in the fight to get this monkey off of my back. I am the one who chose to do drugs, and I had to be the one who chose to turn from drugs. I knew nothing about what some call a Higher Power, even though I felt a strong influence enter my life when I cried out for help in that motel room. The motel room was not to be my last encounter with this Higher Power.

During this time Golda was visiting her ailing father in another state.

As I looked for angels to deliver me, I thought, *Boy, I sure would like some cocaine. I would like to have a beer and party a little.*

After about a week, my craving for drugs became so strong that I said to myself, "This isn't working at all; tomorrow I am going to go look for drugs and get some cocaine." Having promised myself relief from my drug craving on the morrow, I went to bed and went into an unusually deep sleep.

While I was asleep, I had a dream, and in that dream a voice came to me and said, **"I will help you, but first you must get off of drugs yourself."** Then this statement was repeated to me.

I awakened in a rage. I cursed the voice, I cursed the world, I cursed myself and everybody and everything. I beat my fist against the wall, and I beat myself with my own fists. I beat my face against the wall and screamed, "Damn you! You don't love me; nobody loves me." I fell back into bed and cried until I went back to sleep.

The next morning, I waked up lying in my dried blood and my face stuck to the pillowcase. There was blood on the wall and on the floor, and I sat on the edge of the bed, looking at my swollen hands, afraid to look in the mirror.

When I finally did look, I was a mess. As I stood looking at that pitiful sight in the mirror, I said to myself, "Marty, what has happened to you with drugs is your fault. You have done this to yourself, and you are the one who has to get yourself off of drugs." With those words, the healing process began.

¶#44: The Road to Freedom

I later understood the message in my dream as follows: "If I get you out of trouble every time you get into trouble, what would you learn from the experience?" So, I got myself off of drugs, and then the voice that had spoken to me began to help, just as He said He would. In presenting this, **I now realize that the communication of this voice to me was in fact _a powerful source of hope_,** but it was not the free deliverance that I sought. That same Higher Power is helping me today. **The drug abuse awareness program I am doing is not my program; I am the messenger.**

The path out of drug abuse is long and hard and never ending, because drug addiction develops into an incurable disease. The word "addiction" means "a slavish devotion to; dedication to; obsession with; infatuation with; passion for; love of; mania for; or enslavement to."[7] The fact that addicts are obsessed with and enslaved to their drug of choice is not an overstatement. The drive to use drugs becomes so powerful that turning away from drugs is no longer a choice. The Addict cannot merely choose to turn from drugs; the addict can't turn from drug abuse without hope that a better life lies beyond his addiction. Simply stated, the addict needs help, he needs hope, and he needs support.

It is my belief that traditional drug rehabilitation[8] can be helpful for someone who has inwardly made the decision to turn from drug abuse. However, traditional therapy generally does not enlist the spiritual strength that comes from turning to a power greater than yourself. In my experience, traditional rehabilitation does not provide the hope that Providence provided to me. The addict needs something bigger than himself to hope in, and the Higher Power that I had met in that motel room gave me that hope.

It is my opinion that every person has a spiritual dimension, and addressing that spiritual dimension may provide added insight and support to the addict as he or she attempts to salvage and restructure his life, … free from drugs. My addiction to drugs has lead me to develop

---

[7] This definition is compiled from several dictionaries found on the Internet.

[8] Traditional therapy is a combination of humanistic psychology and traditional medicine without a spiritual emphasis (i.e., it chooses not to address the spiritual dimensions or needs of the addict). Traditional psychology is the attempt to define the problem that made the person open to drug abuse and then find a way to treat any underlying psychological trauma and the drug abuse trauma in such a way that enables the addict to turn from drugs and remain drug free. Traditional medicine is the use of medical drugs and physical therapy as needed to physically rehabilitate the body of the drug abuser.

the opinion that all people have spiritual needs that cannot be met by humanistic-based psychology combined with traditional medicine that doesn't offer spiritual help.

The word "psychology" literally means "knowledge of the soul." However, no one knows what the soul actually is. I think it can safely be said that no one *indisputably* knows what a spiritual need is or why we have it. But experience in drug abuse and recovery from drug abuse tells me that there is a world that lies beyond our world, that is much bigger than the physical world we inhabit and can see and feel.

It is not the purpose of this book to analyze or explain what caused me to turn from drugs or how a power greater than myself enabled that to happen, because I can't explain it. In addition, it is not my purpose to tell anyone what to believe about spiritual matters or which of the purported revelations of God to man are true. The individual will have to decide those things for himself. However, it is my testimony that unless addicts invite a presence bigger than themselves into the restructuring of their life away from drugs, success will be much harder, and perhaps impossible.

Until the decision is made to turn from drugs and to enlist the aid of Providence, I have come to believe that rehabilitation therapy for most people is limited to restoring the physical body and enlarging the addict's philosophical view of the world. Certainly views expressed by traditional psychology may help an addict understand why he does the things that he does; in addition, modern medicine has done much to explain the physiology of addiction. However, experience has taught me that psychology and medicine together are not sufficient to give an addict the inner resolve to turn from the physical and mental craving for his drug of choice. He needs help from beyond himself to stand against his craving.

As noted, the greatest discernable need of the addict is hope for a better life, free of drugs. I had been through drug rehabilitation prior to finding the road to freedom addressed in this book. Before encountering a Higher Power in that motel room, or hearing the voice in my dream a week later, I had not found sufficient strength to turn from drugs. It is my belief that had traditional drug rehabilitation continued, it probably would have been more helpful than it actually was under the conditions that I experienced it; however, it was not traditional psychology or medicine that delivered me from drug addiction in May of 1989.

¶#45: An Invitation To Change My Life

What more perfect excuses would a person need to justify drug abuse? Isolated for two years as a toddler in a dingy room in a foster care home; kicked out of the house at ten by my mother; beaten by school principals, school teachers, my dad and stepdad, and the administrators in the reform school I was sent to; quitting school at eighteen while still in the seventh grade; having an undiagnosed learning disability—are there any other excuses I needed? I believed I had experienced enough rejection as a child to justify my need for drugs as an adult, and so my list of excuses went. I had a list as long as both arms, and I used them to justify my choices in life: oh, woe is me, poor Marty. Feeling sorry for oneself makes it hard to see beyond the pain of life to find hope for a better life.

About a week after attempting suicide, I had a dream. In my dream, I was in an alley behind our apartment, and the wind was blowing. A black cloud filled the entire sky. To my left was a staircase, and there were two boys underneath the staircase, hiding from the black cloud that was scaring them. I ran under the staircase to get out of the wind and hide from the black cloud that was also scaring me; it was an ominous sign I didn't understand. Immediately, the two boys disappeared, and the wind stopped. As I watched, a hole opened in the black cloud, and a beautiful, bright white light shone through the hole. I recognized that light. It was the light that I had seen when I was being electrocuted in Mr. Lawrence's backyard in Lockland, approximately forty-one years earlier.

When I saw the light, I waked up. I knew what this dream meant; it was an invitation to come join with the light. It was an invitation to change my life and to follow that light. I had already experienced a power much greater than me, but I was holding back. Even though I had made a covenant with that superior power, I had not yet made the inner commitment to surrender everything I was to Him (i.e., a drug addict, a liar, a cheater, a burned-out junkie with financial debt I couldn't pay, a junkie fighting the inner demon of drug addiction; I truly had a newfound desire to turn from drugs, but I was lacking the internal strength to make that commitment a long-term reality). I was currently drug free, but I knew a relapse into regular use was on the horizon unless I made some changes in life. I did not have the strength to stay away from cocaine. I was on the verge of losing the battle.

¶#46: The Path To Teaching Drug Awareness

Both Golda and I realized I had to leave Southern California area because I did not have the strength to stay away from drugs; the temptations were just too strong. Because of employment opportunities we made the decision to move to Las Vegas, Nevada. The airline company I worked for transferred me to McCarran International Airport in Las Vegas, where I began work as an airplane mechanic. This has proved to be one of the best decisions I ever made. I had no drug contacts in the Las Vegas area, and I have kept it that way. I do not wish to associate with people who do drugs, and even though staying drug free is a struggle, I have found that being drug free is a primary commitment for remaining on the path to developing a meaningful life. The power that came to me in that roach-filled motel room and the voice that spoke to me in a dream soon after, were beginning to help me find my way through life.

Golda and I moved to Las Vegas so that I could remain drug free. Being Drug free allowed us to get a grip on our financial affairs and we began to move toward what may be called a normal life. Then we were hit with the hardest blow we have ever received. Before we moved from LA, my 20 year old son Christopher had become a very successful store manager in a national Pizza chain and he stayed in Anaheim, California, to pursue his destiny. One night Christopher was killed in a motorcycle accident while high on marijuana and alcohol. Of all the pain Golda and I have experienced, this was the most devastating. The death of a child is the one of the hardest issues that any parents can face.

Our first reaction to the news of Christopher's death was paralyzing guilt. Both of us believed we had failed all of our sons and now our youngest son Christopher had been killed; we felt responsible. I had been the world's worst dad and husband imaginable; I had not enabled Golda to be the mother she desired to be. How can a husband and wife work through the pain and guilt they feel at such a time when they have not even developed their relationship with one another? How could I deal with the fact that I had helped my son become a drug abuser? Overwhelming guilt came rushing at both of us. I held Golda and Gold held me and we cried for our sons and our failures to serve them and train them as parents. At such a time guilt and pain do nothing to help one accept their failures find the inner resolve to deal with them and to change their focus in life.

Somehow we were able to travel to LA for Christopher's funeral. Golda and I found consolation in both the quantity and quality of young friends and coworkers who came to Christopher's funeral and their obvious fondness for our son. We were able to see that Christopher had in many ways moved beyond the model that I, as his father, had provided to him. One of the most painful lessons in life is the realization that a self-centered lifestyle does not prepare one to deal with the onward progression of life, with personal losses, or to support someone that is experiencing a personal loss.

The effect of Christopher's death was to force Golda and me to realize that we can do nothing to change what is past, and that the future will come regardless of our pain and past failures. Self-centered living and arrested emotional and interpersonal development is one source of great pain in life, and Christopher's death caused us to look for fulfillment in meaning that is larger that the here and now. Christopher's death was the shock that allowed me to see beyond myself to my responsibilities as a husband and as a dad.

After Christopher's funeral we returned to Las Vegas with an emptiness that soon produced a desire to find a larger meaning for life. I realized that my life had been completely self-centered and that serving self was a meaningless pursuit. I realized that every person needs his family and fellow man and that if parents can catch that vision and transfer it to their children, we can build one another up rather than using one another for self-centered personal gain. I had a lot to learn and I did not know where to begin. But that was to come. The Higher Power I had discovered while attempting suicide was to show me the way; my pledge to teach teenagers about the evils of drug abuse was to become my path into a meaningful life.

I had no idea where to begin, but I knew that if I was to help kids avoid drugs I needed to learn more about drugs that just having abused them. I cannot explain how I knew what to do, I can only say that the path I was to choose was chosen for me by the Higher Power that entered my life in May of 1989. I had a passionate desire to develop a program designed to inform teenagers about the horrors of drug abuse. I was to begin this process by enrolling in a program called Project Alert.[9] I was taught the Project Alert curriculum, and become a

---

[9]   Project ALERT is a nationally recognized, evidence-based program that gives seventh and eighth grade students insight, understanding, and actual skills for resisting substance use. Project ALERT addresses tobacco, alcohol, marijuana, and inhalants, the substances teens are most likely to use. The Project ALERT curriculum was developed and field tested over a ten-year period by Rand, a leading think tank on drug policy. Rand research demonstrates that teens have a mind-set about drugs. By shifting a teen's pro-drug mindset to become anti-drug, this program can help teens avoid drugs. (Developed from information on http://www.projectalert.com/about/highlights)

certified project alert teacher, along with a whole room full of Clark County school teachers. Because of my limited education, I found this learning environment very intimidating. In addition, I soon discovered that I did not have the time to teach this curriculum, because it took too many sessions to present it. I got many good ideas from that program, but I soon began to develop my own approach to teaching drug awareness.

Because of my limited education, I was very inept at using the various tools such as overhead projectors and PowerPoint. I bought a three-foot by two-foot easel and sketch pads as my first teaching aids and developed the program to be presented through this medium. As I look back on my first attempts, I am almost embarrassed at how primitive my methods were, especially when compared to professionally trained teachers.

The whole time I was doing this, I was aware that something was missing; I knew there was another step in the process that I was somehow overlooking. I was called to teach drug awareness to teenagers, and I knew it, but something was holding me back. I had given nearly forty-five years of my life to learn the horrors of drug abuse first hand; this is the kind of training that I would not wish on anybody, not even my worst enemy. But I soon realized that there was one cog in the wheel of effective communication that I did not wish to explore because I knew it would produce a great deal of pain in my life.

The missing cog was that I had to forgive everyone in my life that had ever done wrong to me. I inwardly realized this was what I had to do, but I kept resisting. I think that my resistance was based on the fact that I believed that I had a right to hate these people. This hate also included the driver who illegally turned in front of Christopher, when he was riding his motorcycle at one o'clock in the morning, causing the accident in which Christopher was killed.

One night while alone at home my rage boiled over. In a crying, raging passion, I began to curse everyone who had ever hurt me. After a while, my emotional anger was spent. It was at this time that I said out loud to each person I could remember, as if they were standing before me, "I forgive you," and I meant it. It was like a huge weight was lifted from my shoulders. Many of these people by this time were deceased, but I became like a new person by forgiving them through an act of my will. It was at this time that the voice that had spoken to me in my dream spoke to me again, saying, "Now you're ready."

¶#47: The Program Takes Shape

From that time, things moved rapidly in developing this program. There were times when I would reach stumbling blocks on how to say something or how to present myself, and the answers would come to me in dreams. It is impossible for me to explain just how much the superior power that called me to tell teenagers of the horrors of drug abuse has been involved in developing this program.

At this time, I was attending a large church in Summerlin, Nevada (twenty miles northwest of the Las Vegas Strip). I made plans to present this program to their youth group. Finally they gave me a date and the announcement was placed in the church bulletin. It was scheduled for a Sunday evening in early December 1992. I was as nervous as a cat on a hot tin roof; this would be my first presentation. True to the way I normally do things, I went early and got set up in the youth room. One parent and two teenage boys came to hear the presentation.

In the next room, about twenty teenage boys were practicing tumbling. It seemed in this youth group there was very little interest in a drug awareness presentation.

This was the only presentation that I did at that church. In the years since doing this first presentation, I have come to realize that in general, church leaders, including pastors and youth ministers, simply do not recognize the problems their young people face with drugs. They have actually told me that their youth are "born again Christians, and because of their dedication to Christ, they choose to avoid doing drugs." I agree that religious teaching may be a help in avoiding drugs and coming off of drugs, but unless the individual is wise to the dangers of drugs, he is not equipped to resist the allure of drugs. I realized that the church was going to be a tough audience to play to, although I did not give up.

I had flyers advertising this program professionally printed, and I distributed them to numerous churches. I had interviews addressing this program with ministers from most Christian denominations all across Las Vegas. I found that church leaders just didn't want this program in their church. They simple did not believe their kids were susceptible to drug abuse.

However, I have done numerous presentations in churches in Las Vegas that were well attended and where I was called back to repeat the presentation to the youth group. However, as stated, it is my opinion that the church in general does not believe such a program is needed by their youth. In these first years, I was actually spending more time promoting the program than I was presenting it.

I did this for a couple of years and was getting very discouraged. It was in 2001, that a friend, a retired airline pilot, asked me to speak to his Rotary club about the danger of drug abuse.

As human beings, we want everything now, but it is very obvious to me that Providence has its own schedule. That Rotary club included civic leaders, doctors, and a large assortment of people from all across the community. I did about a twenty-minute presentation and answered questions afterward.

As we were talking afterward, a gentleman came up to me and introduced himself as a math teacher from Silverado High School. He asked me if I would come and do a presentation for his class. I accepted his invitation, and my first experience at Silverado High went much better than I believed it would.

When I arrived at Silverado High, I expected there would be many volunteers doing various programs, but I was the only speaker scheduled that day. Classes started at seven o'clock so, as usual, I got there at six, but the school office door was locked. I went back at 6:15 and the door was unlocked, so I went in and stood in front of the receptionist's desk until she came at 6:30. I explained why I was there and she issued me a visitor badge and told me how to find the correct classroom. I was surprised that there weren't other volunteers waiting to speak. I went to the classroom, scared to death of those kids.

The kids responded well, and I was invited by another teacher to speak to his class. I asked for letters of recommendation from both teachers and received them. I used the letters of recommendation to solicit other schools, and I spoke at three or four high schools per year for the next two years.

¶#48: My First Bump in the Road

One day, I got a response from a teacher at Lied Middle School. By that time, I had changed to a two-day program because one day is not enough (and now I am finding that two days are not enough). This teacher invited me to speak to her health classes. The first day went very well. During the second day, a boy raised his hand and asked me, "How did you get off of drugs?" I responded that I had received Jesus into my life, and that if it hadn't been for Jesus and God, I had no idea where I would be today.

The rest of the second day went well (I thought), but apparently another student had gone home and complained to his parents that I had used the words "God" and "Jesus" in my presentation. While I knew that religion and God were touchy subjects in public schools, I did not believe that my answer in response to a direct question was a violation to the US Constitution. I had asked the teacher for a letter of recommendation, but after two weeks it had not come. So I called her, and she agreed to write me a letter. Here is the text of the letter I eventually received:

> Dear Mr. Gruber,
> Thank you for the time you spent with my class. After your last visit my supervisor met with me in the office in regards to a current complaint he had received concerning your presentation. Although much of your presentation was appropriate for middle school students, due to the references to religion, I am unable to continue to have you as a guest speaker.
>
> I appreciate the drive that you have to educate students about the dangers of drug abuse, and I wish you the best; however, I do not feel comfortable writing a letter of reference to other middle schools.
>
> It was a pleasure meeting you; good luck in your future endeavors.
>
> Sincerely
>
> The Teacher's Name
> Lied Middle School
> Health Education Educator

This letter absolutely devastated me. It was the closest I have ever come to terminating this program. The old "poor Marty" syndrome kicked in, and I began to feel sorry for myself. I had gone to a great deal of personal effort and expense to help kids avoid a major pitfall in the modern world, and my efforts were being rejected because I referred to God and Jesus as a source of help in turning from drug abuse.

The message here was that God and Jesus were not appropriate resources to help kids avoid the very thing that can destroy their lives. It was apparent that I was welcome to come to this school at my own expense and tell kids about the dangers of drug abuse, but I was not allowed to respond to a question by telling them that God and Jesus gave me the inner resolve to turn from drugs, and stay away from drugs, even though it is a fact that most drug addicts do not have the inner strength to turn from drugs and stay away from drugs on their own.

If it is true that humans are caught in a conflict between spiritual powers of good and evil that are at war in a dimension that lies beyond our physical senses, then certainly drug abuse in children must be hard evidence of that war. In researching the issue of religion in public schools, I have not found any legal restrictions that say I can't help kids find ways to love their parents better or turn away from something as wicked as drug abuse, and I can't find anything that indicates that I can't tell them that God and Jesus were sources of power that helped me turn from the absolute destruction that drug abuse had done to me and my family. What I have found is that I cannot seek to draw students into a specific religion. However, it is apparent that the school administration believed that what I had said was a threat to them, and they merely reacted to eliminate that threat.

Let me emphasize that I am open to instruction about how I can present this material in an acceptable manner; certainly it is not my desire to be a problem to school administrations, who I realize will go to great lengths to avoid a lawsuit. In addition, I am in full agreement that they should make all efforts to avoid such problems with parents, and I would not try to indoctrinate any child with my personal views of religion. However, instead of informing me that my statements could have been made in a more acceptable way, I was simply being excluded from this school, with the implication that what I had said would be unacceptable at other schools as well.

This letter put me into a deep funk for more than two weeks. However, as I struggled to deal with this rejection, it came to me that I was not the one being rejected by this letter, this letter was a rejection of what I will call divine Providence. Understanding this gave me the inner resolve to find a way to express these issues in a way that is very general and will not offend but at the same time gives the message that power is available to those who have made life-destroying mistakes and are willing to seek a better way of life from a source that is bigger than their drug addiction. This source is referred to in this book as "Providence," "a Higher Power," "a power greater than yourself," and "a superior power."

By the time this incident occurred, I was already speaking at some large high schools in Clark County. Because drug usage is a prevalent problem in the lives of many middle school students, I believed middle schools could benefit from this program as well. So I resumed sending letters out, offering to present this drug awareness program for free to any middle school in Clark County.

In 2002, I received a response from a health teacher at Leavitt Middle School to come and speak to her health classes; I came as requested. Another health teacher suggested that I take the information I was presenting on the easel and put it on transparencies and project it onto a larger screen. This suggestion revolutionized how I was to present drug awareness information from that time on.

I spent the entire summer putting all the pictures and letters that I was presenting on transparencies. When the next school year began, I was prepared. While there were some flaws in the presentation, it was significantly improved and easier for students to comprehend. This program is not static; I am always adding to and deleting from it in order to improve the flow and content, with the goal of making it student friendly but still present a punch.

¶#49: Why I Teach Drug Awareness Training

As a volunteer in public schools, I was very naïve about how I would be viewed by the school administration, especially teachers. Guest speakers are in the classroom at the invitation of the teacher, with the approval of the principal, and teachers have the authority to bar a speaker from their class at any time, for any reason. I have a tendency to be very direct about what I think and believe, and this certainly comes across in my presentations. Most of the problems that I have encountered in schools have been as a result of my directness. The first requirement in getting along in the school district is, don't make waves in the chain of command, and this means not challenging the judgment of teachers or doing anything that would undermine the status of the teacher in any way.

Volunteers are at the bottom of the school hierarchy, and they should not do anything without approval. At one middle school, a student asked if she could contact me, and I made the mistake of putting my e-mail address on the bulletin board so that the kids could write to me. When a parent saw this, he contacted the school and asked if I was attempting to contact kids outside of the classroom. As a result of this mistake, I was barred from presenting at that middle school; I have not been able to return to that school since. An innocent mistake, but certainly a serious "no-no" that the administration felt it had to proactively deal with. I've learned from my mistakes, and I have learned to accept the judgment of teachers and administrators and move on.

It is a fact that some people are not what they seem to be, and I've come to realize that teachers can be placed in a politically difficult position if I were to violate school administrative protocol. For that reason, I go out of my way to avoid placing a teacher in any kind of administrative jeopardy. It is a miracle of Providence that I am even able to do this program at all, and because I believe that Providence has called me to do it, I try to not make any waves. As indicated, I am learning that there are ways to communicate truth that is not offensive.

To date (February 2012), I have presented my program to over 160,000 kids in grades five through twelve, and I have received over 80,000 letters from kids that have been passed to me through the school chain of command. Some of these letters are presented in "Letters from Orr Middle School" and "Letters to Marty."

For me, the hardest part of this program is driving to the schools. It is more than thirty miles from one side of Las Vegas to the other, and traffic is horrible. I often drive more than sixty miles round trip, and at this writing, gasoline is above $4.00 per gallon. Sometimes I speak as many as seven times a day (usually forty-five-minute periods, with about a ten-minute break between classes). I usually present four days each week (taking Wednesdays off) during each week of the school year (mid-September through mid-May). The presentations I do are like a full time job that is done for free. During the school year, I put a minimum of forty hours per week into this program. As noted earlier, I continually revise what I present to keep it fresh and timely.

In the nearly twelve years I have done this program in public schools, I have not had one parent contact me and thank me for what I have done for their children. It is also worthy of note that I am called to do this program in the public schools by a superior power, and I am primarily doing it to help kids stay away from drugs in obedience to that calling on my life. My rewards will come later.

While some of the handouts I use are furnished by the federal government, about half of what I present I wrote and printed at my personal expense. Some of my friends know what I do and believe this a worthwhile program, and from time to time they give me small donations, but I do not receive regular financial support of any kind from any source. In the ten years that I have presented this program in Clark County School District, I have not seen another volunteer in any class. I have, however, seen teachers that go far beyond the call of duty in the performance of their jobs. Some teachers put in hours significantly in excess of forty hours per week, and some purchase materials for use in their classrooms at their own expense. I have learned that working with kids in the public arena is both heartbreaking and very rewarding at the same time. It seems that drugs are in our culture to stay. Many of the people who teach as a profession do it for something greater than the money they receive as their salary.

¶#50: Final Comments

After doing this program for nearly twelve years, my commitment to do it is still increasing. At this writing, I am seventy-five years old; I have been told that I have a gift to communicate the content of this program with teens, because they listen to what I have to say. This book is my attempt to continue communicating the horrors of drug abuse to kids after I am physically unable to present it in classrooms. The original manuscript for this book was developed entirely by volunteer labor, and it is my intention to use any profit realized through the sale of this book in ongoing support of this program. I see no lessening in the commitment within the drug culture to reduce their exploitation of the American teenagers (and even younger children), for the financial gain of the drug dealer. As long as I have breath, I intend to speak against the abuse of drugs.

As a final comment, it is my opinion that the decriminalization of drugs, or the legalization of drugs, will only increase the damage that drugs inflict on America's young people. My advice to politicians is the same as it is to teenagers contemplating drug and alcohol usage: **DON'T DO IT! DRUGS SEEM TO HOLD PROMISE <u>BUT THEY ARE A TRAP!</u> ONCE THAT MONKEY IS ON YOUR BACK, <u>IT WILL BE THERE FOR THE REST OF YOUR LIFE.</u>**

DRUG AWARENESS PRESENTATION: DAY #1

By
Marty Gruber

In 2011 Marty recorded a DVD presentation covering two forty-five-minute classroom periods at Orr Middle School in Las Vegas. These presentations include projection of information onto a large screen by an overhead projector. In Day #2 of this presentation Marty shows videos of juvenile prisons and police activities dealing with drug offenders, which graphically show the consequences of drug abuse on the person. The following written presentations of Day #1 and Day #2 are transcriptions from live presentations made in the classroom. One 90 minute long DVD of Day #1 and #2 is available for showing in drug awareness presentations and may be obtained as stated under the introductory paragraph "About This Book." The information presented on video in the classroom is not transcribed below.

DRUG AWARENESS PRESENTATION: DAY #1

Good morning! [Class in unison: "Good morning"] That's weak … that doesn't qualify … the sixth graders sound better than you do. **GOOD MORNING!** [class in unison: **GOOD MORNING!**] Thank you.

I read someplace that the teenage brain doesn't start functioning until nine o'clock; is that true? [Heads nod in agreement.]

Well, I ask every class that, and some of the kids tell me their brain doesn't start functioning until noon; do we have any noon-functioners in here? [several hands raise.]

I've only had one class where no one raised their hands to indicate that they were noon-functioners.

My name is Marty Gruber. I am a drug awareness presenter in Clark County School District. I am a volunteer. I do not get paid for what I do. This is my tenth year doing this program. I have never asked Clark County School District for one cent for doing this program—and never will. This program is my contribution to you, the young people of Clark County.

If I can get one person in this class to listen to me, just one, and get you to stop doing what you are doing to yourself or to keep you from getting hooked on drugs, I'll leave this school happy.

Young people, don't start your adult life a chemical freak—**don't do it!**

What a label we put on ourselves at twelve, thirteen, fourteen years old: a druggie, a doper, a chemical freak. If you don't think they laugh at you behind your back—they do! They tell me all the time they do. "Here comes another druggie—tee hee hee. Look at that doper, how he walks; stay away from him." And they do laugh at people who get hooked on drugs.

Now the rules of the class are simple. No cell phones, no i-Pods, no electronic gizmos; if I see you with them, I will take them and give them to your teacher, and he can do what he wants to with them.

We are on a roll at Orr Middle School. This is what, year six? ["**YEAR SEVEN!**" exclaims the teacher in the back of the room.] Year seven that I have set up in this school and presented both semesters, to eighth grade students, and we haven't stopped one class, one time, in eight years, for discipline problems. There is no other school in Clark County School District that I go to that can even come close to that record, not even close. Now we want to keep that record going, because when we are done with this presentation today and tomorrow, that will be seven years in this school without stopping one class for discipline problems.

[Laser pointer to top of screen.] The theme behind this program is right here on top. "Searching for the truth about drugs." What that means is that I'm not going to get up at four o'clock in the morning, like I did this morning, drive all the way from Northwest Summerlin, pay four bucks for a gallon of gas, to come to your school to lie to you, tell you Cinderella stories, because it won't happen. What you'll hear from me today and tomorrow about drugs will be the truth.

As it says up here [Laser pointer to screen.], for a lot of teens, one time is forever; that is also true. You can experiment with some of these drugs one time, get hooked on them, and be a drug addict for the rest of your life. And it says up here [Laser pointer to screen.] drug addiction is for life, it's noncurable, and that is also true.

The recovery rate for drug addicts in America is 15 percent. That means that the other 85 percent of people who choose to get hooked on drugs are hooked for life. The only exceptions to that rule are the people who get hooked on methamphetamine—their recovery rate is about 7 percent.

If your parents and teachers and this old man can keep you off the gateway, or step drugs—alcohol, cigarettes, and marijuana—then there is a 95 percent chance that you won't come down here and start doing the white powder drugs.

I am a drug addict. I've been hooked on chemicals since I was eight years old. I was hooked on cocaine for ten years; I smoked marijuana for over twelve years; I smoked cigarettes for forty-two years; and I got drunk for the first time when I was eight years old.

All three of my sons were drug addicts, most of their friends were drug addicts, and I have seen over and over and over what drugs do to teenagers, and I can guarantee you one thing: it's not the life you want to live.

My first line of cocaine was free. I walked into a drug dealer's house one day to buy some marijuana, and I noticed in the living room on the coffee table a mirror of lines of white powder, and a cut-off straw sitting there, and the drug dealer asked me, he said, "Have you ever tried cocaine before?" I said, "No. I've heard about it, and I curious about it." And he walked over and picked that mirror up and that cut-off straw, and he handed it to me, and he said, "Here, your first line of cocaine is free."

Before I had finished sucking that first line of cocaine up into my nose, I was so addicted to that drug that that addiction lasted for ten years, and it cost me everything that is near and dear to me in my life; ***EVERYTHING!***

So the question I have for you right now is this:

How much are you willing to pay?

What are you willing to give up in your life so that you can feel good with chemicals?

Are you willing to shoot the works and give it all up?

Are you willing to give up all your hopes and dreams for your future? Everything that you are working for in your life right now so you can feel good with drugs?

You can do that, a lot of people do—I did! I gave up a beautiful 3,000-square-foot house on a cul-de-sac. I kicked my family out on the street because they were interfering with my drug use. I gave up the job, the career, the bank accounts. I gave up everything because of drugs.

How much are you willing to pay? What are you willing to give up so you can feel good with chemicals?

And the first things that leave you when you start doing drugs [Laser pointer to screen.] are right here: your decency and your self-respect fly out the window like a flock of geese flying south.

Now let me give you an example of decency. When you go home from school this afternoon and you walk into your kitchen, and your mother's purse is sitting on the kitchen table, would you go into her purse and steal her money? Of course not, that's because you're decent people. But if you're hooked on drugs, you would think nothing of it. It would be a moment of opportunity for you.

The next thing that leaves you is this word, love [Laser pointer to screen.]: L-O-V-E. Because when you get hooked on drugs, the only thing in this world that you love is your drug of choice. The people in this world who care about you, and the people who you care about, suddenly mean nothing to you. Are you willing to give it all up so you can feel good with chemicals? You can do that, a lot of people do that—I did.

How can this happen? What is so powerful in a teenager's life that somebody can get you to shove needles into your veins and pump dope into your body? Is it peer pressure? Pressures at home? The lack of knowledge of what drugs can do to you? Is it because you don't care and just want to feel good?

The reason that I found is just underneath peer pressure, there are a lot of teenagers out there, and maybe some in this room right now, **who simple do not <u>believe</u> what their parents and teachers are telling them about drugs**. Just because your parents and teachers have never done drugs, that doesn't mean that they are not telling you the truth, because they are. I'm going to tell you exactly the same thing that your parents and teachers have been telling you, but only in a slightly different way.

[Laser pointer to screen.] Here's what the letter up here says:

> Dear Marty,
> It was early on Sunday morning. I went into my bathroom and locked the door. I cooked up a batch of heroin. I filled my syringe and pressed the needle against the vein in my arm. I heard a noise and looked up into the mirror, and you were standing behind me, Marty. Then I heard your voice say, "Don't do it. Ask your parents for help. I care about you." I walked into my parents' bedroom and dumped all of my drugs and stuff onto their bed … I was crying … I told them about my terrible drug problem and asked for their help. I am receiving the help that I need … I am drug free … thank you, Marty, for saving my life.

This letter is from a sixteen-year-old high school girl that I received two years ago. If you ask me if I get a lot of letters from teenagers, I would have to say, "Yes, I do." In fact, I could put it to you this way: "In the ten years of doing this program, I've received over 80,000 letters from high school and middle school students from all over Clark County. And they tell me a story, they tell me what is going on in their life, and some of it isn't too good."

[Laser pointer to screen, indicating a picture of a toddler bending over, with the top of her head flat on the ground looking back between her legs.] This one says, "Does it seem like your world is upside down? … It's never too late to change." And it is never too late to change. If I can change after doing drugs for over forty-five years, you can change too. And if you are looking at this world upside down like this little baby is, then maybe it's time for a change in your life.

It doesn't necessarily have to be about drugs, it can be about anything. If there is something going on in your life right now that needs to be changed, change it. When you go home from school this afternoon, and if you're lucky enough to have a bedroom, go into your bedroom and close the door, or go into the bathroom and close the door, and walk right up to the mirror and look yourself right into the depths of your eyes, and if you see something in there that you don't like, then maybe it's time for a change in your life. It doesn't have to be about drugs, it can be about anything. Change your life and become better people.

[Laser pointer to screen.] These young people did. These young people changed their lives and became better people, and they wrote me about it, and they told me about it. And I get a lot of letters from teenagers like this. I get a lot of letters from kids telling me that they went home and looked into the mirror, and they realized that there were things going on in their lives that they needed to change, and they changed them. And you can do the same thing. I did that.

I did that this last summer. There were things going on in my life that I wasn't happy with, and I went home and I looked into the mirror and I saw things that I wanted to change, and I changed them, and I became a better person. And so can you.

Now we don't have time to read the letters, so I'm going to move on.

[Laser pointer to screen.] For this young man, the party ended when he was fifteen years old. This is David. [A picture of a handsome young man in a wheelchair with his feet tied into the wheelchair stirrups.] The party ended for David in Sunrise Hospital Pediatrics Intensive Care. When I heard that David was in the hospital, and he had a problem with drugs, I went to Sunrise Hospital but I couldn't get up into his room because there were too many people up there.

And I was still down in the lobby; I thought, "When I get up to David's room, he'll be sitting up in bed and he'll have that silly grin on his face; he'll wave and say, 'Hi Marty', and everything will be okay."

Well, when I finally got up into David's room, everything wasn't okay. When I finally got up into David's room, his whole family was there around his bed; most of them were crying.

90

They had David strapped down in bed with these big wide straps because his whole body was in convulsions from brain damage from doing so-called "cool" drugs; they had drilled a hole through his throat and put tubes down into his lungs to treat his lungs from the damage he did from smoking cigarettes, from smoking marijuana, and from huffing household chemicals; they had drilled a hole into his side and put tubes into his stomach to feed him; they had placed tubes and sensors in every cavity of his body because his own brain couldn't regulate his body temperature. They had to have a machine to do that; a fine, decent person. David's good people; wrong choices in life.

[Laser pointer to screen.] Because of the wrong choices that David made at twelve, thirteen, fourteen years old, he'll never be out of that wheelchair that he's sitting in, in this picture. He'll never walk again as long as he lives because of brain damage from doing drugs.

This young man spent fourteen months in three different hospitals, and in that fourteen months suffered more pain than a normal human being would suffer in a lifetime. I know, I was there, and I saw what they had to do to him because of drugs, and it wasn't nice. Fourteen months, three hospitals, and a million dollars later, they wheeled him out of a hospital and sent him home.

David's hospital bills, doctor bills, and rehab bills are up to $1,250,000 because of drugs. Let me ask you a question: Do your parents have $1,250,000 that they can soak into your brain-dead brain because you chose to go out and pickle it in alcohol and drugs? Do they? [Numerous kids shake their heads no.] Of course not, and neither do David's.

It ruined them financially, because of his bad choices in life, his parents will never be able to get out of debt as long as they live.

[Laser pointer to screen.] Here's David a week out of the hospital. I put this picture up there to show you how they have to tie David's feet to the wheelchair, because if they didn't do that and somebody pushed the wheelchair, his feet would just flop down to the ground and drag along the ground, because he has no control over his feet or his legs because of brain damage from doing drugs. He made the wrong choices.

Don't you make those wrong choices. And don't you dare wind up looking like the people you are going to see in the video I will show you tomorrow. They made wrong choices too.

[Laser pointer to screen indicating a picture of a very handsome young man.] For this young man, the party ended when he was twenty years old; this is Christopher. The party ended for Christopher on the streets of Anaheim, California, with motorcycle parts strewn up and down the street for fifty yards. He hit the back of a van on his motorcycle at high speeds; he wasn't wearing a helmet, and his head went through the back window of the van, and it cut him to pieces.

This is Christopher.

Two ladies got off work at one o'clock in the morning and drove by and found this young man laying face down in the middle of the street; he was drowning in a pool of his own blood. They made a very gallant attempt to try to save this young man's life. One of these ladies sat down right in the middle of that pool of blood and was cradling his head trying to keep him from drowning in his own blood while her girlfriend ran up and down the street, pounding on doors trying to get someone to call 911. The smell of alcohol was overwhelming because the whiskey bottle he had in his jacket pocket broke when he hit the back of the van. And he lay there in middle of the street at one o'clock in the morning, dying, with his body soaked in whiskey and his own blood.

The next day, after Christopher died, they did a toxicological test on his blood, and they found a large amount of marijuana and alcohol in his system. This is Christopher, twenty years old; this was my youngest son.

Like you, at one time Christopher had a very bright future ahead of him. At one time he was the youngest manager that a national pizza chain had in their system; he had his own store at seventeen years old—unheard of. And they were grooming him to be West Coast district representative of this pizza chain when he reached the age of twenty-one, but drugs and alcohol took care of that at twenty.

Young people, don't wind up becoming a picture. Don't wind up like David in a wheelchair because of brain damage. Don't wind up like Christopher: dead, because of drugs and alcohol.

When Christopher died and we buried him, we buried part of us too, and the horror will never end. When you lose a child, you lose part of yourself too; don't do this to the people in this world who care about you, because when you die, part of them dies right along with you, and when they bury you, they bury part of them too, and for them, the horror never ends.

[Marty is forced to blow his nose.] Now you'll see me do this quite often, and the reason I have to do this is because I destroyed my sinuses with cocaine. I've already had one major operation that cost over $30,000, and it didn't do any good. Now a few summers ago, they wanted me to go back into the hospital and drill holes in my skull to get to the area that I've destroyed, but I'm not going to let then do that. I'll be seventy-five years old my next birthday, May 20, 2011, and I'm just going to have to live with it for the rest of my life.

David had a girlfriend by the name of Jessie. David and Jessie were boyfriend and girlfriend for three years. Two days before David went into his coma, they buried Jessie. They buried Jessie from an overdose of cocaine given to her by her mother. At Jessie's burial, after all the adults had left, her so-called friends surrounded her coffin before they lowered it down into the ground, and they sprinkled cocaine all over the top of it as their tribute to her; they thought it was okay to do that, but it wasn't.

I've been to Jessie's grave with David, and I can tell you it's not a pretty sight; it's not a pretty sight when you see a teenage boy crawl out of a wheelchair and drag his dead legs across the grass because of brain damage from doing drugs, and then lay on his dead fifteen-year-old girlfriend's grave, who died from an overdose of cocaine, and lay there and cry. David lost his lifelong partner to drugs at the age of fifteen. Fine person; wrong choices in life. And for the wrong choices that David made, he will have to pay for them for the rest of his life. But know this, if you have made wrong choices, it is not the end of the world; don't you ever let anybody tell you that. If you have made wrong choices, if you will let it, it can be a new beginning for you.

[Laser pointer to screen, indicating a picture young man approximately thirty-five years old.] For this gentleman, the party ended five summers ago in a courtroom in Orange County,

California, when the judge sentenced him to prison because of so-called cool drugs. This is Gary, this is my oldest son. Because of prescription painkillers, Gary lost his family, he lost his home, he lost his plumbing business, he lost all of his work trucks, all of his work tools, they went into his huge storage unit the size of this classroom; they cut the lock off it and auctioned off everything he had in this world. When he walked out of prison, he walked out of there with the clothes on his back and has nothing—***NOTHING***—because of drugs.

We don't know where he is; we never hear from him. Our family has been split up because of drugs, and it will never be a family again. You should see what his mother looks like when she looks at this picture; you should see what his mother looks like when she looks at the picture of her dead son. Now we've lost two to drugs, and we don't want to lose you. We really don't.

Every person sitting in this room right now is important to me, and that's what counts. If you weren't, I wouldn't be here I'd be home with my wife, who sits at home alone every day, because I'm not home because I'm here. I don't get paid for this. I'm here because I want to be here. … I'm here because I don't want you to wind up looking like this, and neither do your parents and neither do your teachers. But when you go out on that street and start listening to the wrong people in your life, when you start listening to the druggies, the drug dealers, the chemical freaks, the gang members, that's when you start having problems in life.

Look up here; look this old man right into his brown, bloodshot eyes; listen to the people in this world who care about you, and you won't go wrong. **LISTEN TO THE PEOPLE IN THIS WORLD WHO CARE ABOUT YOU, AND YOU WON'T GO WRONG!** Listen to your parents, they care about you the most. They're not perfect, they make mistakes in life, but you're not perfect either. And neither am I. Listen to your teachers; they don't want you to wind up looking like this [Laser pointer to screen.], and neither do I.

Destroyed lives because of drugs? Here's a destroyed life because of drugs. [Marty points to himself.]

[Laser pointer to screen.] I'd like to introduce you to my niece, Chere. Here's Chere when she was eleven years old. Here she is as a young adult; she's already on methamphetamine in this picture; she's already so skinny she almost looks anorexic. It wasn't too long after these pictures were taken that she developed large pus and blood weeping sores all over her face, arms, and legs from all the methamphetamines she was doing, that had poisoned her blood system, and here is Chere's prison badge picture, for the second time because of drugs. Now if you want to look like that, you can; all you have to do is go out there and listen to the wrong people, make the wrong choices in life, and you will. And if you are sitting there thinking, "Well gee, that can't happen to me because I'm cool and macho and unique and different," well, you might be cool and macho, you are unique and different, but you can get hooked on these drugs just as easily as anybody else; don't ever think you can't.

Now let me introduce you to her family. [Laser pointer on picture of Chere's kids on screen.] This is Jacob, fourteen, and Nicky, ten. Now the life that these two children have lived … the only way I can describe it to you is they have lived a life of horror. They never lived in a home, or an apartment, for the most part of their lives; they lived in filthy dirty motel rooms that catered to druggies, all their lives, with rodents and bugs running all over the place. When they tried to eat a bowl of cereal in the morning, they'd have to dump the roaches out of the box first to get to the cereal and then put water in the bowl because there was no milk in the motel room.

Jacob has been mother and father to Nicky and has protected her more than once against the druggie predators. About a year and a half ago, Chere had to make a big decision about Jacob. She had to decide what was more important in her life: drugs or Jacob. Unfortunately, the drugs won, Jacob lost, because she gave him away for the second time, and this time permanently. She traded her son in for drugs. She got rid of her fourteen-year-old son so she could have money to continue to buy drugs.

Chere cannot find a job; nobody will hire criminals. Chere and Nicky are living with her mother, Nicky's grandmother, in a trailer outside of Little Rock, Arkansas, and they have nothing. And the only thing that Chere has is the handouts that her mother will give her. Now if you want to look like that, you can; all you have to do is go out there and make the wrong choices in life and listen to the wrong people, and you will.

When you go home from school this afternoon, I want you to do something, and I really mean it; when you go home from school this afternoon, I want you to walk up to your parents and put your arms around them and give them a hug and tell them thanks for doing all the stuff they do for you; whether you want to admit it or not, they do. I don't know if you know it or not, but your parents are out there struggling right now. There may be homeless teenagers sitting in this room right now.

When I was at Martin Middle School the first semester of this school year, they told me that there were more homeless teenagers in that school today than there has ever been since the school has been open. And your parents are out there struggling, and they need your help. They need to know that you care about them too, because they care a great deal about you. Go home and give them a hug because they deserve it. And they deserve more. Not only will this change your life, but it will change the lives of your parents.

[Laser pointer to screen on several letters from teenagers.] These young people did. These young people went home after this presentation and gave their parents a hug, and they wrote me and told about it. And I get a lot of letters like this. One of my favorites is the letter from a boy from Von Toble Middle School, and he says:

> Dear Marty Gruber,
> I want to thank you for helping me get closer to my father, I really appreciate
> it. Now he and I are best pals

What else in the world could you ask for in life but to be best pals with your father or your mother?

Go home and give them a hug and tell them thanks. If you are having differences with your parents now, resolve those differences and become a family again. And don't pay back the people in this world who care about you by winding up looking like this [Laser pointer to screen.]; don't do it. Don't wind up with a cigarette in your mouth and an alcoholic drink in your hand.

[Laser pointer to picture of young woman drinking and smoking with an obvious attitude.] Here is where drug addiction starts, right here: alcohol and cigarettes.

Now I'm going to entertain you. Some of you look like you need to be entertained. I'm going to play a broken CD. You know what a broken CD is, you put it in the machine and it sits there and says the same over and over and over and over again. Well, I'm going to sound like a broken CD and here is how it goes: alcohol, cigarettes, marijuana, white powder drugs … alcohol, cigarettes, marijuana, white powder drugs … over and over and over and over again like a broken CD.

Why do we have to subject ourselves to this before we learn? Why can't we learn from other people's mistakes? Learn from my mistakes and don't wind up with a cigarette in your mouth and an alcoholic drink in your hand; don't do it. It is a smart person who learns from other people's mistakes.

[Laser pointer to picture of healthy lung that has been removed from a human body.] This is the picture of a nonsmoker's lung. Everybody sitting in this room who is a nonsmoker, this is what your lungs look like right now. This deli-bob you see over here is the inside of a foil marijuana pipe opened up and transposed onto this picture, and if you are smoking marijuana now and you think that your lungs still look like this [Laser pointer to picture of healthy lung.], well, welcome to Disneyland—because they don't. And if you don't believe that, the next picture you see is exactly the same picture, only with a little something added to it. Every one of these black spots that you see on here is an actual hit off of a marijuana pipe. [Laser pointer to screen.] Not phony, not made up, but an actual hit off of a marijuana pipe. The smoke was forced through a wet paper towel, the paper towel was dried and cut up, and I pasted it onto this picture, and I made another picture out of it.

If you think that you can get by in life by putting garbage like this into your lungs and your body, and you're not going to pay for it someday, you will. And there's a name for that, it's called play now, pay later. And if you're playing now, you'll pay, guaranteed. I'm paying, why shouldn't you? I'm paying because I can't breathe anymore after smoking cigarettes for forty-two years and marijuana for over twelve years.

Now listen carefully: in the scientific world, there is a little saying I'm going to pass on to you, and I want you to remember it. Because the first time you're standing over a mirror with lines of white powder, or you have the coke or meth pipe in your hand for the first time, or you have the first joint hanging out of your mouth, I want you to remember this, and it goes like this: "**Garbage in, garbage out.**" Now when you choose to put nothing but garbage into your brain and your body, there is only one thing that you can expect to get out of it, and that's garbage. And that is another broken CD, and it goes like this: I get letters from teenagers all the time that go like this:

> Dear Marty,
> I used to be good in basketball, but I can't run from one end of the court to the other because I can't breathe from smoking weed …

> Dear Marty,
> I used to be good on the tennis court, but I can't play tennis anymore because I can't breathe anymore from smoking weed …

> Over and over and over again … it's like a broken CD.

[Laser pointer to screen.] This is a picture of a cigarette smoker's lungs. Everybody sitting in this room, and I certainly hope no one here smokes cigarettes, this is what your lungs look like right now. And if you smoke hookah and/or marijuana on top of it, your lungs no longer look like this, they're about the color of this band that you see up here on top. [Laser pointer to top of screen.] You're using your lungs as a garbage dump.

But you know what? You don't have to worry about all this bad stuff, all this bad stuff only happens to old people, grandmas and grandpas; am I telling you right? [Kids shake their heads no.] No, I'm not. Because the next letter is from a fourteen-year-old boy; at the time that he wrote it, he was dying from lung cancer from smoking cigarettes since he was ten.

Basically what you are going to read right now is a death letter from a fourteen-year-old boy. And here's what he says:

> Dear Mr. Gruber,
> I am fourteen years old and I have smoked cigarettes since I was ten. I first started when I lived with my grandma. She smoked a lot, and I've been hooked ever since. A month ago I found out I have lung cancer. My brother is the one who took me to the hospital. But when you came to the school and talked to us, I called my brother and told him all about what you talked about. I told my parents how I smoked and how I have lung cancer, and they're really helping me to quit. I'm going to an appointment to see if I can get surgery.

> Thank you so much for coming to our school. You too have saved my life.

NOT ME!

I didn't save his life; nobody did. Shortly after he wrote this letter, they operated on him, and they removed one of his lungs, trying to save his life, but the cancer had spread beyond his lungs, and he died that summer, a few days short of his fifteenth birthday. He never even made it to high school—from smoking cool cigarettes since he was ten.

[Laser pointer to screen.] I often wonder if the lung they took from him looked like this lung.

Garbage in … [Kids in unison:] garbage out … **You got it!**

[Laser pointer to screen.] This is a picture of a cigarette smoker's lungs. This lung was removed from a man who died at the age of sixty-two; he smoked cigarettes for forty years. This is nothing but one big hunk of cancer. Now up here it says, "Read the fine print." Well, let's go over here and see if we can read the fine print. The fine print says:

> Surgeon General's warning: Smoking causes lung cancer, heart disease, emphysema, and may complicate pregnancy.

That's on every pack of cigarettes that you buy, and it's not on there because the cigarette manufacturers want it on there; it's on there because the government makes them put it there.

[Laser pointer to screen.] Now if you'll come over here, and if you can see this, it says:

> There are 16 milligrams of tar in each cigarette.

T-A-R in every cigarette that you smoke; 16 milligrams of tar. Young people, you don't pave the inside of your lungs with tar; you pave the street with tar. Tar is what they use to repair the street with, and when you pave the inside of your lungs with tar, here is what you wind up getting: lung cancer [Laser pointer to picture of cancerous lung on screen.], and you can't breathe anymore.

[Laser pointer to screen, showing picture of man with fifty cigarettes in his mouth.] And if you don't listen and you get hooked on garbage, maybe you can wind up looking like this guy; would you say that this man might have a nicotine problem? He's got fifty cigarettes in his mouth, and some of them are actually lit, and you can see the curl of smoke coming up there, or maybe he just has a big mouth. I don't know. I threw that picture in there; I wanted to show you what an idiot looks like. Well, now you've seen him, and we'll bury him, and we will move on.

[Laser pointer to screen.] Here is one of the most important things that I can say to you in the two days that I'm going to be here with you, and listen carefully: prescription painkillers, pills, are everywhere; pills are in this school; pills might be in this room right now; I don't know. To be addicted to prescription painkillers is as bad as being addicted to heroin. **TO BE ADDICTED TO PRESCRIPTION PAINKILLERS IS AS BAD AS BEING ADDICTED TO HEROIN!**

Is there anybody in here that doesn't understand that, or doesn't believe it?

[Laser pointer to screen.] And here is what it says up there: "Prescription painkillers and over-the-counter cough medicines are very addicting, and they can kill you dead." Don't listen to uninformed people; stay informed, make good choices in life, stay away from taking pills and over-the-counter medicines and medications to get high; some of these pills are as addicting as heroin. Some of them can cause brain damage and do severe damage to your internal body parts (heart, lungs, liver, and stomach); pill addiction is as bad as being addicted to cocaine, methamphetamine, heroin, and steroids. When you mix alcohol with pills, you are walking a thin line with your mental and physical health.

Listen to the people in this world who care about you. If you have a problem with pills or over-the-counter medications, ask for help. Painkiller addiction does not go away by itself, it only gets worse.

[Laser pointer to screen.] And then down there on the bottom I put, "Pill poppers go nowhere in this world except to jail and six feet under. If you are going to 'pharm parties'—and pharm is the abbreviation for pharmaceuticals—and you're sitting around somebody's table dipping your hand into a bowl of pills and popping those pills into your mouth, and you don't even know what they are or what the strength of them is, and then washing them down with alcohol, you're on your way. Because a lot of these people who die from an overdose of prescription painkillers mixed with alcohol die a very horrible, horrible, painful, excruciating death; don't you be one of them.

In fact, it's so bad that when the police get there, they declare it a crime scene because it looks like somebody murdered them. Stay away from pills and over-the-counter medications to get high.

The bottom line is this, young people: make good choices out there, and you have a choice; it's your choice, your life; what do you want to do with it?

[Laser pointer to screen.] This is what you call a setup. This young lady was invited to a party; they knew she was coming, they had it all set up for her, they let her drink all the alcohol she wanted to drink, do all the drugs she wanted to do, then when she got to the point that she could no longer defend herself—and I'll use her terminology—she said, "They did bad things to me."

Well, young men, when you see the video tomorrow, I going to show you where they put "THEM." I'm going to show you the inside of genuine prison for teenage boys, and it's not a nice place, and they have genuine prisons for teenage girls too that aren't nice either; when you go out on the street and you do stupid things, that's where you wind up.

There are some key words in this letter: "friend choices," "they" (meaning more than one), and then she goes on and says, "I'm really glad you came and changed my thinking … from a girl that has learned her lesson." Well, young ladies, that's a mighty dangerous way to learn a lesson, and if the wrong predator is at that party, you won't be going home—at all.

Not good choices for the young lady, and certainly not good choices for the young men.

When you come into class tomorrow, I want somebody to raise their hand and ask me if I ever did drugs with my sons, and we'll talk about that. If nobody asks that question, then I'll go right on with the presentation, but if one person asks that question, we'll talk about it. And if we have time tomorrow, and I hope that we do, I will describe what it was like being sixteen years old in a man's jail in downtown Cincinnati, where I was, where you don't want to be—guaranteed.

Handouts: Now listen carefully, I'm going to point out what is over here. [Marty points to a table with literature on it.] On this side there are eleven tips for teens on all different types of drugs. Ten are on drugs, the eleventh one is HIV and AIDS, and at the end of this presentation you are more than welcome to come over here and pick up any, or all, of this drug information that you want. But keep this in mind: this paper that I have in my hand right here—somebody donated seventeen cents apiece so you could have the proper information and make good choices in life; if you want them, take them, but if you do not want them, do not take them and throw them all over your campus.

There are also six handouts, the back row are all in English, the front row are all in Spanish; they are the same.

Now: The first white handout that I have here is "A Message from Marty." It's a message from me to you about drugs. When you read this message, keep this in mind: I did drugs all of my life, and I know what I am talking about. And on the flip side of "A Message from Marty" is a paper on "Prescription Painkillers," "Over-the-Counter Cough Medicine," and "Steroids."

The next white paper over there is "The Marijuana Myth"; if you want to learn the truth about marijuana, pick up "The Marijuana Myth." On the flip side of that is a "Teen Help Telephone List." If there is a drug or alcohol problem in your family, pick up the "Teen Help Telephone List."

The very top ones up there, Al-Anon and Alateen, are there for you and are free, and if there's an alcohol problem in your family, call Al-Anon or Alateen and ask for help. Don't sit there and suffer in silence. Do something about it.

The pink paper is on "Secondhand Smoke." If you are living in a secondhand smoke environment at home, pick up the pink paper and take it home and ask the people who are smoking in front of you to stop, because they are hurting you.

Young ladies, it is particularity bad for you, because they have linked secondhand smoke with breast cancer; it's not under research, it's not maybe, it's a done deal. And depending upon how long you as a child, and as a young lady, have been subject to secondhand smoke, the risk factor can go up to as high as a 90 percent chance that at sometime in your life you will have breast cancer.

Young men, if you have sisters at home, pick up the pink paper and take it home and ask whoever is smoking in from of them to stop. And on the flip side of the "Secondhand Smoke" paper is a paper on "Cutting." If you are a cutter, stop cutting. Cutting is just as addicting as doing drugs, and it is another dead end street to nowhere. When you cut yourself, your body produces heroin-type chemicals to combat pain, and you get addicted to the feeling that these heroin-type chemicals give you.

If you are doing snappies, stop doing snappies. If you don't know what snappies are, these people who are self-abusers have found a way to abuse themselves all day in the classroom. They put these large rubber bands around their wrists or around their ankles, and they sit there and snap themselves all day to get their bodies to produce these heroin-type chemicals. I've heard it both ways; I've had snappers tell me they stopped snapping and went to cutting, and I've had cutters tell me they stopped cutting and went to snapping.

The yellow paper front and back is the poem, "My Name Is Meth," about methamphetamines, and everything in this poem about methamphetamine is true.

The green paper is on hookah. If you want to find out the truth on hookah, pick up the green paper. Keep this in mind: if you smoke hookah out of a hookah pipe for forty-five minutes, you've smoked the equivalent of one pack of unfiltered cigarettes, and for every cigarette that you smoke, you lose eleven minutes off of your life. On the flip side of the hookah paper is a paper on "Playing the Choking Game." If you're playing the choking game, you're playing a game all right, but it's a very deadly game, and it's killing young people here in Clark County School District. When you choke yourself to the point of passing out to feel good, two things happen: (1) You can go too far and die, and (2) you can get brain damage so severe that you'll wind up in bed for the rest of your life with somebody spoon feeding you and changing your dirty diaper.

The blue paper is a poem, "I Went to a Party, Mom," about a teenage girl that was hit by a teenage boy who was driving drunk, and on the flip side of that is a paper on "How To Help Somebody Stop Smoking Cigarettes."

[All of these handouts can be found in the back of the book under the Section Heading entitled "Marty's Handouts."]

SECTION TWO
DRUG AWARENESS PRESENTATION: DAY #2

By
Marty Gruber

Does anybody have a question for me?

Yes? [Student asks, "Did you ever do drugs with your sons?"]

All right, we have a question already: Did I ever do drugs with my sons?

The answer to that question is, "Yes, many times."

Now, why doesn't somebody raise their hand and ask me if I feel guilty about that?

[Student raises hand and asks question.]

I'm glad you asked that question. No, not at all, in fact.

What is the next obvious question? [Student asks, "Why?"]

If I felt guilty about doing drugs with my sons, would I be living in the past or in the future?

[Student responds, "In the past."]

Make no mistake about this, young people: I am not proud of the things that I did when I was on drugs. I'd give anything if that didn't happen. But it did! I cannot go back into my life and change things that are over and done, and neither can you. If you are sitting there feeling guilty about something that you have done in your past life, and you don't have the capability of going back and changing it, then learn from your mistakes in life. We're not perfect; we make mistakes in life; learn from those mistakes and don't keep making the same mistake over and over again, then bury it and move your life forward into the future, because the future is where it's at; the past is over and we cannot change it; yesterday is over and tomorrow is yet

104

to be. For every day that you live in the past, a little bit of you breaks off and dies, and if you live in the past long enough, your past becomes your future.

Now please don't write me nasty letters about this; I've learned from my mistakes. I will not repeat them, I've buried it and I've moved my life forward into the future, and you do the same thing.

[Laser pointer to screen.] If you have chosen this form of drug addiction—huffing of household chemicals—you've chosen the worst form of drug addiction known to man. Every time you go through a huffing session, you kill hundreds of thousands of brain cells, never again to be replaced.

When you go underneath the sink at home, or you go out into the garage, and take a chemical and spray into a rag and put that rag over your face and breathe the fumes, what you are doing is replacing the oxygen in your brain with chemicals that stay in there long after you quit huffing, and continue to kill brain cells for years to come.

Since huffing has become so popular in our society, a little phenomenon has crept up: seemingly healthy, happy young people between the ages of eighteen and twenty-four go to bed one night and die in their sleep. They perform an autopsy on these young people and cannot determine the cause of death; in the ones that they could, they went into their backgrounds all the way into grammar school, and they discover in 100 percent of the cases that they were huffers of household chemicals in their early teenage years.

This tells the researchers that these chemicals stayed in their brain long after they quit huffing, continuing to kill brain cells up to the point that the brain simply shut down and died. If you are huffing Sharpies or the computer cleaner called Dustoff, you're on your way.

[Laser pointer to screen.] This young man happened to choose two of the worst chemicals that you could possible huff: gasoline and bleach; we got to him and got him the help he needed to stop doing what he was doing to himself. If you have friends who are huffing chemicals, do everything that you can to get them to stop.

I have never stood up in front of a youth group and told anyone to go tell on people who do drugs; that is not the purpose of this program, but if you have friends who are huffing chemicals, let somebody know because they are destroying their brains with chemicals.

[Laser pointer to pictures showing progressive effect of drug usage on a young woman.] Maybe one of these days you could wind up looking like this person. There is ten years of methamphetamine use; here is year one, and here is year ten, and young men, if you think that you look better than they do after doing methamphetamine for ten years—you don't.

[Laser pointer to screen.] This is powdered methamphetamine, here is crystal meth, and then down here on the bottom I threw in two of my drugs of choice: I threw in cocaine and marijuana, and if I was to throw a dart out at a dollar figure on how much money I spent on cocaine over the ten years that I was hooked on that drug, I would guess that I spent over $250,000 on cocaine alone (allowing for inflation, that would be approximately $540,000 in 2010 dollars). That doesn't include the field of marijuana that I smoked or the brewery full of alcohol that I drank or the boxcar full of cigarettes that I smoked—that is $250,000 on just cocaine alone.

[Laser pointer to screen.] Now take a really good look at this last picture; do you notice how her jaws are sunken in and her lips are tightly closed together? She's got her mouth like that for a reason; she's got her mouth like that because she doesn't want you to see what she has in her mouth. Well, I'm going to show you what she has in her mouth, and some of you may not like it, and I don't know what you think about it, but I certainly wouldn't want to kiss somebody who looked like this. That's what you call a "meth mouth." [Picture shows teeth rotted off at the gum line.] It doesn't take methamphetamine too long before it does that to you either; now if you want to look like that, you can; all you have to do is go out and start doing methamphetamine, and you will.

Now there is one thing I didn't tell you about my niece; I saved it for this part of the presentation. About three weeks ago, she had to go the dentist, and in one sitting, they removed twenty-four teeth out of her mouth; they pulled all of her teeth because this is exactly what her mouth looked like from doing methamphetamine for years.

[Laser pointer to screen.] I've been asked a number of times by teenagers, "Why do I get high when I do drugs? What goes on in my brain and my body when I put high-power white powder drugs like cocaine, methamphetamine, ecstasy, heroin into my body? Here is the answer to that: every time you put high-power white powder drugs into your bloodstream, it tricks the pituitary gland, right here at the base of your brain, right before the brain stem; here it is blown up [Laser pointer to screen.]; it tricks the pituitary gland into releasing large amounts of dopamine and other chemicals into your bloodstream. When this happens, the other hormone-producing glands sense all of the chemicals that have been dumped into your bloodstream, and it tricks them into flooding your body with your own hormones.

Basically what happens to you is you get addicted to the feeling that your own chemicals give you, your own hormones, you get hooked on them, and the white powder drugs that you use to make this happen are nothing but a triggering device; you get hooked on your own chemicals.

Now while the pituitary gland and the other hormone-producing glands are flooding your body with hormones, it's also flooding your body with sex hormones. And then you run the risk of getting hooked into the sex-drug trap. There is no worse addiction in this world for any human being than to be hooked on sex and drugs at the same time. It's an addiction that people get into from which it is difficult to escape.

[Laser pointer to screen.] This is a picture of a human liver that is in the early states of cirrhosis, and how you can tell that is the uneven lobe sizes; these are called lobes; they should be more even than they are. It's surrounded by a huge amount of fatty tissue; this would tell us that whoever owned this liver was consuming huge quantities of alcohol, and if left to continue, eventually it would look like the liver that you see on the bottom. This is a female liver that was destroyed by cirrhosis from chronic alcohol consumption; once the process of cirrhosis starts in the liver, it is not reversible. Cirrhosis of the liver is nothing but scarring in the liver. When the liver becomes forty percent contained with scars, it starts to shut down. And the people this happens to, the whites of their eyes turn fire red, their skin turns yellow, and the next step for them is death.

Obviously, whoever owned this liver is not with us any more because we are looking at her body parts, and if you don't listen to the people in this world who care about you, one of these days, this old man might be back at this school talking to another group of eighth grade students, and we might be looking at your body parts.

[Laser pointer to screen.] This is a comparison picture between male and female livers; the top picture is the male liver, and the bottom one is the female liver, and they both have been destroyed by alcohol. The other thing that will destroy your body parts is taking handfuls of pills and tossing them into your mouth to feel good, because a lot of those pills are time release pills, and they stay in your body parts for a long time, even after you have stopped tossing them, and continue to do damage to your body parts.

Now if you want to know where I get my cool body parts pictures from, I get them from the coroner's office. And you know who the coroner is: they process dead bodies, and they cut these dead body parts out of people who listen to the wrong people and have made the wrong choices in life and destroyed themselves with chemicals.

Graphic picture coming up …

Every time you take and put high-power white powder drugs—like cocaine, methamphetamine, ecstasy—into your bloodstream, it makes your blood pressure go to dangerously high levels … every time you take the drug. If your blood pressure goes high enough, it can cause the blood vessels in your brain to explode; it's called a massive stroke, and whoever this happens to is dead before they hit the ground; dead is dead. The picture you are about to see is that of a human brain that exploded on the inside from high blood pressure from doing the cool drug methamphetamine; graphic picture coming up …

[Laser pointer to screen.] This brain literally bled to death internally; that is a big blood clot right in the middle of the brain, and whoever owned it was dead before they hit the ground; dead is dead. Now if you think that it is okay to destroy your body parts with chemicals, and destroy your brain like this so that you can feel good with drugs, then go out into the world and destroy every relationship with people in this world who care about you and who you care about, so you can feel good with drugs, you've made the wrong choices in life.

If you have a problem with drugs right now, do something about it. When you go home from school this afternoon, sit down with Mom and Dad and say, "Hey, I made a mistake. I have a problem with drugs and I need help." They're not going to be happy; they're not supposed to be happy, but they'll help you. Judging by the letters that I get from teenagers who did exactly that after this presentation, Mom and Dad weren't as mad as they thought they would be.

Young people, don't take the only life that you will ever have and destroy it with drugs; don't do it.

Don't join this group; don't join the "three strikes you're out" group (1) if you don't have a high school diploma, (2) if you have a drug problem, and (3) if you have a felony conviction on your police record, you have severely reduced your chances of getting a good job.

Being cool is staying in school, staying drug free, and staying out of trouble; these are the cool people, these are the people who go out and get the good jobs; they live in nice places, they drive nice cars, they meet nice people. Mr. Right meets Miss Right; they get married; they have lots of babies and live happily ever after.

The druggies are too busy being cool to worry about this stuff.

Stay in school, and at the very, very least, get your high school diploma; do not become a high school dropout. If you walk out of high school and turn your back on your education, you have reduced your job market by sixty percent; Seventy-five percent of the people in prison today do not have a high school diploma, and that included my oldest son.

If you'll stay in school, stay drug free, and stay out of trouble, you'll do fine out there in this very tough world that we have created for ourselves—and it's getting tougher every day. Just talk to your parents and they will tell you.

GARBAGE IN, GARBAGE OUT!

SECTION TWO
LETTERS FROM ORR MIDDLE SCHOOL

The following five letters were part of the package forwarded from the students at Orr Middle School. These letters are representative of the letters I get from almost every group I address. Virtually every letter I receive expresses appreciation for telling them that chemical abuse is damaging to their bodies. I know the parents and teachers of these students have already told them what drug abuse will do to them, but I believe hearing about the horrors of drug abuse from somebody that has experienced those horrors first hand, while showing pictures of kids and adults who have been damaged by drugs, and then relating personal experiences, is much more powerful than just cold hard facts about what drugs do to your brain, body, and relationships. When facts are combined with pictures and stories from real life, there is a multiplied impact on the student.

It is my opinion that prevention is far more effective than treatment after the fact, and NIDA estimates that every dollar spent on prevention saves up to ten dollars spent on treatment.

Dear: Mr. Gruber

ORR M/S
09/29/30/10 GIRL

"Hi, I'm a student from Orr Middle School." I'm really happy that you came to our School, because I really paid atention to everything that you said. I have never done drugs, or drink, and I'll never will. After all the things that you told us about drugs, made me happy because I was making the right choice by not doing drugs, or drink.

I hope that I was not the only person that really was lisening to everything that you were saying, because you would really change their lifes, like you did to mine!

So thank you Mr. Gruber for everything that you have done for me, and more Kids.

Sicerely:

110

Dear Mr. Gruber

ORR M/S
09/29/30/10   BOY

Orr Middle
school

Thank you very much for talking to our school. It's what I really needed because now I'm sure that I will say no to smoking. Before, I wasn't sure if I was going to smoke or not and I thought later on in the future I was. I thought that because I live around so I had no hope. Then when you came and showed us the mistakes of others and the consequenses. I learn from the mistakes of others and now I see my future.

Dear Mr. Gruber,   Boy

Thank you for taking the time to talk to our school. You really touched me with all you said. I've always wanted to know how it would feel to smoke, do drugs, or drink but all it took were those two days you talked to us too change my mind. You've made an impact in my life, and i'm never going to forget Mr. Gruber.

Your Pal,

██████████

Dear Mr. Gruber   ORR M/S 09/29/30/10
                                              GIRL

thank you for coming here and teaching
us about what would happen to you if you
do drugs it really help me to know I could
die if I smoke or drink. I have really
learn alot and my brother drinks alot of
beers I took one of the papers you told
us to grab and. I told him to read it
he is making progress of trying to
quit drinking sorry about your son's
but thanks for helping me..

Dear Mr. Gruber,   Boy

Thank you for visiting our class B
informing us about the effects of drugs.
You also informed us about tobacco. Also the
effects of tobacco. The same day you told
me about marijuana one of my old friends
or so I thought he was my friend, offered
me some. When he asked me I thought of
you B your family. And what happened to
your son stopped me from smoking.
                                    sincerely,
                        ██████████████

                        Ps: you saved
my life. Thanks
                        you!!!!

SECTION TWO
<u>DAVID AND ME</u>

<u>¶#51: Allostasis</u>

As noted in the "Drug Awareness Presentation: Day #1," the recovery rate for drug addicts in America is approximately 15 percent.[10] That means that the other 85 percent of people who choose to get hooked on drugs, are hooked for life. The only exceptions to that rule are the people who get hooked on methamphetamine; their recovery rate is about 7 percent. In addition, there may be another exception that is addressed under the main heading entitled "Teen Challenge Success in Drug Abuse Treatment as Verified by the National Institute on Drug Abuse." Teen Challenge has had remarkable success in dealing with teens trapped in drug abuse. This will be discussed in the next section.

The next section, entitled "National Institute on Drug Abuse Information and Facts," reveals that drugs change the brain of the drug addict in ways that make it difficult for him to turn from drugs. As is stated throughout this book, hard experience demonstrates that turning from drug addiction is not a simple decision for an addict; that is why it is called addiction. Through the use of drugs, the brain and body of the addict develop what I will call a "new

---

[10] In his presentation on Day #1, Marty tells us the recovery rate from addiction is about 15 percent for drugs other than methamphetamines (the rate for meth addicts is about 7 percent. However, the report cited below in the report from the National Institute on Drug Abuse (NIDA) indicates that the recovery rate is from 1 to 15 percent. It is difficult to find accurate recovery rates addressing drug addiction recovery rates. The recovery rate cannot be measured accurately because rarely do the records kept by the various organizations that treat addictions track the lives of those who graduate from their programs after they leave the program. Based on this, Marty's estimated recovery rate may be very generous. The following statement is found on website http://www.wisegeek.com/does-drug-rehab-work.htm (bold and underline is added).

The question of whether drug rehab works relies on several factors, such as the type and length of addiction, the duration of the rehabilitation program, and what kinds of long-term support are provided to the recovering addict. Not enough research has been concerned with evaluating, in a controlled setting, programs in comparison with each other. Therefore, **raw numbers are unreliable but suggest that <u>addicts rarely quit without any relapse</u>. <u>Most addicts have the potential to recover.</u>**

All studies agree that the longer an addict participates in a treatment program, the more likely it is that drug rehab works. Therefore, it is logical that lifetime commitments to recovery, as the philosophy of twelve-step programs dictates, help the addict to maintain their pledge of abstinence. Also, when the addict's goal is complete abstinence, drug rehab works better than for those who believe moderation is an acceptable goal.

For some reason, there appears to be a leap in the success of recovery at the three-month mark. Many intensive, inpatient programs offer residential treatment for up to three months. In this kind of supportive, drug-free environment, people can more easily transition to living by themselves. When residential support lasts only a month, success rates plummet. The cooperation of family, friends, and employers are crucial in helping drug rehab work well.

normal," where the drug of choice has become an integral part of the physiological stability of the addict. The result of this new normal is that the addict's physiological and psychological well-being depends upon the repeated utilization of the drug of choice. The physiological change that accompanies addiction is termed "allostasis."

Allostasis is the process by which the body responds and adjusts to stress (or any stimulation); it is self-regulation of the physiological processes of the body by its own internal regulatory system. In allostasis, the psychological processes of the addict's body first adapt to "accommodate" the drug of choice, but with repeated drug use, it rapidly adapts to require the drug of choice for the addict to just function in life. After a period of drug use, **the body will crave the drug of choice <u>so powerfully that the addict cannot function without it</u>**. Here is a nontechnical medical explanation of allostasis:

> **Allostasis:** The process of achieving stability through changes in behavior as well as physiological features. As a person progresses into drug addiction, he appears to enter a new allostatic state, defined as **<u>divergence</u> from <u>normal</u> levels of change which persist in a chronic state**. Addiction to drugs can cause damage to a brain and body as an organism enters the **<u>pathological</u>** state; the cost stemming from damage is known as **<u>allostatic load</u>**. The **<u>dysregulation of allostasis</u>** gradually occurs as the **<u>reward from the drug decreases</u>** and **<u>the ability to overcome the depressed state following drug use begins to decrease as well</u>**. **<u>The resulting allostatic load creates a constant state of depression relative to normal allostatic changes.</u> <u>What pushes this decrease is the propensity of drug users to take the drug before the brain and body have returned to original allostatic levels, producing a constant state of stress.</u>** Therefore, **the presence of environmental stressors may induce <u>stronger drug seeking behaviors</u>**.[11]

In plain language, an addict takes drugs to make him feel euphoric, but his body (i.e., his endocrine system of glands that secrete hormones or other products directly into the bloodstream) can't physically recover fast enough to produce the hormones needed to maintain the level of euphoric feelings that the addict desires. Therefore, to maintain the desired euphoric feelings, the addict takes more drugs, attempting to get higher. In time, the addict's physiological and psychological processes are altered to require the drug to enable him or her to maintain daily physiological and psychological stability.

---

[11] This definition of allostasis was taken from website http://en.wikipedia.org/wiki/Drug_addiction

The inability of the body to produce hormones fast enough means that an addict can no longer produce the euphoric feeling that the drug originally produced (the drug does not directly produce the feeling of euphoria; it is the addict's own hormones that produce euphoric feelings). This causes the addict to crave more of the drug to produce the desired effect that his body can no longer achieve. If an addict does not obtain the desired effect, which his endocrine system can no longer produce, he may lapse into depression and his body cannot react to produce the hormones needed to cause the depression to lift. As this process continues, the addict will enter an increasingly depressed state because the normal chemical balance produced by his own glands has been severely disrupted.

The addict will do whatever is needed to get the drugs his body demands to make him feel good, but his body cannot produce the desired effect no matter how many drugs he puts into it. If an addict does not get the euphoric effect his physical and psychological well-being demands, he will be unable to function (i.e., he will lose his physiological and psychological stability). It is this pattern that leads to crashing and burning, and overdosing on drugs. Crashing and burning is also discussed under the main Section Heading "Getting to Know Marty the Recovering Drug Addict."

For many years, people have spoken about the two prongs of drug addiction as being physical addiction and psychological addiction. However, allostasis demonstrates that physical addiction and psychological addiction are so closely interrelated as to become virtually indistinguishable from one another. Because of this fact, addicts are essentially condemned to use ever increasing quantities of drugs until something stops the process. Allostasis explains why few addicts are able to quit drugs for good on their first attempt, even when they want to do so.

¶#52: My Adopted Grandson

David is the son of a former coworker. David is a demonstration of how difficult is to stay away from drugs once you become addicted, even after a near fatal overdose that left him confined to a wheelchair for the rest of his life.

Golda and I have one grown grandson, who lives in California. After I turned from drug abuse and my daily life began to return to what most people consider "normal," I began to realize just how much my addiction had robbed my and me family of interpersonal relationships. I have already mentioned my sons; my youngest son was killed in a motorcycle accident involving his use of drugs, my oldest son was incarcerated and lost his plumbing business because of drug abuse (and we do not have ongoing relationships with him now that he is out of prison), and my middle son lives in California, and we have reestablish interpersonal relationships, including my relationship with my grandson Brandon, who is now grown.

After turning from drugs, over time I developed a desire to have a grandchild that I could have ongoing relationship with. I had missed many beautiful things in life because of my drug addiction, as had my family. In time, I began to seek ways to experience some of the things that I had missed because of drug abuse; to that end, I wanted to experience grandchildren. For over two years, I diligently prayed that God would bring a child into my life that I could adopt as a grandchild. It did not matter if that child was a boy or a girl.

David's dad and I worked together at McCarran Airport in Las Vegas, Nevada, and it was through this coworker that I met David when he was about ten years old. In the course of time, David and I became close, and we began doing numerous activities together such as a grandfather and his grandson would naturally do. This included going to the mountains and snow tubing, going to movies, and just hanging out together. This was fine before David began to discover girls. However, after David discovered girls at about the age of twelve or thirteen, his time became more limited, and our time together suffered severely.

As David got older, we naturally drifted apart. Most young men develop interests that consume their out of school time, and certainly David was no exception. I later realized that in addition to girls, drugs had become one of David's main interests in life. One day a friend told me David was in Sunrise Hospital in Las Vegas, in a coma from brain damage caused by drugs. I went to the hospital, but it took me more than an hour to get into David's room because of the number of family members there. As much as I have been around drug abuse, I was naive enough to believe that when I finally reached David's room, he would be sitting up in bed with a silly grin on his face; he'd wave and say, "Hi Marty." However, that was not to be.

¶#53: David: Drugs, Recovery, and Length of Life

When it was finally my turn to visit David, all I could see were two feet sticking up in bed, and both of them were shaking. All of a sudden, reality penetrated my mind; a voice deep

116

within me said, "Here is your grandchild. See what you can do for him. He is going to need a lot of help."

In the coming weeks, I spent hours upon hours with this boy, wiping away his tears, bending his arms and legs, and helping the hospital staff tend to his physical needs.

David was in a coma; sometimes his eyes were open, and sometimes they were closed, but there was no indication that he even knew he was alive. David had tubes running into his lungs; he had damaged his lungs severely from smoking cigarettes and marijuana and from the huffing of household chemicals. He also had a tube in his abdomen to feed him; they had tubes and sensors placed into every body cavity to deal with his bodily functions; he could not even regulate his own body temperature—they had a machine to do that. His legs were swollen up to about three times their normal size, and his hands were swollen and bent all out of shape. It did not look good for David.

As I sat there day after day, people would come into David's room and move close to his face and say, "David, move your arm; David, move your leg," but there was no response, not even the flicker of an eye. One day a nurse came into the room to monitor all the machines that were keeping David alive; as she was making needed adjustments, she remarked that they were seeing more and more teenagers coming in, "looking like that." She said, "He reminds me of a person much older who has suffered a catastrophic stroke." She continued, "Look at his hands and his legs, all deformed. I'm afraid that what you see is what you've got." It was quite apparent that this nurse had no hope that David was going to recover.

What this nurse did not know was that over a period of about eight years, David was going to move from being brain dead to graduate with an associate of arts degree in drafting and then attend engineering school, and for a time, he was near the top of his class. Was David a miracle? His doctors thought so, and so do I, but there was more to come in the story of David and me—more joy, more pain, and certainly more of the consequences of doing drugs.

David was a trusting and unsuspecting adolescent that did not consider the pitfalls of the choices presented to him at the ages of thirteen and fourteen, and he made some bad choices.

One Sunday evening, I went to visit David. When I got to his room, the lung therapist had just arrived, and he asked me to hold David on his side so he could use the vibrator to break up fluid that had accumulated in his lungs. I had done this many times before and knew the routine; as usual, there was no discernable response from David. After the therapist left the room, David was laying on his back with the covers up to his chest, with his arms out from under the covers. I got out of my chair, went to David's right side, and tapped his elbow and said, "Move your arm, David." Up came the arm and plopped down on the bed.

I was stunned; I stepped backward and almost knocked over one of the machines attached to David. Excitedly, I moved in closer to his bed and tapped his elbow and said, "Do it again, David." Up came the arm a second time.

This was the first inkling that there was hope for David. He heard, he understood, he responded. There was still a connection between his brain and the rest of his body. I ran out of the room to tell anyone I could find what had just happened, but the hall was empty.

I went back into the room, proclaiming thanks to the intelligent power I knew had heard our prayers. However, I was soon to discern that just because we now had hope for David to experience some degree of recovery, the actual process of recovery was to involve more pain than any of us were prepared to imagine at that time. The long painful healing process had started; before it was over, David was to experience more pain than a normal person would suffer in a lifetime, and his friends and family were to experience some of that pain as well. But for the moment, we were elated. David was to have another chance at life.

David progressed so rapidly that within a few days, he was showing signs of coming out of his coma. The first step was to move him from intensive care to guarded care in the hospital. Within a few days, David was transferred out of guarded care to a nursing and rehabilitation home in Henderson, Nevada, where he could receive the care and rehabilitation therapy that he was to need in the coming months.

It happened that David's high school, where he had been a very popular student, was just down the block from the nursing home. Day after day, I sat and watched as a parade of kids filed into his room. As some of them came up to his bed, they broke into tears. They weren't prepared to see the effects that the cool drugs they were personally curious about had done to David. I know that many of David' friends had personally tried drugs themselves. Many of them would ask, "How did this happen?" My response was always the same: "**This is what drugs do to people**."

One day, a boy about fourteen came to the door of David's room. I watched as the boy stood outside and looked in, then he abruptly turned around and started down the hall to the exit. I rushed to the door and called after him, and he returned to just a few feet from the door. I asked, "Do you know David?"

He replied that they were best friends, and he didn't want to see David like that.

I put my arm around his shoulder and led this young man to the side of David's bed. Just before the tears started to flow, I asked him, "Do you do drugs?"

He replied quietly, "Not any more," and hurriedly left the room, crying.

Perhaps the most painful physical therapy for David came as a doctor and his nurse came to straighten out David's fingers and wrists. The doctor looked at me and said, "I'm not sure if you will want to stay in here for this." He then turned and said, "David, this is going to be painful, but it is necessary. The longer we wait, the harder and more painful it will get."

The doctor had brought two sets of splint casts for David's fingers and wrists. The nurse closed the door, and they began to straighten out the fingers and wrist of his left hand. David started screaming and crying. The pain was intense. After they got the fingers and wrist straightened, they clamped on a cast that went halfway up to his elbow.

I thought they were finished for the day; surely they would wait awhile and give David a chance to rest and prepare for the right hand, but they began immediately on the right fingers and wrist, which produced the same level of pain. The story of David is a classic illustration that feeling good with drugs comes at a very high price.

So went convalescence with David. After months of extensive therapy, the machines were removed one by one. Eventually David was transferred to another facility for advanced therapy. After fourteen months, three hospitals, three physical therapy facilities, and $1,250,000 had been spent on his health care, David was sitting up in a wheelchair; he was ready to go home, but he was never to walk again without a walker to support him.

After David went home, I waited for two weeks before contacting him; I knew he had a lot of catching up to do. He also was still going through home therapy. I spoke regularly with his dad at work, and he kept me up to speed on David's progress.

Finally I called David and asked him if he wanted to go for a ride, which of course he did. When I went to pick David up for this ride, I was amazed at the initial difficulty I had in handling him. David weighed about 150 pounds, and it was necessary to physically manhandle him just to get him into my truck. But we would soon master this, and our rides became a routine. David's dad also instructed me in how to help David with his bodily functions; David could not yet use his hands well enough to do these things for himself. **I include this detail only to emphasize that <u>feeling good with drugs comes with a price</u>.**

It is interesting that David wanted to attend church with me, and I pushed that wheelchair many miles, going to various churches in Las Vegas. I had begun speaking to youth groups about the dangers of drugs, and together, David and I would speak to youth groups about the horrors of drugs. David was a willing example of what drugs do to people.

In 2002, I began speaking in public schools, presenting what we now call Drug Awareness Training. David soon began accompanying me to church youth groups and he and I began presenting this program in middle schools. Having David speak openly and matter-of-factly about his experiences with drugs was an instant success. David is a natural speaker, and he looked forward to each presentation. I had to work hard to connect with students; David did not. To say the least, David has a way with girls, and many of these teenage girls seemed to find their guy with David; he was an instant hero. I believe David's story about his experiences with drugs helped a lot of kids avoid the mistake he had made.

In time, David moved to California, where he lived with his grandmother while he studied drafting, and at this writing, he is still living with her. He earned an AA degree in drafting. He then went on to study engineering; after one year of study in an engineering curriculum, he was near the top of his class academically.

I lost touch with David for several years after he moved to California, but I learned that while in engineering school, he suffered a relapse and began to do drugs again. This time, his drug of choice was heroin. As will be presented in the next section, it is quite common for recovering drug addicts to regress at some point after willingly entering into rehabilitation. David has since turned away from heroin, but like me, David will always have a desire to feel the sense of euphoria that drugs cause your body to produce.

You may recall from my Drug Awareness Presentation on Day #1, David's drugs of choice were smoking cigarettes, smoking marijuana, and huffing of household chemicals and prescription painkillers. Then on Day #2, I said:

> If you have chosen this form of drug addiction—huffing of household chemicals—you've chosen the worst form of drug addiction known to man. Every time you go through a huffing session, you kill hundreds of thousands of brain cells, never again to be replaced.
>
> When you go underneath the sink at home, or you go out into the garage, and take a chemical and it spray into a rag and put that rag over your face and breathe the fumes, what you are doing is replacing the oxygen in your brain with chemicals that stay in there long after you quit huffing, and continue to kill brain cells for years to come.
>
> Since huffing has become so popular in our society, a little phenomenon has crept up: seemingly healthy happy young people between the ages of eighteen through twenty-four go to bed one night and die in their sleep. They perform an autopsy on these young people and cannot determine the cause of death; in the ones that they could, they went into their backgrounds all the way into grammar school, and they discovered in 100 percent of the cases that they were huffers of household chemicals in their early teenage years.
>
> This tells the researchers that these chemicals stayed in their brain long after they quit huffing, continuing to kill brain cells up to the point that the brain simply shut down and died.

David is now in his early twenties and has experienced a series of small strokes. His doctors have informed him that it is simply a matter of time until a larger stroke takes his life; doctors do not believe that he has long to live. However, as of this writing, David is dedicating his free time to performing drug awareness training in Palmdale, California, high schools, and he is walking with the aid of a walker. David is living proof that if you want something badly enough, the obstacles will eventually be removed. David's story is an inspiration to me to continue this program as long as I can.

Will David be another victim of his early choices to do drugs? Apparently there is nothing that medicine can do to free him from the trap he prepared for himself through the choices that he made at thirteen and fourteen years of age, and that he also made a second time later in life. However, as with me, there is a power beyond this world that is in control of time and space and matter; only in time will we learn if Providence has provided David an opportunity to share what he has learned about the detrimental effects of illicit drugs.

Is the price of feeling good on drugs for a short time worth the price you will pay later?

Under the paragraph heading "Questions To Think About," my writing assistant wrote:

> It is also our desire to caution young people to avoid certain pitfalls that will destroy their life before they even get started. Drug abuse is one of those major pitfalls. **It is a wise person who can learn from his or her mistakes, learn from the mistakes of others, <u>and learn to proceed into the world of the unknown with educated caution</u>.**

Learn from David's mistakes. Young people, don't start your adult life a chemical freak;

<u>don't do it!</u>

SECTION THREE
NATIONAL INSTITUTE ON DRUG ABUSE
INFORMATION AND FACTS

Except as otherwise noted, the information in this section was taken from the National Institute on Drug Abuse (NIDA) and their affiliates. The various information designated is available at the website listed in the appropriate footnote.

¶#54: Understanding Drug Abuse and Addiction [12]

Many people do not understand why or how other people become addicted to drugs. It can be wrongfully assumed that drug abusers lack moral principles or willpower and that they could stop using drugs simply by choosing to change their behavior. In reality, **drug addiction** is a complex disease, and quitting takes more than good intentions. **In fact, because drugs change the brain in ways that foster compulsive drug abuse, quitting is difficult, even for those who are ready to do so**. Through scientific advances, we know more about how drugs work in the brain than ever before, and we also know that **drug addiction can be successfully treated to help people stop abusing drugs and lead productive lives.**

Drug abuse and addiction have negative consequences for individuals and for society. Estimates of the total overall costs of substance abuse in the United States, including productivity and health and crime-related costs, exceed $600 billion annually. This includes approximately $181 billion for illicit drugs,[13] $193 billion for tobacco,[14] and $235 billion for alcohol.[15] As staggering as these numbers are, they do not fully describe the breadth of destructive public

---

[12] The information under in paragraphs #54, #55, #56, and #57 was taken the National Institute on Drug Abuse on July 25, 2011, in verbatim form, from website http://www.drugabuse.gov/infofacts/understand.html#Anchor-References-47857. This website was last updated in March of 2011. This information is supplemented by similar information found at website http://www.nida.nih.gov/scienceofaddiction/. The information on both websites is in the public domain and may be reproduced without permission. Paragraph numbers, bold, and underline have been added by the author.

[13] Office of National Drug Control Policy (2004). *The Economic Costs of Drug Abuse in the United States, 1992–2002.* Washington DC: Executive Office of the President (Publication No. 207303). Available at www.ncjrs.gov/ondcppubs/publications/pdf/economic_costs.pdf

[14] Centers for Disease Control and Prevention, National Center for Chronic Disease Prevention and Health Promotion, Office on Smoking and Health, US Department of Health and Human Services. Best Practices for Comprehensive Tobacco Control Programs—2007. Available at http://www.cdc.gov/tobacco/stateandcommunity/best_practices/pdfs/2007/bestpractices_complete.pdf.

[15] Rehm, J., C. Mathers, S. Popova, M. Thavorncharoensap, Y. Teerawattananon, and J. Patra. "Global burden of disease and injury and economic cost attributable to alcohol use and alcohol-use disorders. *Lancet* (373)9682, 2223–2233, 2009.

health and safety implications of drug abuse and addiction, such as family disintegration, loss of employment, failure in school, domestic violence, and child abuse.

¶#55: What Is Drug Addiction?

Addiction is a chronic, often relapsing brain disease that causes compulsive drug seeking and use, despite harmful consequences to addicted individuals and to those around them. **Although the <u>initial decision to take drugs is voluntary</u> for most people, <u>the brain changes that occur over time challenge a person's self-control and ability to resist intense impulses urging them to take drugs</u>.**

Fortunately, treatments are available to help people counter addiction's powerful disruptive effects. Research shows that combining addiction treatment medications with behavioral therapy is the best way to ensure success for most patients. Treatment approaches that are tailored to each patient's drug abuse patterns and any co-occurring medical, psychiatric, and social problems can lead to sustained recovery and a life without drug abuse.

Similar to other chronic, relapsing diseases, such as diabetes, asthma, or heart disease, drug addiction can be managed successfully. And as with other chronic diseases, **it is not uncommon for a person to relapse and begin abusing drugs again**. Relapse, however, does not signal treatment failure—rather, it indicates that treatment should be reinstated or adjusted, or that an alternative treatment is needed to help the individual regain control and recover.

¶#56: What Happens to Your Brain When You Take Drugs?

Drugs contain chemicals that tap into the brain's communication system and disrupt the way nerve cells normally send, receive, and process information. There are at least two ways that drugs cause this disruption: (1) by imitating the brain's natural chemical messengers and (2) by over stimulating the "reward circuit" of the brain.

Some drugs (e.g., marijuana and heroin) have a similar structure to neurotransmitters, chemical messengers that are naturally produced by the brain. This similarity allows the drugs to "fool" the brain's receptors and activate nerve cells to send abnormal messages.

Other drugs, such as cocaine or methamphetamine, can cause the nerve cells to release abnormally large amounts of neurotransmitters (mainly dopamine) or to prevent the normal recycling of these brain chemicals, which is needed to shut off the signaling between neurons. The result is a brain awash in dopamine, a neurotransmitter present in brain regions that control movement, emotion, motivation, and feelings of pleasure. The over stimulation of this reward system, which normally responds to natural behaviors linked to survival (eating, spending time with loved ones, etc.), produces euphoric effects in response to psychoactive drugs. **This reaction sets in motion a reinforcing pattern that teaches people to repeat the rewarding behavior of abusing drugs.**

As a person continues to abuse drugs, the brain adapts to the overwhelming surges in dopamine by producing less dopamine or by reducing the number of dopamine receptors in the reward circuit. The result is **a <u>lessening</u> of dopamine's impact on the reward circuit, which reduces the abuser's ability to enjoy the drugs, as well as the events in life that previously brought pleasure. <u>This decrease compels the addicted person to keep abusing drugs</u> in an attempt to bring the dopamine function back to normal, <u>except now larger amounts of the drug are required to achieve the same dopamine high</u>—an effect known as <u>tolerance</u>.**

Long-term abuse causes changes in other brain chemical systems and circuits as well. **<u>Glutamate</u>** is a neurotransmitter that **influences the reward circuit and <u>the ability to learn</u>**. When the optimal concentration of glutamate is altered by drug abuse, the brain attempts to compensate, which can impair cognitive function. **Brain imaging studies of drug-addicted individuals show changes in areas of the brain that are critical to <u>judgment</u>, <u>decision making</u>, <u>learning</u> and <u>memory</u>, and <u>behavior control</u>. Together, these changes can drive an abuser to seek out and take drugs <u>compulsively</u> despite adverse, even devastating consequences—<u>that is the nature of addiction</u>.**

¶#57: Why Do Some People Become Addicted While Others Do Not?

No single factor can predict whether a person will become addicted to drugs. Risk for addiction is influenced by a combination of factors that include individual biology, social environment, and age or stage of development. The more risk factors an individual has, the greater the chance that taking drugs can lead to addiction. For example:

❖ **Biology:** The genes that people are born with—in combination with environmental influences—account for about half of their addiction vulnerability. Additionally, gender, ethnicity, and the presence of other mental disorders may influence risk for drug abuse and addiction.

❖ **Environment:** A person's environment includes many different influences, from family and friends to socioeconomic status and quality of life in general. Factors such as peer pressure, physical and sexual abuse, stress, and quality of parenting can greatly influence the occurrence of drug abuse and the escalation to addiction in a person's life.

❖ **Development:** Genetic and environmental factors interact with critical developmental stages in a person's life to affect addiction vulnerability. Although taking drugs at any age can lead to addiction, the earlier that drug use begins, the more likely it will progress to more serious abuse, which poses a special challenge to adolescents. Because their brains are still developing in the areas that govern decision making, judgment, and self-control, adolescents may be especially prone to risk-taking behaviors, including abusing drugs.

¶#58: Prevention Is the Key

Drug addiction is a <u>preventable</u> disease. Results from the National Institute for Drug Abuse-funded research show that prevention programs involving families, schools, communities, and the media are effective in reducing drug abuse. Although many events and cultural factors affect drug abuse trends, **<u>when youths perceive drug abuse as harmful, they reduce their drug taking</u>**. Thus, education and outreach are key in helping youth and the general public understand the risks of drug abuse. **<u>TEACHERS, PARENTS, MEDICAL PROFESSIONALS, AND PUBLIC HEALTH PROFESSIONALS MUST KEEP SENDING THE MESSAGE THAT DRUG ADDICTION CAN BE PREVENTED IF ONE NEVER ABUSES DRUGS.</u>**

¶#59: Other Information Sources

For information on understanding drug abuse and addiction, please see our booklet, *Drugs, Brains, and Behavior—The Science of Addiction*, at www.nida.nih.gov/scienceofaddiction.

For more information on prevention, please visit www.nida.nih.gov/drugpages/prevention.html.

For more information on treatment, please visit www.nida.nih.gov/drugpages/treatment.html. To find a publicly funded treatment center in your state, please call (800) 662-HELP or visit www.findtreatment.samhsa.gov.

TABLE 1: Monitoring the Future

Study Trends in Prevalence of Various Drugs

for Eighth-Graders, Tenth-Graders, and Twelfth-Graders

2007–2010 (in percent)[16]

DRUG ABUSE PERCENTAGE BY SCHOOL GRADE LEVEL

	8th-Graders				10th-Graders				12th-Graders			
	2007	2008	2009	2010	2007	2008	2009	2010	2007	2008	2009	2010
Any Illicit Drug Use												
Lifetime	19.0	19.6	19.9	**21.4**	35.6	34.1	36.0	**37.0**	46.8	47.4	46.7	**48.2**
Past Year	13.2	14.1	14.5	**[16.0]**	28.1	26.9	29.4	**30.2**	35.9	36.6	36.5	**38.3**
Past Month	7.4	7.6	8.1	**[9.5]**	16.9	15.8	17.8	**18.5**	21.9	22.3	23.3	**23.8**
Marijuana/Hashish												
Lifetime	14.2	14.6	15.7	**17.3**	31.0	29.9	32.3	**33.4**	41.8	42.6	42.0	**43.8**
Past Year	10.3	10.9	11.8	**[13.7]**	24.6	23.9	26.7	**27.5**	31.7	32.4	32.8	**34.8**
Past Month	5.7	5.8	6.5	**[8.0]**	14.2	13.8	15.9	**16.7**	18.8	19.4	20.6	**21.4**
Daily	0.8	0.9	1.0	**[1.2]**	2.8	2.7	2.8	**[3.3]**	5.1	5.4	5.2	**[6.1]**
Inhalants												
Lifetime	15.6	15.7	14.9	**14.5**	13.6	12.8	12.3	**12.0**	10.5	9.9	9.5	**9.0**
Past Year	8.3	8.9	8.1	**8.1**	6.6	5.9	6.1	**5.7**	3.7	3.8	3.4	**3.6**
Past Month	3.9	4.1	3.8	**3.6**	2.5	2.1	**[2.2]**	**2.0**	1.2	1.4	1.2	**1.4**
Hallucinogens												
Lifetime	3.1	3.3	3.0	**3.4**	6.4	5.5	6.1	**6.1**	8.4	8.7	7.4	**8.6**
Past Year	1.9	2.1	1.9	**2.2**	4.4	3.9	4.1	**4.2**	5.4	5.9	[4.7]	**5.5**
Past Month	1.0	0.9	0.9	**1.0**	1.7	1.3	1.4	**1.6**	1.7	[2.2]	[1.6]	**1.9**
LSD												

16 Data in brackets indicate statistically significant change from the previous year. This table was taken from Website http://www.nida.nih.gov/infofacts/HSYouthtrends.html. This information is in the public domain and may be reproduced without permission.

TABLE 1: Monitoring the Future

Study Trends in Prevalence of Various Drugs

for Eighth-Graders, Tenth-Graders, and Twelfth-Graders

2007–2010 (in percent)[16]

DRUG ABUSE PERCENTAGE BY SCHOOL GRADE LEVEL

	8th-Graders				10th-Graders				12th-Graders			
	2007	2008	2009	2010	2007	2008	2009	2010	2007	2008	2009	2010
Lifetime	1.6	1.9	1.7	1.8	3.0	2.6	3.0	3.0	3.4	4.0	3.1	4.0
Past Year	1.1	1.3	1.1	1.2	1.9	1.8	1.9	1.9	2.1	2.7	[1.9]	[2.6]
Past Month	0.5	0.5	0.5	0.6	0.7	0.7	0.5	0.7	0.6	[1.1]	[0.5]	[0.8]
Cocaine												
Lifetime	3.1	3.0	2.6	2.6	5.3	4.5	4.6	3.7	7.8	7.2	[6.0]	5.5
Past Year	2.0	1.8	1.6	1.6	3.4	3.0	2.7	2.2	5.2	4.4	[3.4]	2.9
Past Month	0.9	0.8	0.8	0.6	1.3	1.2	[0.9]	0.9	[2.0]	1.9	[1.3]	1.3
Crack Cocaine												
Lifetime	2.1	2.0	1.7	1.5	2.3	2.0	2.1	1.8	3.2	2.8	2.4	2.4
Past Year	1.3	1.1	1.1	1.0	1.3	1.3	1.2	1.0	1.9	[1.6]	1.3	1.4
Past Month	0.6	0.5	0.5	0.4	[0.5]	0.5	0.4	0.5	0.9	0.8	0.6	0.7
Heroin												
Lifetime	1.3	1.4	1.3	1.3	1.5	[1.2]	[1.5]	1.3	1.5	1.3	1.2	1.6
Past Year	0.8	0.9	0.7	0.8	0.8	0.8	0.9	0.8	0.9	0.7	0.7	0.9
Past Month	0.4	0.4	0.4	0.4	0.4	0.4	0.4	0.4	0.4	0.4	0.4	0.4
Tranquilizers												
Lifetime	3.9	3.9	3.9	4.4	7.4	6.8	7.0	7.3	9.5	8.9	9.3	8.5
Past Year	2.4	2.4	2.6	2.8	5.3	4.6	5.0	5.1	6.2	6.2	6.3	5.6
Past Month	1.1	1.2	1.2	1.2	2.6	[1.9]	2.0	2.2	2.6	2.6	2.7	2.5
Alcohol												
Lifetime	38.9	38.9	[36.6]	35.8	61.7	[58.3]	59.1	58.2	72.2	71.9	72.3	71.0
Past Year	31.8	32.1	30.3	29.3	56.3	[52.5]	52.8	52.1	66.4	65.5	66.2	65.2
Past Month	15.9	15.9	14.9	13.8	33.4	[28.8]	30.4	28.9	44.4	43.1	43.5	41.2]
Daily	0.6	0.7	[0.5]	0.5	1.4	[1.0]	1.1	1.1	3.1	2.8	2.5	2.7
Cigarettes (any use)												

TABLE 1: Monitoring the Future

Study Trends in Prevalence of Various Drugs

for Eighth-Graders, Tenth-Graders, and Twelfth-Graders

2007–2010 (in percent)[16]

DRUG ABUSE PERCENTAGE BY SCHOOL GRADE LEVEL

	8th-Graders				10th-Graders				12th-Graders			
	2007	2008	2009	2010	2007	2008	2009	2010	2007	2008	2009	2010
Lifetime	22.1	20.5	20.1	20.0	34.6	[31.7]	32.7	33.0	46.2	44.7	43.6	42.2
Past Month	7.1	6.8	6.5	7.1	14.0	[12.3]	13.1	13.6	21.6	20.4	20.1	19.2
Daily	3.0	3.1	2.7	2.9	7.2	[5.9]	6.3	6.6	12.3	11.4	11.2	10.7
1/2-pack+/day	1.1	1.2	1.0	0.9	2.7	[2.0]	2.4	2.4	5.7	5.4	5.0	4.7
Smokeless Tobacco												
Lifetime	9.1	9.8	9.6	9.9	15.1	[12.2]	[15.2]	16.8	15.1	15.6	16.3	17.6
Past Month	3.2	3.5	3.7	4.1	6.1	5.0	[6.5]	7.5	6.6	6.5	8.4	8.5
Daily	0.8	0.8	0.8	0.9	1.6	1.4	[1.9]	2.5	2.8	2.7	2.9	3.1
Steroids												
Lifetime	1.5	1.4	1.3	1.1	1.8	1.4	1.3	1.6	2.2	2.2	2.2	2.0
Past Year	0.8	0.9	0.8	[0.5]	1.1	0.9	0.8	1.0	1.4	1.5	1.5	1.5
Past Month	0.4	0.5	0.4	0.3	0.5	0.5	0.5	0.5	1.0	1.0	1.0	1.1
MDMA												
Lifetime	2.3	2.4	2.2	[3.3]	5.2	4.3	5.5	6.4	6.5	6.2	6.5	7.3
Past Year	1.5	1.7	1.3	[2.4]	3.5	2.9	3.7	[4.7]	4.5	4.3	4.3	4.5
Past Month	0.6	0.8	0.6	[1.1]	1.2	1.1	1.3	[1.9]	1.6	1.8	1.8	1.4
Methamphetamine												
Lifetime	1.8	2.3	[1.6]	1.8	2.8	2.4	2.8	2.5	[3.0]	2.8	2.4	2.3
Past Year	1.1	1.2	1.0	1.2	1.6	1.5	1.6	1.6	[1.7]	1.2	1.2	1.0
Past Month	0.6	0.7	0.5	0.7	0.4	[0.7]	0.6	0.7	0.6	0.6	0.5	0.5
Vicodin												
Past Year	2.7	2.9	2.5	2.7	7.2	6.7	8.1	7.7	9.6	9.7	9.7	[8.0]
OxyContin												
Past Year	1.8	2.1	2.0	2.1	3.9	3.6	5.1	4.6	5.2	4.7	4.9	5.1
Cough Medicine (nonprescription)												
Past Year	4.0	3.6	3.8	3.2	5.4	5.3	6.0	5.1	5.8	5.5	5.9	6.6

Revised 8/2010

¶#60: Additional Statistics Addressing Drug Abuse:[17]

- ❖ The number of people who died as a result of a cocaine overdose was 699 in 2004. In 1992, that number was 223.

- ❖ Between the years 2001 and 2005, the number of Americans between the age of fifty and fifty-nine who were using illegal drugs rose from 2.5 percent to 4.7 percent.

- ❖ Over six million children in America live with at least one parent who has a drug addiction.

- ❖ Since 1980, the number of deaths related to drug overdoses has risen over 540 percent.

- ❖ The most commonly abused drug (other than alcohol) in the United States by individuals over the age of twelve is marijuana, followed by prescription painkillers, cocaine, and hallucinogens.

- ❖ Each year, drug abuse and drug addiction cost employers over $122 billion in lost productivity time and another $15 billion in health insurance costs.

- ❖ Baltimore, Maryland, has more per capita individuals living with heroin addiction than any other state [sic] in the United States.

- ❖ Since 1990, the number of individuals who take prescription drugs illegally is believed to have risen by over 500 percent.

- ❖ Marijuana is the most widely used drug in the United States. Over three quarters of all drug addicts use or have used marijuana. [This apparently does not include tobacco.]

- ❖ Every year, over 20,000 individuals die as a result of illicit drug use.

---

[17] This information was taken from http://www.michaelshouse.com/drug-addiction/drug-addiction-statistics/ and is reproduced in verbatim form below. The date this information was compiled was unavailable but it was last updated on May 27, 2011. These statistics show general trends rather than specific and quantified trends.

❖ In the past twenty years, the number of people with drug addictions in the United States has skyrocketed by over 500 percent.

❖ Over 15 million Americans use illicit drugs each year. Of these individuals, many become addicts but few seek the treatment they need.

TEEN CHALLENGE SUCCESS IN DRUG ABUSE TREATMENT AS VERIFIED BY THE NATIONAL INSTITUTE ON DRUG ABUSE; <u>SIGNIFICANT RESEARCH THAT EVERYONE SHOULD KNOW</u>[18]

¶#61: National Institute on Drug Abuse (NIDA) Report

Teen Challenge claims of a 70 percent cure rate for the drug addicts graduating from their program attracted the attention of the US federal government in 1973. Most secular drug rehabilitation programs have <u>a cure rate of 1 to 15 percent</u>. The National Institute on Drug Abuse, part of the US Department of Health, Education, and Welfare, funded the first year of this study to evaluate the long-term results of the Teen Challenge program.

This study focused on **all students** in the class of 1968 that entered Brooklyn, NY, Teen Challenge and then transferred to **Rehrersburg**, PA, for the second half of their training. **This follow-up study seven years later (1975) sought to determine <u>six variables</u>: what proportion of the program participants (1) were still drug free, (2) had no legal involvements, (3) were employed or pursuing education, (4) were a part of a family unit, (5) were participating in church activities, and (6) were of good physical and mental health.**

The survey was conducted under the leadership of Dr. Catherine Hess, MD, the former assistant chief of the Cancer Control Program of the US Public Health Service, who had previously served as the medical director for the New York Hospital Methadone Clinic. **The main premise of the study was to demonstrate that <u>introduction of a religious component</u> into the treatment of drug addicts <u>is the one aspect that produces the largest success rate</u>.**

---

[18] The below report was taken from website http://www.acadc.org/page/page/2495014.htm from the Association of Christian Alcohol & Drug Abuse Counselors Institute. This information was paid for in part by the National Institute on Drug Abuse and is in the public domain. See also website http://teenchallengeelpaso.com/teen_challenge_el_pasao___nida_report. For a similar report made by the University of Tennessee in 1994, see website http://www.beholdministries.org/STUDIES-HTML/University-of-Tennesee.html.

The National Opinion Research Center of the University of Chicago developed the survey instrument, located survey participants, conducted the personal interviews, and obtained a urine sample to test for drugs. The drug screening detection for this population was conducted by National Medical Services of Philadelphia.

¶#62: Research Results Were Categorized into Three Groups:

- ❖ **P1** were students that entered Brooklyn Teen Challenge but dropped out and never attended the Rehrersburg program.

- ❖ **P2** were students that completed the Brooklyn program who later dropped out of the Rehrersburg program.

- ❖ **P3** were graduates of the Rehrersburg Training Center program.

A total of 186 persons were interviewed for this project, **P1=70**, **P2=52**, and **P3=64**. **The P3 group of 64 represented 97 percent of the total population possible.** The results of this survey clearly indicated the success of the Teen Challenge program in the following areas:

- ❖ The Teen Challenge definition of **"drug-free" means abstaining from all use of narcotics, marijuana, alcohol, and cigarettes; 67 percent of the graduates (P3) are drug-free as indicated by the urinalysis test [86 percent stated they were drug-free on the questionnaire].**

- ❖ **72 percent of the graduates (P3)** continued their education upon completion of Teen Challenge. The areas include getting their GED or pursuing college-level education.

- ❖ **75 percent of the graduates (P3)** indicated their current status as employed; 73 percent of the graduates are self-supporting by earning their own salary. **Of those who are currently employed, 58 percent have been at their present job for over one year.**

- ❖ **87.5 percent of the graduates (P3)** did not require additional treatment in drug treatment programs after leaving Teen Challenge. Over 90 percent considered themselves addicted to drugs before entering Teen Challenge.

❖ **67** percent **of the graduates (P3)** are regularly attending church; **57** percent **of the graduates** are involved in church work.

❖ **92** percent **of the graduates (P3)** report good to excellent health, whereas the numbers are significantly lower for the other two groups: **P1=59% and P2=75%**.

For a more detailed report on these and other research projects on Teen Challenge, contact: http://mygtct.org/STUDIES-HTML/Northwestern%20University%20Study.html

The above report also illustrates that nearly 66 percent of the people who entered the program dropped out before finishing. The reason for this are not listed, nor are the statistics for the dropouts provided, nor is the dropout rate of other programs available for comparison. It is also noted that the kind of statistical information available in this report is not readily available for other recovery programs, nor is more recent information available for Teen Challenge. It is assumed that the cost of maintaining statistical follow-up data is cost prohibitive for chemical abuse programs. In addition, up to the present time the data collected in the various programs has not been of a uniform nature, which prevents accurate comparison to access the effectiveness of various programs.

The above report raises a question: **Why have the results of Teen Challenge not received greater attention in the public discussion of drug abuse?**

For information about Teen Challenge in the United States, contact Teen Challenge International, USA, 5250 N. Towne Centre Dr., Ozark, MO 65721; phone: (417) 581-2181; http://www.teenchallengeusa.com.

For information about Teen Challenge around the world, contact Global Teen Challenge, P.O. Box 511, Columbus, GA 31902; phone: (706) 576-6555; http://www.globaltc.org

As of January 2012, the above addresses, phone numbers, and websites addresses were valid.

SECTION FOUR
QUESTIONS ABOUT
THE DECISION MAKING PROCESS OF LIFE

¶#63: Questions for the Twenty-First-Century Teen

When the decision making process is examined to determine what drives some of the critical decisions individuals make in life, such as the decision to experiment with drugs, without question we recognize that they are looking for something to make their life more fulfilling. It is also true that few young people understand that their search for fulfillment is a search for meaning and purpose in life. In writing about my friend Marty Gruber, it is clear that his struggles were based in a search for meaning, and chemical abuse was a very real part of that search. Marty the child (or even Marty the adult) may not have understood his escape into drug abuse as a search for something to bring purpose or meaning into his life. However, Marty knew that he was unhappy, and he was reaching to bring fulfillment (some kind of joyous experience) into his life, and he used drugs to help him do this. This was evident at eight when he got drunk for the first time and then, as a minor, continued to drink at every opportunity to escape the boring existence of life lived without fulfillment. After discovering alcohol, Marty sought fulfillment through a chemically induced euphoria, and he was searching for something more exciting when he tried both marijuana and cocaine the first time.

In preparing Marty's story for presentation to the reader, it is apparent that Marty was shaped in his youth through a very dysfunctional social environment, and this environment did little to prepare him to answer, or even ask, the basic questions of life. Because of this, it is very clear there were several great nuggets of wisdom that Marty had to grapple with before he came to recognize that the foundation of wisdom rests in the purpose of divine Providence, which is beyond the world we live in. Marty first recognized this when he realized that divine Providence was calling him to share the dangers of chemical abuse with young people. Somehow, Marty has specifically been prepared to share his life with young people, and he has sought to be obedient to that calling since that day in 1989 when he attempted suicide and encountered a power greater than himself.

Marty didn't find wisdom in the school classroom, he found it by being open to what he now recognizes as his calling in life. As presented herein, it was through the pain that began in the home he was born into, and then progressed through the pain he experienced because of the bad choices he made over the course of his personal life, that Marty was prepared to fulfill his calling, which he recognized at the age of fifty-three—immediately after attempting suicide in a roach-filled motel room in the depressed state that followed repeatedly crashing and burning on cocaine.

Before Marty could answer his calling to become a drug awareness presenter, he had to willingly change his focus in life, and before he changed that focus, he had to hit the end of the pity party he found so easy to engage in.

As Marty's story has unfolded through the narrative of this book, we saw him attempting to end his life before crying out to someone bigger than himself. Marty cried out because he knew that he was unable to turn from drugs without help and ultimately he would succeed in killing himself if he didn't find help. It is also true that when he cried out for help in that motel room, he was calling out to the unknown. **But that call was answered by allowing Marty to see how his life could have meaning; when Marty saw his personal need, he realized that other junkies had this same need. He immediately realized that <u>kids needed to understand the necessity of avoiding the trap of drug addiction at all costs</u>. <u>Marty quickly realized that his life could have meaning by telling his story to help others avoid the pitfall of drug abuse that he had fallen into.</u>**

This flash of insight opened Marty's eyes to the startling fact that he was not alone; he was not living in a vacuum. This is the meaning of the expression, "No man is an island." Through his experience in that motel room in 1989, Marty has come to know that there is more to life than the here and now and that this world is designed to demonstrate that each person requires help from divine Providence in finding the purpose for his personal life. Marty did not learn this until he was fifty-three, but when he encountered divine Providence that day, he realized that if teenagers could learn what he had learned at the age of fifty-three, essentially their entire lives could be full and rich. They needed to learn how to make good decisions, and choosing to avoid drugs and understanding why it is imperative to leave illicit drugs alone throughout life is a good place to begin this process.

Over the years, Marty has learned to see this world from a completely different perspective than he developed growing up. This world is designed to teach the observer that we are not alone. Marty's multiple near death experiences, as presented earlier, were designed to teach him this.

In support of this, there is design and purpose behind the world we physically inhabit. Those who explore the physical world and seek to understand what they observe are perplexed by the extremely high orders of organization and complexity they see everywhere they look. As scientists examine this organization and complexity, they soon discern how the microscopic world is complex beyond description. As they look at the macro world, they find complexity beyond human understanding. If they look into our solar system, they soon find complexity far beyond their ability to comprehend it. If they look into the cosmos, they also discern that the interstellar and intergalactic worlds are exceedingly complex. It is interesting to note that there are numerous theories of origins, all of which cannot be true, but almost all of them have been presented as being true at some time. However, there is one thing that is very clear: the world did not produce itself. This leaves us with an open question: What is the first cause of what we can see and experience with our senses?

When we as human observers examine the world we all inhabit, we see that the human creature is at the top of all that is accessible to him through his five senses. Our observations seem to cause some to ask several simple questions, such as, Who am I? Where did I come from? Why am I here? These are fundamental questions about life that many observant people ask in one way or another.

In the second decade of the twenty-first century, we are told by theoretical scientists that the structure of the universe is vastly more complex than human observers historically have believed or have been able to explain. As we grow and observe more of the world we live in, we recognize the interrelatedness of all things that we can see. As we begin to explore our world, we see that complexity and organization are observed everywhere we look and that all we can explore is interrelated. This recognition generates additional questions such as, What caused all this? Where is my journey through life taking me? Is there a purpose for the organization and complexity I see all around me?

In school we learn that many very intelligent people have spent their lives trying to understand how the structure and organization of the physical world came into being, only to learn how new discoveries frequently show us how little we actually know and reshape what we thought we knew. A primary question the modern observer struggles with is, Did our world happen by chance or is it intelligently designed and engineered to work together? Regardless of how we believe it originated, the close observer innately knows there must be a foundational reality for what is, or there must be a first cause that initiated and holds together the complex world we see and experience. Very intelligent men and women have labored for millennia to answer these questions, and now the questions come to the twenty-first-century teenager in America.

¶#64: The Drug Trap

If something is true, it will work well when applied where it is intended to work. This is true in engineering design and construction principles, and learning engineering principles has allowed engineers to harness the physical world and use it for beneficial purposes. The same is true in the social world humans live in: the application of truth to life works well. Thus, if truth becomes the foundation for making decisions in life, the decisions we make will work well, and if something is applied improperly, or is not true, it may not work well or it may not work at all. With this thought in mind, look around you; American society has produced the greatest culture the world has ever seen, but today it is in decline, and drug abuse is a very real part of that decline. The question we need to ask is, Why is this happening to America?

The reality is that in the American culture, many people have turned from applying truth to the decisions of life. I believe the reason for this is that few parents and educators are attempting to answer the basic questions of life and then help young people build on those answers. As a result, children are overwhelmed by life because they have few answers to the basic questions of life that they are struggling with. However, in all probability they have not yet put these questions into words. This contributes to the world without purpose they are living in.

Many chemical freaks find their lives empty and boring, and most of them were looking for something to give them excitement and hope when they found drugs. It doesn't take drug abusers long to discern that drugs are not supplying what they hoped to find, but by the time some of them come to this conclusion, they are addicts. They were looking for purpose and fulfillment, right up to the point in their lives when they discovered drugs and made a very bad choice, and now they look for increased fulfillment through more powerful drugs. However, addicts soon discover they are looking for fulfillment in the wrong place; but by then, it is too late.

The drug trap is specifically designed for teenagers who are bored with life and are looking for something to fill an emptiness they feel, or they have been hurt and are looking for something to help them escape the pain they feel. Most teenagers today have little knowledge of how illicit drugs will affect them over time, and so they proceed blindly into the trap prepared for them. Upon trying drugs for the first time, the only thing many teens knew about them is that "drugs make me feel good and make me look cool," and the euphoria of drug usage causes them to be fulfilled—for a while. Drugs cause them to feel acceptable when they are high, but they all must come down into the world they are trying to escape—they can't stay high 24/7.

Down through time, almost all people have asked the basic questions of life, and some of them have sought to write down their answers and then communicate those answers to coming generations. I believe it is this quest for answers by the teenager, and the lack of answers provided, that cause many to struggle. It is a lack of answers that sometimes manifests itself as the generation gap. Many times teens realize that their lives are not working, but they also realize that the lives of their parents or guardians are not working either, and so they reject the values of their parents and go in search for their own answers to the questions of life. The answers individuals who are engaged in a quest for meaning formulate to the basic questions of life will have far reaching implications on the choices they make in the options that life presents to them. Teens are fledgling adults searching for their identity, and teenage drug addicts are teens who made bad choices in their search for meaning.

¶#65: The Controversy Over Meaning

The answers to the meaning of life that many very intelligent people have found and communicated to others through the passing millennia can be quite controversial. To avoid problems over conflicting answers, American educators in the twentieth and twenty-first centuries have thought it prudent to leave controversial topics such as origins and eternity to parents or legal guardians. In order to diffuse controversies, legislators have attempted to address and enforce this issue through law. **The effect of this is the dearth of answers** presented to teens at home and in school, and this sometimes leaves them in an intellectual vacuum, and the human mind does not like a vacuum.

Teens are going to look for answers to their questions about life with or without guidance from the adults in their lives. They are looking for something to bring life together; teens looking for answers to their questions are trying to integrate their life into something meaningful and fulfilling. This is why they experiment with the various dimensions of life that adults sometimes tell them are best left unexplored until they are older and can make decisions based on a broader range of knowledge. It is hard to be obedient to someone whom you do **NOT** believe has the answers you have been searching for.

In studying what motivates a teen to choose a drug-free life or what causes a drug addict to turn from drugs, one thing is very clear: the teen struggling with the questions of life needs intellectually satisfying answers and hope for a future that has purpose, and a drug addict trying to find a motivation strong enough to turn away from drugs is looking for the same things. It is the teen's search for meaning that sometimes leads to curiosity about drugs, about sex, about the occult, and just about everything else. It is the unanswered question that draws the teen to experiment with what is unknown, like a moth to a flame. And like a moth that flies into the unguarded flame, many get burned in a way that produces life changing, or life ending, damage.

In order to prevent being drawn into the flame or to retrieve someone who has been burned, individuals have to see an alternative that is real, and they have to find hope for something that is better than their current condition. The question for parents who are seeking to help their child find fulfillment in life is, How can I steer my child into a healthy lifestyle with his full cooperation? The answer is (1) by demonstrating a fulfilling life to your children in the home, and (2) by helping them ask pertinent questions about life and then answer their unanswered questions.

¶#66: The Limitations of Public-Funded Education

Education through high school is designed to educate the child in the basic areas of knowledge and provide the intellectual tools he needs to become a continuous learner after high school. However, formal public education, up to and including high school, is not designed to address the basic questions of life we all begin to ask as we grow up and encounter the world we live in. If we have learned anything about worldviews and personal values, it is that the ideas children accept from birth to approximately eight years of age become the foundation of their values, and this foundation shapes their worldview throughout their life. The worldview of the individual is laid upon the foundation of ideas that are presupposed to be truth, that most people simply accept from their home environment and then build on throughout life.

¶#67: The Foundation of Truth and Values

As we mature, we realize from personal experience that it is increasingly difficult to change attitudes and habits that were formed at a younger age. Most of us realize that the older we are when we desire to change a personal habit, and the longer we have had a specific habit, the more difficult it is to change. The presuppositions that we accept as basic truth and build into our views of life are very similar to habits. The basic ideas we presuppose to be truth during childhood, and reinforce in adolescence, are difficult to change in adulthood. Because of this, children are like arrows shot from the bow of the family unit.

Thus, if parents have not answered the basic questions of life for themselves and discovered how to build a fulfilling life as they matured through childhood and adolescence, and then continued in this process as a married person with their spouse, then they cannot demonstrate to their children how to do something they have not learned to do for themselves. And if they marry someone who has not answered the basic questions of life, as a married couple, they will have a bumpy relationship as they sort out the rules for life in marriage. A marriage built in this way cannot function in harmony until the couple works out how they will adjust to the new pattern of life, nor can the parents in such a marriage provide a secure environment for raising their children and demonstrating how to build a successful family. The importance of worldviews cannot be overstressed in the building of a successful and functioning family unit that will produce secure and mentally healthy children.

Children catch what parents demonstrate to them, because values are caught rather than taught. The result is that children raised in dysfunctional families encounter a bewildering world that they are not equipped to deal with in childhood, adolescence, or adulthood. In addition, when grown children from such homes accept life changing truth as adults, they

141

find that it is difficult to alter their worldview in a significant manner. And the older they are when they encounter life changing truth, the more difficult it is to change their worldview and to consistently implement that truth in their lives. Changing our worldview takes time and can be difficult to accomplish.

People who have been raised in a home modeling traditional values sometimes discover a different foundation for truth, such as a divine revelation that they consider to be truth, that is different than the foundation of truth they had accepted earlier in life. These people may find that even though their behavior is consistent with their new understanding of truth, the basic reasons they behave in a certain way is now different. Their presuppositions of truth have changed. People living under traditional values who discover foundational truth in this manner find that the changes they must make are more mental (i.e., their pattern of thinking is altered) rather than being both mental and external (i.e., adjusting to a new pattern of thinking that also requires a change in behavior).

This happens when people accept the truth that their forefathers had accepted and built into their pattern of life, but in the progression of their culture, the foundational truth had been lost. People who encounter truth in this manner may find that there is an internal struggle for a time as the new pattern of thinking is applied to their established memories, mental processes, and habits. They have a new intellectual foundation for decision making, and they may discover **WHY** they have done things as their forefathers did. These are ideas of truth that were not communicated to them in childhood as the foundation of truth establishing traditional values that establish behavior. The foundational reason had been lost, but the tradition remained. This can actually be difficult for a person to work through as they realize their mental processes were not consistent with the foundation of truth they have now come to accept. As difficult as this may be to work through, it is much easier than discovering life changing truth that produces significant changes in behavior, causing the person to wrestle with the changing intellectual processes simultaneously with behavioral changes. Both conditions can be stressful, but the second condition is significantly more stressful than the first.

¶#68: Social Drift

Publicly funded schools and society regulate behavior through rules rather than attempting to teach presuppositions of truth that undergird mental processes. Thus, children who have not begun to answer the basic questions of life at home will bring what they have learned to school, and they will control their behavior at school the way they learned to behave at home. If the rules at home are similar to the rules at school, adjustment to the new environment is much easier for the child than if they are different. If behavioral rules are different, the child may become confused. To minimize confusion in a child, it is very important that parents provide a consistent demonstration of values that work in the public arena to their very young children and explain these values and the root of these values to their maturing children in the daily grind of life as their children grow up.

However, if parents have not answered the basic questions of life for themselves and do not have a working understanding of who they are and what is important in life, they cannot communicate these values to their children, and their children must grow up in the same bewildering world their parents grew up in. Even if parents have carefully trained their children, if the environment at school is significantly different than the values demonstrated by parents in the home environment, the child may be caught in a cross fire of conflicting values and become confused. This is the condition produced in any social environment when the values of society begin to drift from traditional values (i.e., social drift). When children observe social drift and do not have an adequate foundational reason supporting the values they are taught at home, they have no anchor of absolutes, and the result is that they may begin to question what they have been raised to believe; the result is increasing social drift.

¶#69: What Works in Life Is Built Upon Foundational Truth

There is one thought that most people who search for truth in a serious way are compelled to agree on: "**Because the world that we observe**[19] **operates in obedience to physical laws that we can observe and understand, we may confidently believe that we inhabit a grand kingdom of truth just waiting to be found.**" In fact, this is the basic presupposition of science, and formal education is well designed to teach science. But this is also the presupposition of divine revelations, and public educators are forbidden to present discussions of divine

---

[19] The world that we observe is the ecological system of life, which clearly operates under established laws. It is also clear that we sometimes have a difficult time understanding how those laws function and we get into ecological trouble from time to time. The same is true in social laws. The reason we have difficulty with social laws is because we as individuals build our lives on ideas that are not true, and we attempt to build our societies on ideas that are not true. When everyone attempts to do what is right in their own eyes, social drift is the result. Social turmoil frequently accompanies social drift.

revelations (i.e., religion) in the classroom, and many refuse to address this when questions are asked. This makes it impossible to compare what some claim science teaches to what divine revelations teach and to evaluate one in terms of the other. This makes it impossible to evaluate how consistently either view actually meets what works in the world of experience and to analyze why one works better than the other.

However, the above facts do not prevent kids from asking the basic questions of life; they want to know what truth is and why it can be accepted as truth. They want to know, Is man really at the top of all we can see? Is there an unseen hand that guides the activities of mankind? In the dearth of answers provided to them in the conflicting views of our world, they are confused and growing up in a confused world, where the adults in their lives have not answered the basic questions either.

In working through what works in life and why it works, we (the writers of this book) have come to understand that truth is like the pot of gold at the end of a rainbow, and that the rainbow is comprised of nuggets of wisdom to be found in the individual's search for the mother lode of wisdom. The mother lode of wisdom provides the one searching for meaning with a consistency that is based in reality. This mother lode presupposes that there is real truth that can be found and understood, if the individual will persist and is willing to turn from self-centered pursuits and pursue the questions of meaning to their logical end. If allowed to pursue questions to their logical end, there are intellectually satisfying answers to be found. This is what kids are looking for. They want to know why they feel the way they feel and why some things hurt them in life and why some things are wrong in one context and right in another. The place to begin answering these questions is not with the adolescent (twelve to eighteen years of age), it is with the child from birth onward in the family atmosphere. In this atmosphere, values are not only taught, they are caught.

This book is not attempting to tell anyone what to believe about science, religion, or any proclamation of truth claiming divine origin, but <u>hopefully it will encourage the reader to engage in a personal search for truth and meaning and to ask Providence to guide them in that search</u>.[20] Most certainly it is our desire to cause prospective parents and young parents to anticipate and answer the questions their children will be asking as they grow up.

---

[20] How this can be accomplished is the primary subject addressed under the next main section heading.

It is also our desire to caution young people to avoid certain pitfalls that will destroy their life before they even get started. Drug abuse is one of those major pitfalls. **It is a wise person who can learn from their mistakes, learn from the mistakes of others, <u>and learn to proceed into the world of the unknown with educated caution</u>. If truth exists, it will not change from place to place or over time; therefore, real truth will be the same for all people in all places at all times.**

¶#70: I Think, Therefore I Am

Rene Descartes penned the astute observation, "I think, therefore I am." This thought opens the human mind to a world of never-ending wonder if we will pursue our thoughts to their logical conclusions: Where did life come from? How am I capable of understanding that I exist, and that others like me also exist and are asking the same kind of questions? Did the mud rise up and become conscious of itself? Does good and evil really exist, or is everything relative? Is drug abuse wrong? If we answer, "**<u>YES, DRUG ABUSE IS WRONG,</u>**" to that last question, then we must ask, **<u>WHY IS IT WRONG</u>**? As we pursue these thoughts, at some point we finally ask, What is the meaning of life? Is man just an intelligent animal, or is there more?

Once we begin the pursuit of this question, we have found the golden rainbow leading to the mother lode of truth. Now we must pursue our thoughts from one golden nugget to the other. There really is a pot of gold at the end of that rainbow that will supply answers that will allow us to discern purpose in our personal life. If we mine the golden nuggets of truth, we find along that path, they will lead us to the mother lode. But we must be open to change as we progress through our observations of life. Hopefully the person on a quest for truth will persist and follow the rainbow of golden thought nuggets to the mother lode of truth that is waiting to be discovered.

Every honest question and every honest answer to that question will open the door of our personal pilgrimage a little wider. You are on a trek that countless numbers before you have trod, but that does not make your journey any less exciting. In fact, discussing our journey into truth with others on this pilgrimage is quite exhilarating, and discussing our journey with others along the way makes it progressively more exciting. Cleary there is a foundation for truth, and the quest to find this foundation is the most exciting pilgrimage imaginable. In the personal experience of the writers, finding the foundation of truth has opened our minds to see from this world into eternity, but that is the result of our search for truth. Each of you are on your own personal quest, and in time the product of your quest will become as unique as your fingerprints.

Regardless of where your pursuit of truth leads you, as you develop a more consistent understanding of the world, what you observe will begin to make more sense. In time you will be aware that what you believe basic truth to be has become the foundation of your intellectual life; it allows you to discern your basic purpose in life. This foundation is made up of your intellectual presuppositions that you use for evaluating all incoming information. In time, everyone who undertakes the quest for truth will develop a personal understanding of truth that is their intellectual base supporting all of the answers they develop to their questions of life.

If you are willing to pursue truth, you will find answers that are both intellectually satisfying and experientially fulfilling in the practice and application of what you learn in the processes of life. Even a casual observer must discern that there is more to life, and the meaning of life, than what we see in the here and now. What we can see is incapable of producing itself. Thus, there is a much larger world beyond what we can see, and the world that we can see points us to that unseen world.

¶#71: Questions Lead to Answers and Answers Lead to Eternal Fulfillment

The questions posed above may not be well formed in the minds of many young adults, or even older people, but they are very real nonetheless. The answers we find for our questions will help us find a satisfying path through life. Based on our personal experience, it is the unanswered questions of meaning that lead to a sense of meaningless existence, and this leads many young people to seek a level of fulfillment through chemical abuse that they have not found elsewhere. However, observations of the illicit drug world clearly demonstrate that drugs are at best a temporary diversion; their destination is increasing pain in life, ending in death—not exactly a future or a destination that most people will find fulfilling.

It is a feeling of emptiness coupled with a sense of hopelessness that may not be clearly formed or recognized in the minds of many people, especially young people, that leads them to experiment with mind-altering chemicals. The person drinking alcohol, experimenting with white powder drugs, or puffing marijuana may feel more fulfilled under a chemically induced euphoria, and so they experiment with chemicals, and many become addicted. This drove Dr. Timothy Leary in the 1960s and 1970s to experiment with hallucinogenic drugs. It is also a large part of what drives teenage kids in 2012, and it certainly is what drives college kids in the twenty-first century. As the statistics immediately following Table 1 demonstrate, older people are also increasingly experimenting with mind-altering drugs. This indicates that some older people have not answered the basic questions of life in a way that is fulfilling to them, and they are looking for fulfillment through drugs.

Regardless of what drives a person to experiment with drugs, once an individual has begun the long downhill slide called chemical addiction, it is very difficult to turn back to a drug-free life. Once ensnared, if drug abusers are to successfully turn away from mind-altering drugs, they must find a source of encouragement that will help define who they are and give them an incentive to seek a better way of life, and then to begin living a better life. We must learn to encourage kids to express and to clarify their ache for meaning and acceptance and show them how to find answers to the questions they have about who they are and about the life they are experiencing.

This book has been written to stir the minds of both young and old alike to search for the answers to their questions with willing minds and hearts that are open to recognize foundational truth whenever and wherever they find it. Training to avoid the pitfall of drug abuse must begin as a toddler and continue through adolescence, rather than beginning with teenagers who are seeking to define themselves through some form of personal pleasure or looking for escape from the pain of their young life. Purpose in life is to be anchored in the foundation of real truth; a substitute truth will not produce lasting meaning. This world is greater than the individual, and the first cause of this world is greater than the world we can see. Thus, truth will be found in a reality bigger than the individual and bigger than the world we see with our eyes.

No one has to be afraid of truth; truth will always produce greater freedoms than money, power, or intellectual achievement can produce in and of themselves. The reason I can make this statement so boldly is because experience teaches that every person will pass from this world; we are all going to die. **Thus, long-term meaning cannot be found in this world.**

No matter what you believe about origins and eternity, we are only passing through the here and now.

The old adage "Eat, drink, and be merry, for tomorrow we die" is a formula promoting hedonism.[21] **It is this thought that leads young people to seek meaning through pleasure, which includes drugs.** But if someone turns to the excesses of hedonism (i.e., pleasure) as their foundation of meaning, they have turned to a horrible living death, rather than to a life with zest and filled with promises of things to come, promises that all humans desire and are seeking in life. In the world of hedonism, pleasure is only as lasting as your current experience, and in normal life, your ability to experience pleasure is going to be diminished, and then you will die. Thus, our hope for lasting meaning must lie beyond the here and now. You can only experience freedom within form, and the promise of life throughout eternity produces an eternal format for understanding ongoing purpose through eternity.

¶#72: Why

Many of us will remember when we first began to ask why. As toddlers, we asked why to almost all things we were learning, and sometimes the adults in our lives actually attempted to answer our question. As children, we were sometimes as entertained by the adults who tried to answer our question as we were baffled by their answers. I have come to believe that children should never cease to ask why, because that is the first question on the path to a great many very valuable discoveries that will serve them well in life and provide them with meaning. There is so much to know about life that no matter how educated we become, we are still like that child asking why. Through the process of age and experience, some of us have come to believe that many answers are yet to be found, even though we have already found meaning in life by sincerely asking why and then seeking to answer that question for ourselves to our own satisfaction. When life becomes a personal quest for meaning, it seems to take on a richness that it did not have before; it is through asking why that life may become an adventure.

The individual begins to experience life at conception. After gestation, comes birth. At birth, infants are separated from their mother and introduced into the world as an individual,

---

[21] Hedonism is the philosophical view that pleasure is the supreme value in life. The value system of the hedonist is centered on pleasure as the ultimate good.

almost completely empty of knowledge. At birth the infant begins to gain knowledge through his five senses, and as he grows his mind develops the ability to remember what he has experienced. Eventually, the person arranges what he remembers into some kind of order, and that becomes the pattern for his continuing intellectual development. Gradually, the person learns to recognize sounds and shapes and to identify people who are important to him. Then he learns to speak and communicate with others like himself. In time, the world he experiences becomes larger and larger, and soon he grows to the point that he must begin to make choices, and then he begins to define good versus evil essentially based on what he wants at the moment (i.e., what he thinks is good for himself). In time, the person will learn that what is good for him may hurt someone else, and this realization opens up a whole new realm of right versus wrong to be explored.

Small children have no concept of the many choices to be made in life or of the consequences that flow from the choices they make. Guardians of those children realize that right choices can bring great rewards over a lifetime, and wrong choices can bring pain, and some choices may bring pain that may last for a lifetime. The idea is to make choices that will benefit you over your lifetime. However, young children can't grasp this because they do not know what a lifetime is. The experiences of a child are limited to the short time they can recall, but what they can recall grows with each passing day, and their understanding of what they have experienced is also growing and continually being shaped.

¶#73: Fire

Those who are responsible for raising children watch as their children grow and begin to make decisions for themselves. Those who care about young people and are charged with parenting them frequently agonize over how they can help those children learn to act wisely. Guardians recognize that there are many choices that lead to pain and a damaged life while there are substantially fewer, but much wiser, choices that lead to a fulfilling and pleasing life. Children learn how to make decisions by watching the primary adults in their lives and imitating the decisions they have watched parents or guardians make.

Children having parents in life who have asked and answered the difficult questions about life, and who know how to share what they have learned in the formation of boundaries they set, are exceedingly fortunate. James Dobson has summarized these thoughts by observing, "Values are not taught, they are caught."[22]

One illustration of this process is that we desire for children to learn about fire and how to use it to heat their house, instead of burning their house down with it. For example, many children are fascinated by a fire in the fireplace, and they usually want to play with it; they are curious about it and want to find out about it through personal experience. Until they are burned, they have no fear of the harm uncontrolled fire can do, even though they have been told it can burn them. They may understand that a burn may be painful, but until they have experienced a little of this pain, they really do not understand it. Therefore, it may be healthy for a child to get a minor burn in order to learn to respect fire and to control it to benefit himself and those around him. The child who has not learned to respect fire, in ignorance, may start a fire that damages or destroys his house and/or the house of others.

Electricity, which is used for so many good things in our modern world, is generated by controlling fire to make it beneficial instead of burning out of control. A great deal of effort has gone into learning how to control fire to generate electricity, and those who design, build, and operate electric power plants study how to do so. Engineers diligently study what has worked in the past, learning from mistakes, projecting what will work better, and refining what is known about electric power generation with the intention of improving how we generate and distribute electric power.

Frequently mankind is more dedicated to the study of controlling fire than to what will improve the decisions that humans make in the processes of our personal lives. We are finding ways to build power plants more simply and make them more effective. At the same time, as the world becomes more technical and affluent, we tend to make the decision making processes of life more complex and less defined, and we sometimes insist on making decisions in our own limited wisdom, even though we are told that doing things our way will bring a bad result. Over multiple generations, older people have observed that many people go through their teenage years fighting against those having authority over them, only later in life to become like the adults they were resisting in their teenage years.

---

[22] This quote is believed to come from the film series entitled, "Focus on the Family." We have used this thought, or variations of it, in several places throughout this book.

We know fire burns and we respect it, and there are construction codes written to ensure that fire is used safely. However, as we rebel against authority, we frequently play with a different kind of fire (e.g., sex, drugs, alcohol, etc.) that will burn us bad, but in a different way than the fire that we harness to perform work. It seems that we almost challenge these areas of experimentation to harm us. Teens tend to think that bad things will not happen to them, because they have never seen the long-range conclusion of their choices. Many of us seek freedom by throwing off traditional restraints, but many who do this have not counted the potential cost to themselves by learning how others in the past have fared by ignoring the experiences of the people who have made the very choices they are considering.

How many of us have ever stopped to realize that virtually every moral decision that can be made has been made by somebody else in the past? The fact is that many times, the adults around us know what happened to the people who made the choices we desire to make. Do we know the outcome of what we desire to do when it has been practiced within historically defined boundaries? Do we know the outcome when practiced outside of historically defined boundaries? Young people frequently are moved to act on impulse, and impulse may bring pain and damage into their lives if not acted on within wisely established boundaries. It is a fact that people, both young and old, who are burned by impulsive decisions are surrounded by people who could assist them in making a better decision if they would only ask for guidance. The things we see and want to posses, the things we pursue to experience before we know how to make wise decisions and deal with consequences, and the things we believe will make us important or fulfill us in our journey through life are the things that we must learn to make wise choices about.

So it is with almost everything in life that is important. The good things that bring the most fulfilling experiences into life can be practiced in a way that is good and that history demonstrates is good. These same things can also be practiced in a way that will bring pain and destruction into our experiences of life, and there may be ample evidence to demonstrate this as well. Those having the best interests of children in mind desire for them to experience what is beneficial, and we desire for them to know why things should be done in a certain way.

This is what parenting skills are all about; we want our children to heat their house, but we do not want them to play with fire and burn their house down. So we teach them about fire. The quest for what works in life is a pursuit that is needed in every dimension of life, because every person engages in the pursuit of what works.

¶#74: The Present Connects Our Future with Our Past

It has been said, "Those who have not learned from history are doomed to repeat it." Another proverb is, "A wise choice in youth serves for a lifetime," or "Too soon old ... too late smart."[23] All of these sound bites assume that we can learn from instruction, from our personal mistakes, and by observing the mistakes of others. One mistake that almost all young people make is their failure to realize that time is a nonrenewable asset. When time is gone, it is gone forever; the life of every person is moving toward the final moment of life, and no person can change the past. Many older people look back over life and realize that they wasted their early years on things that were insignificant when they could have used their time to much greater advantage by learning things that would benefit them as adults (i.e., "Too soon old ... too late smart").

These observations teach us that every choice we make is a midcourse alteration in life, and the summation of our choices determines our overall path through life. In addition, each choice we make influences not only ourselves, but other people, and the choices other people make influence us. When we look at life in this manner, it is apparent that we can learn to imagine our future, and if we can imagine our future, we can learn to make good choices. If we can learn to make good choices in youth, we have taken a giant step toward maximizing our enjoyment of life and minimizing our pain. However, we must be willing to imagine the consequences that flow from our choices and then make decisions based on what we feel is the best choice.

No one can unscramble eggs; this means that what is done sometimes cannot be undone. This is true for both good and bad choices. The long-term quality of our personal life, the lives

---

[23] These three proverbs apply to the individual, but in a very real sense, they also apply to the United States of America. America is in the process of growing as a people, and the question facing our nation as I write this is, Are we going to make good choices, or are we going to pursue what will make us feel good in the short term as a people in the absence of foresight? Will America pursue the vision of the founding fathers, or will we pursue of the addiction of affluence? What is meant by this will become clear in the next section.

of our family and friends, and the quality of our culture is the fruit of making good choices, moment by moment, as we travel through time. Every choice we made in the past was like sowing a seed; we cannot change the good or bad we did in the past, but if we sowed bad seeds in the past, we can learn from our mistakes and begin to sow good seed in the future. But the harvest of the seeds we have sown, good and bad, will come in due time.

Note that imagining consequences that come from the choices we make allows us to evaluate good choices from bad choices; this allows us to make better choices throughout life. In the film *The Sands of Iwo Jima*, John Wayne, playing Sergeant Stryker, says, "Life is tough … but it's tougher if you're stupid." Allow me to paraphrase this as, "Life is tough … and it's tougher if you make bad choices."

Good choices begin with realizing that everything we experience in life is interconnected with everything else. When we grasp this thought, the statement that our future is connected to our past through the present tells us that our future is determined by the choices that we make in the present. And this is true for every person, in every place, and at all times. The experiences of my family members, friends, neighbors, and other humans will affect my experience of life, and my choices will affect their experience of life. The choices I make, **matter**: the decisions my friends and family members make, **matter**: **the choices we make collectively determine the course of our life**. The choices we collectively make as a society ultimately determine the course of American society; no person lives in a vacuum. We're going through this life together.

¶#75: Those Who Have Not Learned from History Are Doomed To Repeat It

It is my observation that the moral drift in the American culture over the past fifty years indicates that the individuals of American society are increasingly making self-centered decisions. Previous American generations were more focused on building a secure and prosperous experience in life for their families than they were with being "entertained" by life. In previous generations, financial security, a peaceful existence, and physical health were much more difficult to achieve and maintain; survival was an ongoing challenge. One reason that prosperity was much more difficult to achieve and maintain is because there was no political, economic, technical, or military superpower to provide answers and to enforce peace and offer prosperity to the nations, as America has done in the Western Hemisphere for the past seventy-five years. The result is that people worked themselves to death trying to earn a living and to maintain a stable society. In addition, medicine was not as advanced as it is today, and the average life span was significantly less.

In early America, life was a struggle because machines did not do the physical work involved in producing food or much of the heavy lifting in construction. The heavy lifting was done by farm animals and human labor, and everything took longer to accomplish. In addition, people did not have the free time they have today to pursue their fantasy. However, our forefathers envisioned a culture where individuals respected one another and where the family (Dad, Mom, and children) through hard work and planning could prepare themselves for later life, and families could obtain a secure and prosperous future for themselves and their growing families through diligent and persistence efforts.

After the War of Independence, our American forefathers worked hard within the framework established by the Declaration of Independence and the United States Constitution (including the Bill of Rights), and within the framework of what we may term traditional values,[24] to produce the culture they envisioned. While they did not do these things perfectly, they knew who they were because they had a foundation of truth to build upon. In the course of time, these things came together to produce the American culture we have inherited today.

---

[24] The term "traditional values" is a reference to the values imported into America by the Pilgrims and the Puritan leaders who first came to the New World to establish freedom to worship God according to their personal conscience and to establish a culture where they were free to raise their children according to those values. Among the first American immigrants, it was almost unanimously presupposed that the Bible was the revelation of God to mankind and that biblical revelations were to establish the foundation of values in the culture they hoped to establish. Neither the Puritans nor the Pilgrims desired to establish a state religion formally regulated by the government, but they did hope to establish a form for culture that would give birth to freedom within that form. The vision for this new culture was that the laws of the land were to be derived from biblical revelations, which they believed to be truth. This ideal is clearly stated in the Mayflower Compact (see http://en.wikipedia.org/wiki/Mayflower_Compact).

It is highly unlikely that the Pilgrim or Puritan leaders foresaw the tremendous prosperity their experiment in freedom was to unleash when a free people were empowered to pursue their own interests in a culture built upon the value system given to them by their Creator. These ideals are without question the foundation of philosophical thought upon which the Declaration of Independence and the United States Constitution (with the Bill of Rights) were erected. This ideal is also the presupposition within the Magna Carta and English common law (English common law was built upon the Magna Carta). All of these documents presuppose that God is the author of human rights, and not even the king is empowered to transgress human rights ordained by God (see http://www.fordham.edu/halsall/source/magnacarta.asp).

For additional information, see the trilogy entitled *God's Plan for America* by Peter Marshall and David Manuel. Book One is subtitled *The Light and the Glory*. Book Two is subtitled *From Sea to Shining Sea*. Book Three is subtitled *Sounding Forth the Trumpet*. Published by Revel, a division of Baker Publishing Group, P.O. Box 6287, Grand Rapids, MI 49516-6287; see www.revellbooks.com. The Magna Carta is addressed in Book One on pp. 316, 320, and 386.

The consequence of this is that the founding fathers of America were successful beyond their wildest dreams, and the American experiment gave birth to what has been termed "the American dream." A shining city on a hill has become the symbol of the American dream. This dream frequently became the dream of immigrants coming here seeking a better life, where it was possible for them to work hard and reach financial security, something that was nearly impossible in their home country. In this manner, America has become the imagined city of light on a hill, because it is the most affluent culture the world has ever seen. Traditional America has become an economic, political, military, and technical superpower and has demonstrated the idea of freedom for the masses to the world around us. As noted earlier, fledgling America has made many mistakes in developing and administering freedom, but people having a view of what is right based upon the Judeo-Christian ethic have corrected some of those major mistakes.

¶#76: A Wise Choice in Youth Serves for a Lifetime

The founding fathers of America realized that all men are "endowed by their Creator" with specific rights, which are "life, liberty, and the pursuit of happiness."[25] These words, written to be displayed before a "candid world," envisioned a culture where Americans young and old, in the sight of their Creator, are to be free to pursue peace, prosperity, and security through their personal efforts in building a culture where individuals respect their neighbors and their neighbors respects them. American culture was quite successful in fulfilling the vision of the

---

[25] The first two paragraphs of the Declaration of Independence state:

When in the Course of human events it becomes necessary for one people to dissolve the political bands which have connected them with another and to assume among the powers of the earth, the separate and equal station to which the Laws of Nature and of Nature's God entitle them, a decent respect to the opinions of mankind requires that they should declare the causes which impel them to the separation.

We hold these truths to be self-evident, that all men are created equal, that they are endowed by their Creator with certain unalienable Rights, that among these are Life, Liberty and the pursuit of Happiness. — That to secure these rights, Governments are instituted among Men, deriving their just powers from the consent of the governed, — That whenever any Form of Government becomes destructive of these ends, it is the Right of the People to alter or to abolish it, and to institute new Government, laying its foundation on such principles and organizing its powers in such form, as to them shall seem most likely to effect their Safety and Happiness. Prudence, indeed, will dictate that Governments long established should not be changed for light and transient causes; and accordingly all experience hath shewn that mankind are more disposed to suffer, while evils are sufferable than to right themselves by abolishing the forms to which they are accustomed. But when a long train of abuses and usurpations, pursuing invariably the same Object evinces a design to reduce them under absolute Despotism, it is their right, it is their duty, to throw off such Government, and to provide new Guards for their future security. — Such has been the patient sufferance of these Colonies; and such is now the necessity which constrains them to alter their former Systems of Government. The history of the present King of Great Britain is a history of repeated injuries and usurpations, all having in direct object the establishment of an absolute Tyranny over these States. To prove this, let Facts be submitted to a candid world.

founding fathers, and within a hundred years after its founding, America became the envy of the world. Thus, there was massive immigration to America by people seeking a better life. The Statue of Liberty has become an icon of this phenomenon.[26]

Immigrants were coming to America to escape the social systems they were born under. And most immigrants came here not seeking to reestablish the culture they left but to establish a new life in a new world and to adopt the American worldview and values. In other countries, government leaders (kings and monarchs) and the wealthy social elite frequently took these God-given rights from the larger society by force and subjected the individuals under the rule of the social system the monarchs themselves envisioned and desired. In this way, most of the world's population was confined to serfdom. But the early American immigrant came here seeking to be free and seeking to learn how to be free, and how to produce freedom for their families.

In most countries through the nineteenth century, there were essentially two classes of society: the rich and the poor. This essentially meant if you were born in wealth, you would live and die in wealth, and you were in command of many serfs. If you were born in poverty, you would live and die in poverty; you were a serf under the thumb of the wealthy land barons. Our founding fathers understood this and protested against the king of England, who was

---

[26] The Statue of Liberty, a gift to the United States from the people of France, is of a robed female figure representing Libertas, the Roman goddess of freedom, who bears a torch and a *tabula ansata* (a tablet evoking the law) upon which is inscribed the date of the American Declaration of Independence, July 4, 1776. A broken chain lies at her feet. The statue has become an icon of freedom and of the United States (taken from Website http://en.wikipedia.org/wiki/Statue_of_Liberty). *The New Colossus* is a sonnet by Emma Lazarus (1849–1887), written in 1883, and in 1903, it was engraved on a bronze plaque mounted on the Statue of Liberty. Here is the sonnet:

The New Colossus

>Not like the brazen giant of Greek fame
>With conquering limbs astride from land to land;
>Here at our sea-washed, sunset gates shall stand
>A mighty woman with a torch, whose flame
>Is the imprisoned lightning, and her name
>Mother of Exiles. From her beacon-hand
>Glows world-wide welcome; her mild eyes command
>The air-bridged harbor that twin cities frame.
>"Keep, ancient lands, your storied pomp!" cries she
>With silent lips. "Give me your tired, your poor,
>Your huddled masses yearning to breathe free,
>The wretched refuse of your teeming shore.
>Send these, the homeless, tempest-tost to me,
>I lift my lamp beside the golden door!"

(Taken from website http://en.wikipedia.org/wiki/The_New_Colossus)

essentially seeking to impose his rule of law on the thirteen colonies as a means of financing his empire through taxation. This persisted until the colonies finally found a sufficiently unifying theme in the Tea Act, which had been passed by the British Parliament in 1773. The Tea Act united the leadership of the thirteen colonies to revolt against the king of England. This revolt was formally stated in the Declaration of Independence, which followed the Boston Tea Party, which took place on December 16, 1773. American colonial leaders rebelled, knowing full well it was being done at the risk of their lives, fortunes, and sacred honor. The result was that the American colonies engaged in, and won, their War of Independence from England (the most powerful nation in the world at that time).

Few world leaders thought that America could win their fight for independence. But America, under the leadership of George Washington, did win, and as a consequence, they founded the United States of America. America was founded as a democratic republic, where the American dream took root and flourished. The American dream was pursued by Americans and men and women who immigrated from all over the world, who came to a new land where individuals were free to do what they could do within an overarching form that taught individuals to respect their neighbor within a basic understanding of what was right and what was wrong (i.e., the Ten Commandments and the value system issued by nature's God). It was this basic understanding that gave birth to the American ideal of "Manifest Destiny."[27]

¶#77: Too Soon Old ... Too Late Smart

Today we may ask, Is the affluent America of the twenty-first century what the founding fathers envisioned when they issued the Declaration of Independence? I would answer that the

---

[27] Manifest Destiny was the nineteenth-century American belief that the United States culture was providentially destined to expand across the North American continent and provide a culture where all men were free and where true liberty and justice for everyone was the law of the land. There have been hundreds of history books written about this, which effectively document the harshness (desperation) of those seeking to escape the tyrannical cultures they were born into so that they could establish their own life in a free land. Manifest Destiny captures the thought that when free individuals have something to tell them what they should do (i.e., what is right), they are left to do what they can do . . . Americans did what they thought they should do. Manifest Destiny was an idea that energized the American culture as it swept the North American continent in the seventeenth, eighteenth, and nineteenth centuries. The ideal of Manifest Destiny brings the idea of Providence into the forefront of how America was established. We must ask ourselves, "**If Providence established America, can Providence disestablish America?**" For an extensive discussion of Manifest Destiny and the providential purpose of America, see *the three book series entitled "God's Plan for America"* by Peter Marshall and David Manuel. Book One is Subtitled, "The Light And The Glory". Book two is subtitled, "From Sea To Shinning Sea". Book Three is subtitled, "Sounding Forth The Trumpet". Published by Revel, a division of Baker Publishing Group, P. O. Box 6287, Grand Rapids, MI 49516-6287; see website www.revellbooks.com. See "Manifest Destiny" in Book Two, pages. 391-396.

right to pursue freedom unencumbered by a state-imposed religion is what the Pilgrim and Puritan fathers envisioned, and that freedom to govern themselves is what the writers of the Declaration of Independence and the Constitution envisioned, and that modern affluence is definitely within the vision of both. However, the self-centered values that have grown up as a result of that affluence are not the product of freedom that the founding fathers envisioned. The opening paragraphs of the Declaration of Independence most certainly envisioned a society where the people were interconnected within a social order where the passion for freedom was paramount. However, what we see in much of American society today is not the passion to be free within the form imposed by nature's God upon those He created, but the passion of the individual to do whatever is right in his own eyes, which in many instances places him in defiance of God. If this is true, perhaps we should ask, What has been lost in the pursuit of the American dream?

It is my observation that affluence has become the pursuit of Americans, rather than freedom. What has been lost in our affluence is the idea that we are all interconnected. With this loss, the American culture is increasingly becoming harder to legally administrate. In America, individuals increasingly believe they can make any decision they want to, because they feel it is their "right" to make any decision regardless of how it affects their neighbor. It is my observation that as the American society has moved into greater and greater affluence, individuals have increasingly become inwardly focused on their personal peace and satisfaction, rather than the well-being of their neighbor. This is producing what some refer to as the "Me generation."

As a symptom of this, I believe that it is becoming increasingly difficult to find individuals who unselfishly volunteer to improve their communities and local institutions. In our affluence and self-centeredness, we have somehow lost the awareness that because we are interconnected, we must support each other in our mutual pilgrimage through life.

I believe that there are three errors in how we how pursue the choices open to us in prosperous America:

First

There is a growing indifference to the well-being of our neighbor, indifference that clearly is permeating the American culture and is a direct result of individuals coming to believe that purpose and personal satisfaction in life will be realized only through their self-centered achievement of personal fulfillment. The result is that increasingly individuals are pouring their main energies of life into achieving personal prosperity, believing their efforts will eventually raise them to a higher level of peace and satisfaction. This is essentially trading their life today for a better tomorrow under the idealistic belief that they will achieve what they seek at some point in the future. The flaw in this thinking is that we fail to understand that no one can experience the future; we can only experience the present. In our pursuit of the future, we have forgotten that we live in the present. This error quite logically leads to the second error.

Second

In the pursuit of personal peace and satisfaction, it is very easy to overlook the fact that our most valuable acquisitions in this world are not the things we control but the relationships we form with those we love and those who love us. In the pursuit of financial well-being, we tend to forget this and neglect the building of relationships. Then if we actually achieve financial security, we have no one to enjoy it with. It is necessary to spend time with a wife, husband, son, or daughter to build a relationship, and many who are building for the future fail to recognize this. A relationship does not just happen by chance or because we expect a person to be there for us when we need them. If we don't build relationships in the present, they will not be there when the future becomes the present.

Third

It is quite common for kids to believe that achieving personal satisfaction in their future is out of their reach. One reason for this is that parents, especially fathers, have not taken the time to build a relationship with their own children and to show their children how to live a successful life apart from high financial success. When this happens, it is easy for a child to forget about their future and focus only on the present in their attempts to find personal peace and satisfaction. When a person, young or old, does not feel valued in their relationships, it is natural to try and find something that makes them feel better about their life.

Chemical abuse is a natural trap for people who do not feel valued in their relationships (i.e., to be valued is a large part of what a chemical freak is searching for). Those who feel all alone in this world, or those who are looking for greater fulfillment than they have been able to find through personal relationships, are vulnerable to the trap of chemically induced euphoria. Those who need a place of refuge from the pain of life may believe they have found just such a place through chemical abuse. In the early stages of chemical abuse, individuals frequently feel it is better to pass the moments in a chemically induced ecstasy than feel unloved, unappreciated, or unfilled, and thus they willingly enter into chemical abuse. Those who do this have failed to understand the consequences of drug abuse.

But the future still passes through the present to recede into the past, where it can only be remembered in the present. Failure to grasp this leads chemical abusers to increasingly trade the present moment for what they hope will be a high that will never end. **For addicts, being high IS the future they envision,** but what they actually experience is not the future they imagined when they first began to experiment with drugs. I believe **drug addiction is largely a consequence of not learning to enjoy the present moment or, for those in despair, of not taking the present moment to prepare for the future.**

As previously stated, in a very real way we only have the present moment, so we must learn to turn the passing moment into a beneficial journey through this world that prepares us for, but in the process does not destroy, our future. We do so by learning how to make decisions that protect ourselves, protect others, protect our environment, and then put what we have learned all together to protect our families, our communities, and our environment for the good of all. We do this by making good choices in the present moment that enable us to enjoy life now but will also help secure our future and also enable others to enjoy life and make good choices that help them secure their future. Making good choices addresses virtually everything that we may participate in throughout our total experience of life. Choices are like roads that connect one place to another; once a choice is made and acted on, it has determined a trajectory for the coming moments of life.

The Emotions of Life

Life presents a series of choices that lead to experiences, and experiences mold us and shape us into the people we are continually becoming. A human's path through life is strewn with great mysteries to be explored. Frequently the exploration of great mysteries opens the door to great danger or to great rewards. As with controlling fire, individuals must learn that there are ways to do things that have been proven through time, and a wise course of action is to make choices that yield a predictable result. The maturing teen must be led into discerning how to explore a mystery and avoid the pain that comes from making serious mistakes in the process. Many times, emotions of the moment may cause individuals to make decisions that they would not make in the absence of strong emotions. Because of this, it is wise to evaluate the consequence of choices we know are coming in our future and then make the best choice.

One way of determining if the consequence of a decision will be good or bad is to imagine how something would work in our personal life in an atmosphere devoid of personal emotions. In emotional situations, individuals are so focused on the moment that few can imagine what consequences lie beyond that choice. It is virtually impossible to make a wise decision in the heat of emotions. The result is that individuals who have not determined a course of action before the height of an emotional situation arrives may be coached or pushed into making a poor decision based on the emotions of the moment. For this reason, important decisions should be planned for before we get into that emotional situation. If we can imagine a choice being presented to us, we can also imagine the possible consequence that may come following our choice. These critical moments of life will come whether we plan for them or not, but if we have the presence of mind to imagine specific critical choices that come in life and to imagine when the moment is right for each choice to be implemented, we can predetermine a course of action to deal with that moment when it comes.

If we have the presence of mind to do the above, it will help us choose what is in the best interest of all who will be affected by whatever decisions we are called upon to make in life. In addition, it may help if we imagine the same decision being presented to another person; doing this may help us lay aside the emotions of the moment. For example, it may help to imagine our mother or father making the decision we are faced with. What we think is best for them is probably what is best for us.

It is a fact that we become better at making decisions, by making decisions and then living with the consequences. This is called experience, and experience allows us to project consequences. In fact, this seems to be part of the design of life. It is a simple truth that an older person can see further down the road than a younger person—because of experience. This is why it is important for younger people to ask for input from older, more experienced people.

If we do not have experience in decision making, we may fail to realize that consequences will come, but know this: consequences will follow each decision we make just as sure as tomorrow follows today. People who do not have a firm grasp of this may look at a situation and make a judgment based on the present condition, without looking at the circumstances that may follow their choice. In order to make a good choice, all circumstances must be addressed. Rarely is the right decision made in the emotion of the moment.

Sometimes it is difficult to lay aside raw emotions and look at issues logically. This is particularly true with young people, who have not learned to turn away from raw emotions and imagine possible consequences apart from those emotions. This is why young people need supervision as they learn to make decisions and gain the experience that comes from making decisions and living with the consequences of those decisions. This is also why increasing responsibility for making important decisions is transferred to the maturing young person over time. We must learn how to proceed with the decisions to be made about tobacco, drugs, alcohol, sex, proper nutrition, moral values, education, various philosophies of life, and a host of other issues that we encounter as we grow into adulthood. These are specific areas of life where young people need help in imagining the consequences of their decisions. It is a sad condition when young people grow old without answering the basic questions that enable them to make good decisions in life.

As stated, we learn from instruction, we learn from our mistakes and the mistakes of others, we learn by envisioning the possible consequences of our actions; hopefully our observations will guide us into making increasingly better choices throughout life. So it is with individuals who are probing the mystery of learning who they are, why they are here, and what their purpose in life is.

No person will find meaning in and of himself because the individual, is only a small part of a much larger picture. Over the course of our personal journey through life, it may take a few hard knocks before we realize that all we want in life may not be right for us. Life is an ongoing journey, and there are many people on that journey with us. There is a beneficial way and a harmful way to approach almost any issue in life. In order to have a fulfilling experience along life's journey, we must follow our golden nuggets of learning to the mother lode of wisdom. Meaning can only be found by offering your life to something, or someone, much larger than yourself. This is what the life story of Marty Gruber is all about.

THE ROLE OF PARENTING
IN CONTROLLING DRUG ABUSE

¶#78: One Suggestion To Reduce Drug Abuse

The theme of this section is that parents or guardians are the key to preventing teenage drug abuse. There is an extreme amount of information about drug abuse available on the Internet. The following statements from website http://archives.drugabuse.gov/newsroom/09/NS-02. html#Anchor-14210 are about the National Institute on Drug Abuse (NIDA) research into teen alcohol abuse:

> **Parental Monitoring Reduces High School Drinking, Leading to Reduced College Drinking**: Drinking among college students, especially those that are underage, is a major public health concern. A recent study of more than 1,200 first-year college students revealed that parental monitoring in the last year of high school significantly impacts alcohol consumption. **Interviewers asked students about their living situation in college; alcohol consumption in high school and college; and their perceptions of parental monitoring during the last year of high school, such as being required to tell parents of their evening plans and having consequences for breaking curfew. <u>Higher levels of parental monitoring and supervision were associated with less alcohol consumption in high school, regardless of students' sex or race or the importance of religion in their lives.</u> Moreover, the amount that students drank in high school was a significant predictor for drinking in college. "While parental monitoring did not directly influence college alcohol consumption, evidence for mediation was observed whereby <u>parental monitoring indirectly reduced college drinking through reductions in high school drinking</u>," explain the authors.** Although the study was limited to a single university and did not explore the mechanism by which parental monitoring reduces high school alcohol consumption, **the results <u>"extend support for parental monitoring and supervision during the high school years as a strategy to reduce adolescent drinking,"</u>** conclude the authors. [Bold and underline added.]

The National Institute on Drug Abuse (NIDA) states their mission as follows:[28]

---

[28] This is taken from NIDA's website: http://drugabuse.gov/about/aboutnida.html.

NIDA's mission is to lead the Nation in bringing the **power of science to bear on drug abuse and addiction**.

This charge has two critical components. **The first** is the strategic support and conduct of research across a broad range of disciplines. **The second** is ensuring the rapid and effective dissemination and use of the results of that research to **significantly improve prevention and treatment** and **to inform policy** as it relates to drug abuse and addiction. [Bold and underline added.]

NIDA's Prevention Objectives Include:[29]

1. To identify the characteristics and patterns of drug abuse.

2. To understand how genes, environment, and development influence the various risk and protective factors for drug abuse.

3. To improve and expand our understanding of basic neurobiology as it relates to the brain circuitry underlying drug abuse and addiction.

4. To apply this knowledge toward the development of more effective strategies to prevent people from ever taking drugs and from progressing to addiction if they do.

Note that NIDA's stated **first goal** is to lead in research on drug abuse rather than to prevent drug abuse. The **secondary goal** is to use the research to prevent and treat drug abuse. **While the following information is very informative, it is troubling that the objective of NIDA is not to first prevent drug abuse and then to use science to support that objective.** The reason this is troubling is that it suggests a mind-set of studying a problem instead of solving a problem. In addition, NIDA frequently refers to drug abuse as a disease, and it rarely makes any differentiation in the state of this disease in the person before abusing drugs and after abusing drugs. Thus, I caution you as you read NIDA's material to question if chemical abuse is a disease before the chemical abuser becomes an addict or if it is a disease only after the person becomes an addict after drug abuse. It is my belief that addiction is the disease, but prevention occurs **before** individuals voluntarily introduce the disease to themselves through willing chemical abuse. **Once a person becomes an addict, his addiction may have become**

---

[29] This is taken from NIDA's website http://drugabuse.gov/StrategicPlan/StratPlan10/Index.html#prevention

a disease, but if he had never performed chemical abuse, he would not have developed the disease of chemical addiction.

The information in the fourteen attachments under Section #5 is provided for the individual wanting to research the subject of drug abuse more completely. After multiple hours of searching the Internet for information on drug abuse (almost all of which has been developed through a federal study), I know for a fact that there is so much information that it would be almost impossible for any parent to read and digest it all. It is also apparent that there is more information available informing us about what happens after people abuse drugs (e.g., what happens in the brain and body of a chemical abuser) than is available to instruct us how to prevent drug abuse and addiction from happening in the first place.

With drug abuse increasing, it is obvious that **the approach being taken by the government to prevent drug abuse is not effective**. Table 1 tells us that 48.2 percent of high school seniors indicated that they had used illicit drugs at least one time in their lives, 38.3 percent have used illicit drugs in the last year, and 23.8 percent have used illicit drugs in the last month. From these statistics, it does not seem that the NIDA studies informing the nation about drug abuse prevention are working very well, especially considering that estimates indicate that the annual cost of drug abuse to the United States economy, including lost production, health care, and other costs associated with prevention, are somewhere in the range of $600 billion.[30] This indicates that the cost of drug abuse reduces American GDP by substantially more than 5 percent (i.e., it reduces GDP by more than one dollar in twenty). Drug abuse is an extremely costly problem to every American.

---

[30] See information under "National Institute on Drug Abuse Information and Facts," and see website http://www.drugabuse.gov/infofacts/understand.html#Anchor-References-47857. Finding accurate information on drug abuse costs is difficult. One thing is very clear: drug abuse is a huge problem. The cost of drug abuse in 2000 was reported as follows:

Costs of Substance Abuse

Studies have shown the annual cost of substance abuse to the nation to be $510.8 billion in 1999 (Harwood, 2000). More specifically,

- Alcohol abuse cost the nation $191.6 billion.
- Tobacco use cost the nation $167.8 billion.
- Drug abuse cost the nation $151.4 billion.

Substance abuse clearly is among the most costly health problems in the United States.

Among national estimates of the costs of illness for thirty-three diseases and conditions, alcohol ranked second, tobacco ranked sixth, and drug disorders ranked seventh (National Institutes of Health, 2000).

This information was taken from website http://crimeinamerica.net/2010/03/22/substance-abuse-costs-511-billion-a-cost-benefit-analysis-crime-news/

In reviewing the literature about risk factors for drug abuse, the theme that seems most prominent is that impending change in a young person's life (e.g., puberty, competition for grades, divorce of parents, a death in the family, going into the next grade, moving to a different school) produces stress, and during these times, teens may feel insecure and overwhelmed by life. In times of high stress, they become very vulnerable to bad choices and may yield to an opportunity to experiment with drugs. In addition, peer pressure and unwholesome friendships also contribute to drug abuse. The following quote was taken from website http://www.at-risk.org/teen_drug_abuse.html:

> **Drug Abuse Among Teens:** Teen drug abuse statistics will show that many teens abuse drugs. Some teens start off out of curiosity or peer pressure. But many become addicted and remain on the drugs. It's not hard for your child to get drugs either, no matter where you live, so never think that your teen will not have access. Some teens begin with alcohol and then move into other drugs. If your teen is smoking or drinking, **you need to talk to them** about drugs and drug abuse. If your teen has started to hang with a bad crowd, become irritable and withdrawn, or had a drastic change in personality or grades in school, **you might suspect drug use**. **You should try to catch it as early as possible to get help for your teen.**
>
> **How To Help Your Teen:** The best way to help your teen **is to try to prevent drug use to begin with**. There are different ways of preventing drug use. **You need to try to give your teen alternatives.** [Bold and underline added.]

NIDA's website (http://www.nida.nih.gov/prevention/applying.html) provides a long reading list of material prepared by very educated people about preventing drug abuse. As I reviewed this information, it is apparent that risk factors associated with drug abuse and strategies for prevention include:

1. Police and criminal activity associated with the drug community.

2. Teaching about drugs in the classroom setting.

3. Teaching parents various communication skills with children.

4. Organizing communitywide efforts to work together to prevent drug activity.

5. Intervention methods in dealing with those on drugs.

6. Developing programs to provide assistance to a number of groups involved in preventing or treating drug abuse.

7. Teaching kids about peer pressure and how to say to no to drug abuse.

The NIDA publication entitled "Preventing Drug Abuse among Children and Adolescents" exposes **why** high risk kids get involved in drugs, but **the parental goal is to prevent them from participating in drug abuse**. The following quote is taken from website http://www. nida.nih.gov/prevention/risk.html:

> **What are the early signs of risk that may predict later drug abuse?** Some signs of risk can be seen as early as infancy or early childhood, such as aggressive behavior, lack of self-control, or difficult temperament. As the child gets older, **interactions with family**, at school, and **within the community can affect that child's risk for later drug abuse**. Children's earliest interactions occur in the family; **sometimes family situations heighten a child's risk for later drug abuse**, for example, when there is:
>
> - A lack of attachment and nurturing by parents or caregivers
> - Ineffective parenting
> - A caregiver who abuses drugs
>
> **But families can provide protection from later drug abuse when there is**:
>
> - A strong bond between children and parents
> - Parental involvement in the child's life
> - Clear limits and consistent enforcement of discipline
>
> Interactions outside the family can involve risks for both children and adolescents, such as:
>
> - Poor classroom behavior or social skills
> - Academic failure
> - **Association with drug-abusing peers**
>
> ***Association with drug-abusing peers is often the most immediate risk for exposing adolescents to drug abuse and delinquent behavior.***

Other factors—such as drug availability, trafficking patterns, and <u>beliefs that drug abuse is generally tolerated</u>—are risks that can influence young people to start abusing drugs. [Bold and underline have been added.]

Both of the above websites seems to identify <u>parenting and parental supervision</u> as the most effective way to identify teens that are vulnerable to drug abuse, BUT IT IS MY OBSERVATION THAT <u>THIS EFFECTIVELY TELLS US HOW TO PREVENT DRUG ABUSE</u>. The NIDA publications <u>DO NOT</u> strongly follow up on this finding <u>and tell parents specifically what they can do to prevent drug abuse in their children</u>. It is my view that not specifically telling parents what they can do to become more effective in preventing drug abuse is a weakness in the information NIDA has to offer.

All of this prompts me to ask the same kind of "why" questions that most children ask their parents, such as, Why can't we stop drug abuse? The answer to this question seems apparent. **Drug abuse is not the problem, <u>it is a symptom of the problem,</u> and most of our action is designed to treat the symptom rather than preventing the underlying problem**. Just as fever is a symptom of an infection; the infection is the problem, and fever is only a symptom that reveals the problem. It is the same with drug abuse. I want to suggest a method for significantly reducing drug abuse in the following paragraphs.

¶#79: Perhaps Drug Abuse Is Only a Symptom of a Bigger Problem

My experience in the drug world indicates that the group having the greatest participation in drug abuse is easily young people, and the greatest abuse of drugs is by teens. Therefore, if we are to stop drug abuse, we must teach teens how to avoid drugs. However, this observation also leads me to conclude that the real problem is not with teens; the actual drug abuse may not take place until the child becomes a teen, but perhaps the roots of drug abuse begin earlier. **Perhaps the roots of the drug abuse go back to the basic environment the drug abuser was raised in. <u>Perhaps the root problem is that the drug abuser was raised in an environment conducive to drug abuse.</u> The environment we are raised in provides us with our first demonstration of values and lifestyles that are subliminally programmed into our minds. These are provided to young people by their parents, family, and friends, and this begins when the child is an infant.**

Perhaps the root problem is a climate where children fail to learn they are loved, that they are part of a family culture where people support one another and face problems together and make decisions together. Young addicts tend to be troubled teens and loners who are searching for something to bring fulfillment into their lives, and many of these addicts do not feel they are important to the family, extended family, or community; they are looking for fulfillment wherever they can find it.[31] The family unit, extended family, and community are the logical places where maturing children should find that fulfillment. If children do not find fulfillment in their home and community environments, they will look elsewhere; gangs, alcohol, drug abuse, and promiscuous sex are some of the places they look.

---

[31] The following quote, entitled "Teen Challenge's Proven Answer to the Drug Problem," is from a review of a doctoral dissertation written by Aaron T. Bicknese, a PhD student at Northwestern University. The review was written by Andrew Kenney, a professor at Vanguard University. This eye-opening review may be read in its entirety at website *http://www. teenchallengeusa.com/docs/NW_study.pdf*:

The number of federal dollars appropriated for drug treatment has steadily climbed over the past twenty-five years, from $120 million in 1969, to $1.1 billion in 1974, to $3 billion in 1996. [This quote skips down 3-1/2 paragraphs to continue.] Regarding publicly funded treatment programs, Kweisi Mfume, during his days in Congress, said, "I just get a little pain thinking about the lack of success rates for many of these drug treatment programs and the fact that there are a lot of people, quite frankly, who are in that business to make money and they make their money and they make it off of us."

The concern about low cure rates of treatment programs funded by public dollars opens the door to questions about whether such rates are all one can or should expect of any method of drug treatment, whether or not the program receives public funding. If low cure rates and minimal changes in behavior are all that can be anticipated, does the public have the right to demand that improvement in drug and alcohol treatment programs be made? On the other hand, if significantly higher rates of success do exist somewhere in the world of drug treatment programs, then perhaps the public does have the right to demand action. [This question goes straight to the heart of political correctness in the approach of the federal government to address drug prevention.]

Because of the vast damage done to the individual and society by drug and alcohol abuse, it is crucial that society evaluate the effectiveness not only of publicly funded programs, but also, for the sake of comparison, programs not using public funding. **For these reasons, Aaron Bicknese, a researcher at Northwestern University, decided to explore a drug treatment program which, according to a study done in the 1970s, enjoyed unusually high rates of effectiveness. The program is Teen Challenge International, a Christian nonprofit addiction treatment ministry with 130 centers (2,885 beds) in the United States.**

The study, published in June 1999, is the most comprehensive statistical analysis of its kind to date. **The study surveyed several key areas, including freedom from addictive substances, employment rates, productive social relationships, and other tangible factors that lead to a better quality of life. The study was designed to determine how Teen Challenge's treatment centers, funded primarily by nonprofit contributions, compared to organizations funded by public dollars or insurers' dollars.** Outcomes based on survey data were statistically compared between samples of Teen Challenge graduates and graduates of publicly funded Short-Term Inpatient (STI) drug treatment programs. As the newest type of treatment to capture the attention of addiction program evaluators, 30- to 60-day hospital stays for STIs funded by private or public insurers have become increasingly common since the early 1980s. **The results show that with at least one very popular type of publicly funded secular drug treatment program, Teen Challenge is in many ways far more effective. The study particularly emphasized Teen Challenge's ability TO HELP STUDENTS GAIN NEW SOCIAL SKILLS, so that upon leaving the program, the Teen Challenge student, compared to clients of the secular programs surveyed, is productively employed at a much higher rate and HAS A DRAMATICALLY LOWER CHANCE OF RETURNING FOR FURTHER RESIDENTIAL TREATMENT.**

[Bold, underline, and caps were added.]

¶#80: Values Are Not Taught, They Are Caught

Asbestos workers have learned that it is not wise to wait until workers have asbestosis before they take efforts to shield themselves from the harmful effects of exposure to asbestos, neither do coal miners wait until they have black lung to begin shielding themselves from coal dust; why then do we wait until teens have a problem with drugs to begin training them to shield themselves from drugs? Why do we wait until we think they are old enough to become involved with drugs before we begin to teach them to avoid drugs? Once the cause of asbestosis or black lung became known, the safety training designed to prevent these diseases was initiated before workers entered the environment where exposure was a probability. Can't we transfer this learning into preventing drug abuse?[32]

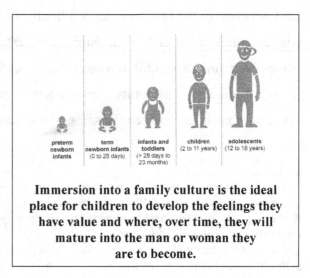

Immersion into a family culture is the ideal place for children to develop the feelings they have value and where, over time, they will mature into the man or woman they are to become.

It is my view that safety training to prevent drug abuse begins with parental influence. The prevention of drug abuse begins with infants and toddlers and continues through the adolescent years, only **the parental influence to avoid drug abuse I have in mind for children is not what to avoid so much as it is <u>immersion in a family culture of caring people where the maturing child has ever increasing responsibility to that culture</u>.** Obviously it is my belief that shielding adolescents from drug abuse begins before children become adolescents. This shielding is not the responsibility of the government, it is the responsibility of the parents and the family, and if drug prevention is going to occur, it will begin with the parents and the family of the child.

Because drug abuse has become a massive social problem involving a high percentage of teens who are experimenting with drugs, and personal experience demonstrates that experimentation leads to chemical addiction and destroyed lives, government officials have become involved in studying drug abuse with the goal of preventing it. This involvement has

---

[32] This picture was taken from http://www.nhlbi.nih.gov/childrenandclinicalstudies/whydo.php.

led to numerous expensive government programs to study and prevent drug abuse. **But the study of drug abuse does not produce results that are effective in preventing it.** **Some of those studies tell parents what I believe should be obvious: it is parenting and family values that prevent drug abuse.**

A knowledge of what drugs do to the body is very important, but if drug abuse is to be prevented, children and teens must believe there is a good reason to refrain from doing drugs, and they must know what these reasons are. Immersion in a family and extended community atmosphere leads to relationships and camaraderie and personal responsibility to the family unit, and IT IS THESE THINGS THAT PREVENT OR CURB DRUG ABUSE. It is these very things that my current drug awareness training is designed to encourage in teens and to promote in families with teens, and the letters I get from teens indicate success in these areas.

¶#81: Building the Community Corral

Clearly those who study drug abuse and recommend ways to prevent it have not found an effective solution for preventing or controlling it, because drug abuse is increasing rather than decreasing. It has become my belief that teaching teens how to avoid drug abuse is like closing the barn door after the horses have run away to answer the call of the wild. While it is a good idea to keep other horses in the barn by closing the door, the goal of effective parenting is to keep our kids from wanting to flee to answer the call of the wild in the first place. Wanting to flee the home environment is an age old problem with teens, and many families have experienced it. Hindsight frequently tells parents that precautions in the form of wise parenting skills could have been taken to prevent this from happening.

When some horses break for the wild, it is certainly a good idea to close the barn door if there are other horses in the barn. However, it is also a good idea to have a horse corral built around the barn so that the spirited horse can't run too far if he decides to flee. The idea of strengthening the family unit, through building the community in the pattern of an extended family, is similar to building a corral around the barn. If the horse bolts out of the barn, there is a secondary fence to stop him from going too far. I am speaking of a communitywide effort to build a network of caring people (parents and extended family) who are willing to network with each other for the specific purpose of developing a friendly place to live and to provide a homey environment for our children to grow up in. It does not take great wealth to produce the atmosphere of community; what it does take, however, is willingness and community volunteers who want to do it. If a community network is to exist, it will be built the old fashioned way; this means knowing each other's names and having one another's phone numbers and planning straightforward steps to reach out and get to know the people who live in our communities.

When drug abuse is seen as a symptom rather than the problem, it becomes apparent that the road to prevention is more than enforcing laws and thwarting the selling of drugs, it begins by reducing demand for drugs by building a community where drugs abuse is not cool. This is the key function of the community corral. The community corral is designed to develop more robust personalities in our children through community involvement, beginning with the interaction of parents and their children with their extended families and the community at large, with the specific goal of preventing drug abuse in the activities of our children. It is not inevitable that almost half of high school seniors will experiment with drugs and that almost a quarter will use illicit drugs once or more each month. The way to prevent drug abuse is to raise kids in an environment (a barn and corral) where drug abuse is not part of the culture; this means that drug abuse is not accepted within the community corral and that the entire community is on drug awareness alert.

Certainly drug abuse is a complex issue, but it has a cause, which leads teens (and some older people) to search for meaning and purpose <u>in drugs</u>, rather than within the fullness of what can life can be, or what life can promise. It is my belief that those who experiment with drugs frequently are seeking the very things that parents, extended family, and community are designed to produce, which is a feeling of acceptance and responsibility to the family and extended family; it was that way with me, but at fourteen, I did not know what I was looking for, and of course I did not know how to find it.

It is ironic that those who experiment with drugs soon discover that drugs **<u>CANNOT</u>** provide the same feeling of acceptance the family is designed to produce, **but many teens become addicted <u>before</u> they realize this**. I believe that experience teaches that we haven't prevented significant drug abuse **because we haven't dealt with the root cause; we can't stop significant abuse because we don't know how to deal with the root cause, which is to be a friend to**

our kids and to provide a family environment for them to grow up in. For that reason we treat the symptom rather than the cause.

In addition, as I write this, many highly educated and highly paid people make their living studying drug abuse and dealing with the symptom of drug abuse; perhaps they have gotten used to studying the symptoms of abuse as a priority rather than preventing abuse as a priority (this seems consistent with the published mission statement and prevention strategy of NIDA). I am not trying to be critical, but this seems to be an accurate observation. The result is that we are not preventing drug abuse, because drug prevention starts in the home, and we seem to dismiss parental responsibility in preventing drug abuse. Our goal has become to study it and make recommendations based on those studies, rather than rolling up our sleeves and preventing it.

¶#82: Parenting Is the Key

With the above in mind, I want to make an observation and a suggestion that may help. Parents are responsible for teaching their children how to build a successful life. As noted, this process of building a successful life begins at birth rather than with the coming of adolescence. The family is the basic unit of society, and it is the failure of this basic unit that has created a condition where drug abuse becomes appealing and can take root in the life of a teen. Thus, it seems that improving parenting skills may be the place to begin serious chemical abuse prevention.

Traditional methods treat the symptom; effective parenting deals with the problem at its root and prevents the problem of drug abuse before an attitude conducive to drug abuse is developed in the child. Perhaps dealing with the symptom of drug abuse for so many years causes us to uncritically allocate federal resources to the study of drug abuse rather than to its prevention. **Perhaps what is needed is to enable parents to become <u>effective parents</u> rather than pouring billions of dollars each year into teaching their adolescents (twelve- to eighteen-year-old children) how to avoid drugs or treating drug abuse once it is established in the child. <u>Many times drug prevention is taught to a child AFTER he or she is already on drugs</u>. This is closing the barn door after the horses have fled to answer the call of the wild.**

With divorce at 50 percent and higher in many places, and with unmarried couples living together and splitting up on a whim, it is quite obvious that many couples simply do not know how to build effective families. Until we are ready to solve the issue of parenting skills and parental values, schools, health care workers, the work environment, and the local community will be responsible for teaching kids and adolescents how to avoid chemical abuse or to turn from chemical abuse after they have already become drug abusers. I believe that the illicit drug abuse problem could be significantly reduced in one generation if parents simply knew how, and were willing, to assume the responsibility of being parents that they took upon themselves by becoming parents. **I am going to be so bold as to suggest that it is possible to seriously reduce drug abuse by strengthening the family within the extended community. This can be accomplished by encouraging and teaching parents to provide a place where children are secure and instinctively turn to Mom and Dad, the immediate family, and the extended family (including friends and community) as the source of answers to their questions about life, rather than turning to drugs and experimenting with them as a way to escape the pain of life.**

The family and the community are the corral around the barn; the **parents are the barn** and the **extended family and community are the corral**. **It is my thesis that the parents, extended family, and the community, are the obvious path to significantly making reduced drug abuse a reality in America.**

Will this be an uphill battle? Of course it will, but so is traditional drug prevention, which obviously is not working well. It may be time to try a little different approach based upon what we already know.

The first two steps in problem solving are (1) **recognizing that a problem exists**, and then (2) **defining the problem**. It is my opinion that NIDA has defined the problem. Perhaps, because of political correctness, we have not yet moved to implement what I think is a possible solution to the problem. It is clear that our efforts are aimed at fixing the symptom rather than fixing the root cause. Drug abuse is like a fever; it is very visible, but like a fever, drug abuse is only a symptom. It is not the underlying problem that has produced the symptom.

¶#83: The First Obvious Problem

In writing this book and looking at the cause of drug abuse in my personal life, it has become my opinion that the first obvious problem leading to drug abuse, as described in Table 1, is that **the family structure has severely been degenerated in American society**. The family structure is out of control because moms and dads cannot control themselves, and marriage today is not a "once for life contract" as was previously true in American culture. If we are to reduce drug abuse, we need to strengthen the family unit. **Those who may become parents must enter marriage with the idea that they will demonstrate how to build a happy life under the ever watching eyes of their children, and then they must do what they set out to do in the course of life, which is to produce a happy and fulfilling life for themselves and their lifetime partner, and the fruit of their marriage, which is their children.**

We go to school and learn tremendous ideas that will enable us to function in life and become productive employees, but **the skills we learn in school do not prepare us morally or philosophically for becoming a socially productive man or woman, husband or wife, or to raise our children to become the same.** <u>We learned social and parenting skills by watching the people who raised us, and our children are learning such skills by watching us, **THEIR PARENTS.**</u> In school, our kids learn how to manage fire and how to become a lifelong learner so that they can continuously improve fire management (see the paragraph entitled "Fire" in the previous section), but they do not learn how to manage their home or how to become a true friend to their neighbor. What are we teaching our children at home and in school that leads so many high school seniors to experiment with drugs (See Table 1)?

¶#84: The Second Obvious Problem

The second obvious problem is closely associated with the first; teen society has spun out of control through drug abuse, primarily because parents are out of control. Parents are busy earning a living or doing whatever occupies their time, to the point that they are not demonstrating how to build a satisfying life before their children. Most parents are simply demonstrating what their parents demonstrated to them. This was partially addressed earlier in Section #4, "Searching for the Truth About Drugs; Questions About the Decision Making Process of Life." In many families, toddlers, children, and adolescents absorb the idea that **family relationships are <u>LESS</u> important than a new car, a new house, the latest electronic gizmo, or season tickets to a sporting event**. In fact, electronic gizmos effectively become baby sitters for many busy parents, and there is growing evidence to suggest that electronic games may contribute to a host of social problems, including addictions. The importance of the family unit must move up in our parental priorities, and the priority of parental involvement in the family unit, the extended family, and the larger community must be very visible to our children.

¶#85: The Third Obvious Problem

It is very apparent that some of the people who have significance influence on the behavior of America's children and adolescents <u>are not the ones responsible for the behavior of the children and adolescents they are influencing</u>. Many teens today are more involved with electronic gizmos, music, and games instead of with parents, siblings, immediate family, and extended family. **The consequence of this condition is that <u>the child is developing no sense of responsibility to the family, and this attitude contributes to the risk of addiction</u>**. Kids simply do not realize what it takes to earn a living and to be an effective parent; how could they? They have never done it, and most of them have never seen it done. **The deterioration of the family structure allows entertainment and peer pressure to become the dominate influence in shaping the behavior of a child**. In the lives of many teens, the influences of entertainment and peer pressure are as powerful as, and perhaps more powerful than, parents and extended families. **<u>Today it is common for children to derive their sense of worth from peers rather than from parents and family, and if they can't do this with peers, they seek other ways to do it, such as drugs.</u>**

Almost all entertainment is built around what sells best to the targeted market, and there is a lot of entertainment aimed at teens and younger kids. It is not a newsflash that children are not specifically interested in learning morality that is pleasing to parents through their electronic games and music, or other forms of entertainment, or from their peers.

The mind of a baby is essentially empty at birth. Therefore, the things that first fill a baby's mind shape that child's developing character. With this in mind, it seems that a lack of parental oversight in entertainment of young children allows those who desire to sell something to our children to appeal to their passions. It is also evident that many times predators are appealing to passions that younger kids or teens have not yet developed the maturity to control; they have not learned the boundaries that will enable them to make good decisions and prevent them from destroying their lives by making poor decisions. The fact that values are caught more than they are taught opens the door for someone you don't even know to shape the mental and moral focus of your child in ways you may not appreciate (in fact, it probably happened to you as a child or a teen, and it is certainly happening to you as an adult). In many cases, parents are unknowingly paying big dollars to the very person who is destroying their home by influencing the judgments of their child or teen.

Electronic games and hit songs are not produced with the idea of providing a demonstration of good values and morals. **Parents must learn how to oversee the things their kids are being entertained by, and <u>the most effective way to do that is TO PARTICIPATE WITH YOUR CHILDREN IN THEIR ENTERTAINMENT</u>.**

Assuming the obvious problems have been accurately stated, what are the obvious solutions? I believe three of these solutions may be stated as follows.

¶#86: The First Obvious Solution

This is the inverse of the first obvious problem; prospective parents need to learn how to enter into lifelong relationships, and they need to know what constitutes effective parenting. Those of us who came from broken homes or dysfunctional families did not learn how to do this. While it may not be politically correct to state this, without question the family is the basic unit of any society, and the degeneration of the family unit has led to increased drug abuse and a host of social problems associated with drug abuse. Neither the government nor the institutions of government are the basic building blocks of society, but in the dearth of parenting skills, the institutions of government are assuming greater and greater responsibilities in raising the children of America. Thus, it seems quite obvious that strengthening the American family would lead to a serious reduction in drug abuse and perhaps a lessening in other social problems and costs as well.

¶#87: The Second Obvious Solution

This is also the inverse of the second obvious problem. Parents (Mom **and** Dad) must recognize and accept that they are responsible for the behavior of their children, including their teens, and begin to influence ongoing behavior by getting intimately involved, and remaining intimately involved, in the lives of their children from birth onward. This means getting involved in their education and getting personally involved with their friends and, in many cases, even the families of their friends. **The goal of this is to build a network of friends and acquaintances that are trusted to have the best interest of each other in mind.**

No matter what kids do, somebody sees them doing it or knows what they are doing. A benefit of building an extended family and community is that they are interwoven, and in an interwoven community every person, including kids and teens, is recognizable to the community of friends and acquaintances. Community networking is developed from the age of a toddler upward. Local civic leadership can function to encourage this kind of community networking to take place in real time and space. If there were community events that children want to participate in with their parents, this would provide opportunities to get to know the families of their children's friends at the same time. **When this happens, there are more people personally involved in attempting to assist everyone in finding their way through life and avoiding stumbling into a life destroying temptation; this most certainly includes teens and young adults.**

Children Are Future Adults Under Construction

As noted under the paragraph entitled "Fire," American society seems more interested in controlling fire than controlling our children; the result is that parents have lost control of their children. This needs to change; building the family unit must become the central focus of what parents are all about. We have learned how to produce effective fire control, and national standards have been written to enable us to safely use fire in generating electric power and to energize American industry with electric power. We use that same power to heat, cool, and light our houses, and we are continually learning to do this more efficiently and inexpensively. Why then can't we learn how to build a marriage and raise children in the home produced by our marriages? I believe that building an electric powerhouse, powering industry, and heating, cooling, and lighting our homes is more complex than building a marriage and raising children who know enough to avoid chemical abuse that will destroy their lives. The difference is that an electric powerhouse does not have a mind of its own, but husbands, wives, and kids have a mind of their own and want to make their own choices, which frequently include unhealthy choices. Many times the goal of parents is to become financially successful rather than to discover and enjoy success in marriage and parenting. It is a problem when we prefer to put time into things other than family; the symptom is suffering families who are learning to make unwholesome choices because of our poor understanding of life.

Because we tend to be selfish, husbands, wives, and children frequently do not yield to the plan that was socially implied when a man and a woman made the decision to become parents. I have come to view my marriage as "**my adult life under construction**" and children as "**future adults under construction.**" The family unit is where children are placed where they can study for their "**future under construction**" as they grow up. We first learn how to function in relationships by watching our parents. **IT IS THE BREAKDOWN OF**

PARENTAL RELATIONSHIPS THAT IS THE ROOT OF DRUG PROBLEMS IN AMERICA AND PROBABLY THE ENTIRE WORLD.

We Are All in Life Together

When a husband, wife, or child bails out on their responsibilities to their family unit (i.e., leaves their position in life to do what is right in their own eyes and goes their own way regardless of consequences), it is the extended family that may come to the aid of the husband, wife or child and help them find their way through the crisis. Large extended families clearly function in this manner, but how can a community become like an extended family? The answer is through a lot of work and planning by community leaders. It takes a lot of effort to build a network of extended family and friends that are willing to render assistance when something bad happens, but it is possible because it happens in large families. Let me also note that it also happens through the formation of long-term associations with friends, but these things have to be initiated and cultivated over time; they do not happen automatically.

One thing we must all realize is that we are in this life together, and if we pull together to help everyone, it becomes more difficult for one of us to wander too far off the established path; the benefactors of learning to pull together will be our children and our communities. In a close extended family and close community atmosphere, a sense of belonging develops in the individual participants over time; belonging to the family and group is very important to each individual in that group. When someone in the group strays, there are family and friends to help pull that individual back into the mainstream of life and away from damaging behaviors. The movie *My Big Fat Greek Wedding* demonstrated this very well. This big Greek family fought, teased, criticized, laughed, mocked, and encouraged one another, and in the process built a community that included everyone (rich and poor, and educated and uneducated, alike).

We laugh at, and sometimes ridicule, those who belong to that kind of extended family or community, but the truth is most of us want to belong to that kind of family or community. It is relationships that make life worth living, much more so than material things or places. In the hierarchy of people, places, and things, people by far are the most important. In our materialistic world, many young parents have lost sight of this fact, because they were raised in homes that had lost sight of this fact.

If local civic leadership would become interested in assisting families in building stronger interfamily and interpersonal relationships that happen in an extended family atmosphere, it seems possible that organizing and participating in community activities could become part of the binding energy that draws and holds American families together into ever larger and intersecting communities that bind our culture together. You laugh and say this would be Mayberry, USA. **That's right, <u>it would be</u>**. If this could actually happen in a community, interpersonal relationships could produce binding energy that binds very diverse people together and builds the community into something like one large extended family. **Building extended community through strong families must become as important as pursuing and arresting drug dealers; building community through strengthening families has the potential to substantially reduce the market where drug dealers sell their product, and this will certainly reduce law enforcement costs in a multitude of ways.**

¶#88: Political Correctness;[33] A Side Note to Obvious Solution #2

This side note is something that is not the specific subject of this book, but it is a topic I feel compelled to address, because it is extremely important to the subject of building community and preventing drug abuse. It is political correctness. I have been an observer of American society for a number of years, and I have observed that many Americans (especially Americans with lucrative jobs) are in a rush to buy things they generally don't need, with money they don't have, to impress people they don't know, and they are giving up relationships with family and friends to accomplish the elusive goal of happiness. In addition, they seem not to recognize what they are actually doing in life. It seems this undefined goal is to look prosperous and successful before a largely undefined audience. **This undefined goal is what we sometimes refer to as <u>the rat race</u>.**

---

[33] Politically correctness is essentially the idea that all values are equally correct, and anything that challenges this assumption is disrespectful. Note however that this idea has a logical flaw: if all values are equally correct, then to be disrespectful is impossible. One may ask the question, How is it possible to truly believe that differences do not matter and still feel the need to enforce your views? In the world of political correctness, morality is impossible because nothing is inherently right or wrong. It is this philosophical opinion that is the goal of politically correct beliefs and actions. Also note that in the world of political correctness, that which is determined to be politically correct is determined by the group that enforces their views. Political correctness is the logical result of the death of absolutes from which morals are defined. The logical result of political correctness is social chaos. It is a fact that as I write this book, I am seeing the implementation of political correctness in the culture all around me, and our culture is suffering because we can no longer discern right from wrong because laws no longer have an absolute base for morality. Political correctness produces social drift because there are no absolutes to anchor society. The implementation of political correctness is essentially each person doing what is right in his own eyes and contending with all who disagree with his views.

Our kids are watching us as we willfully plunge into the rat race. Have we ever stopped to ask ourselves, Is participation in the rat race an addiction? I previously defined addiction as "a slavish devotion to; dedication to; obsession with; infatuation with; passion for; love of; mania for; or enslavement to." This looks very much like many Americans who pursue a new car, an expensive vacation, a new computer, a new video game, and so on. On the surface, the American pursuit of these things looks like an addiction because the people who are running in the rat race are acting like addicts. If this is an addiction, there are large numbers of all ethnic groups who are addicted to running in a race where there is no real way to identify the winner. By definition, the rat race is a competition no one can win because rules to identify the winner do not exist. Why then do we give up our relationships with the people who are the most important to us in life to run in a competition that we cannot win? Has our brain been altered so that we want more than we actually need to be comfortable in life? Are we all addicts in that sense? If those who do these things are addicts, our children are being developed into addicts as they watch Mom and Dad service their personal addiction to the material world.

The information about addictions tells us that when chemical abusers become addicted to an illicit substance, there are changes in their brain that make it difficult for them to turn from their drug of choice, because they now need that chemical to function normally (their brain has established a new normal). It is also evident that it is the hormones secreted by the endocrine system of their own body to which addicts are actually addicted (this is what getting high is; see the information under "National Institute on Drug Abuse Information and Facts"). Are there changes that take place in the brain of people seeking to appear successful at all costs that cause them to make the choices of a "success addict"? My point in asking this is that I believe many parents (including me) are teaching (we are providing a demonstration of), or have taught, our children to make unhealthy choices through the model of decision making that we are presenting to them. We are subliminally demonstrating to them that material success is more important than our relationship with them, and if we are giving them this message, it seems to me that we are preparing them for their future addiction. We want our children to refrain from making bad choices, but many times we demonstrate bad choices before them almost daily. **Our children are watching and learning from us.**

Nowhere is the height of political correctness displayed more vividly than through the modern concept of separation of church and state. This idea has been elevated to the point that many who know how to raise children cannot discuss why they are successful parents in public because someone may be offended by their worldview. This condition has been forced on America and the school systems by the courts. Many parents who know how to build a marriage and raise and nurture children within that marriage, and have actually demonstrated this by successfully doing it, have been silenced by the courts. In addition, public school teachers cannot encourage the discussion of successful parenting in public, and specifically in their classrooms, because they fear a lawsuit. The result is that many individuals having values that are grounded in absolutes have gravitated to private schools, where they are free to discuss who they are and what works in their life, without becoming entangled in politically correct controversies that did not exist as recently as fifty years ago. It is apparent that a vocal few seeking to enforce their view of political correctness have produced an exodus from the public schools by many who have enjoyed tremendous success as parents. Of course, the children of successful parents are now missing from the public schools as well, which means that the influence of these children on their peers is also missing.

One Way Political Correctness Has Damaged American Society

Because their values have been silenced, many successful parents have removed their children from the public schools where the traditional values that made them successful have been essentially rejected. These families were very positive in the influence they had in the public school and on the quality of education in the public school; now that influence is gone, and we have seen that the consequences it has produced is increased chaos in the public school, and increased chaos includes ever increasing drug abuse.

As political correctness has silenced successful parents in public, it is also spreading to the faith-based communities (i.e., churches). Church leaders are increasingly being discouraged from speaking against practices that are obviously destructive to healthy families. The result is producing the secularization of the church just as it produced a valueless climate in the public school. The result of being afraid to teach against harmful social practices, even within the church, has also been that the church has changed to look more like the politically correct society surrounding it, and that is seeking to enforce its views of morality. Is this by design?

An absolute is something that is the same for all people in all places at all times; morals are derived from absolutes. Divine revelations are viewed by many as the only source of

true absolutes. It is undeniable that the philosophical foundation of people who make up a church is divine revelation, and the idea of divine revelation is under attack as never before. However, it is still true that **values and morals are derived from the people's faith in <u>divine revelations, and divine revelations do not change as the culture is changing around and within the church.</u> Divine revelations are therefore the foundational doctrines that produce moral stability within the church. In the absence of divine revelations in the church, the church is just another organization.**

Morals are simply the implementation of values into the complete fabric of life (i.e. morals based in absolutes do not change with situations). Cultural morality is the implementation of values across the spectrum of a culture. The result of political correctness is that within the church and within the school, we have lost the mentoring effect of people who know how to raise kids. The result is that people having values that produce healthy kids and teens have retreated from the community, and the mentoring effect of these people and their children has essentially vanished from the community. Much of this mentoring effect used to take place through the school system and through the many activities involving both parents and children associated with the school system. Now much of that mentoring activity is taking place in private schools, where the influence of political correctness is substantially less pervasive.

Separation of Church and State

I readily admit that I don't want someone holding a different view of God than I hold teaching my children or grandchildren their views of God. However, someone's fear that their child may be influenced by my child, or my parental instructions to my child, should not be the basis of legally forcing me to be silent about the influence that divine revelations have played in shaping my understanding of right versus wrong. Because this is actually the issue in separation of church and state, the parental values that many people cherish are not reinforced through public-funded education. How we shape our families, and how we implement values into society through law, is being demonstrated to be a big deal in American culture. **Open discussion of the foundation of values and morals is strengthening to our culture and community because it strengthens the individuals who make up our communities. The traditional values of traditional parents have been denied in favor of producing a valueless culture in the public arena. The result is the chaos we are seeing in the public arena at multiple levels, including the public school system.**

The battle over separation of church and state has actually taken the things that once made us strong and used the differences as wedges to separate and to silence people who could otherwise become part of the extended community family. It is not necessary to agree with each other, to be friendly toward one another and have an exchange of views, but it is very evident that many people who claim to be tolerant are only tolerant of their views and are extremely intolerant of views they disagree with. But what works is obvious if people will take the time to examine it. It is also this way with conflicting lifestyles. What works, works; there is a predictable and fulfilling result of living under defined values that have been demonstrated for thousands of years. What does not work is obvious because it also has a predictable and unfulfilling result. **Perhaps NIDA should study American traditional values <u>as a strategy to prevent drug abuse.</u>** If civic leaders can find a way to promote discourse between parents within the community as a path to strengthening the family, the faith-based community could, and should, provide creative ideas to support these community efforts. **It is my belief that this can be done in communities in the absence of open aggression by people who willingly participate, and it is also my opinion that *if* this can be done, <u>it *should* be done</u>.**

That being said, the idea of separation of church and state has stifled public discussion about who God is, what morality is, why God-based morality it is important, and why revealed truth must be and remain the foundation of values in society. The consequence of stifling this discussion is that many parents haven't answered the basic questions of life for themselves; therefore, they can't help their children answer those questions, nor can they help their children's children answer those questions. Laws establishing the separation of church and state have discouraged both political and religious leaders from having public debate over God and the foundation of values and the explanation of the historical values upon which our society was founded and has successfully been pursued since 1620 (beginning with the landing of the Pilgrims and the founding of the Plymouth Colony). It is not the purpose of the Supreme Court to establish values for society, but that is effectively what their legal interpretations addressing the freedoms of religion in America (First Amendment) have done.

<u>The Loss of Values in America</u>

The result of turning from historical traditional values has clearly been the visible loss of the personal values and morals that historically were the philosophical foundation of America (the philosophical base that produced freedom as the American society was growing). It is a fact that the founding fathers of the United States government separated from each other over details in church liturgy and interpretation of divine pronouncements. They did this even though the basic values extended from their religious views were remarkably similar (being generally based in the Ten Commandments). **It was Benjamin Franklin who caused the Continental Congress to finally come together and see the destructive consequence of refusing to find common ground and form a federal government. The result was that the Continental Congress, under the leadership of George Washington, as influenced by Benjamin Franklin and others, finally produced and agreed upon the Constitution of the United States, including the first Ten Amendments (commonly known as the Bill of Rights).**

The legal debate over separation of church and state is essentially doing the same thing to our country today that the religious differences did to the Continental Congress. The great majority of Americans still hold remarkably similar values, but we have lost the uniting factors that allow us to overlook our personal philosophical preferences and come together as community. Political correctness has stilled the public debate over the basic questions of life, with the result that many adults have not pursued answers to the basic questions of life. The logical result is that many parents have never developed answers to these questions. Numerous parents do not know who they are, where they came from, or why life has meaning and significance; **the result is that they cannot communicate what they don't know to their children**.

This has led to raising children in families having values that clearly do not work, but they are the values of many parents nonetheless. American culture is witnessing the values of those parents being implemented as broken or dysfunctional homes. While we have always had broken and dysfunctional homes in our culture, this condition is an epidemic in 2012. The offspring from these homes has in turn led to the implementation of values that do not work in their children, and this is snowballing into an increasingly larger portion of American society. As noted, we are seeing the result of this as the breakdown of the family. Perhaps the solution to this dilemma could be as simple as promoting local community activities involving families helping other families. This could be initiated and sponsored as ongoing projects by local civic leaders. This could definitely be coordinated through local faith-based organizations and other civic-minded organizations, but it will require a willingness to work together rather than fighting over philosophical differences. The most difficult part of this will be finding successful parents who are willing to volunteer their time to help struggling families. It is my belief that retired people (i.e. grandparents who have demonstrated successful parenting skills) are the readily available workforce to do precisely this.

Values That Work

If we don't bring America together, <u>we're going to lose it,</u> and <u>drug abuse is an ever growing illustration that alternate self-centered values don't work</u>. Drug abuse rehabilitation that actually works focuses upon promoting values that do work in an extended family community. If this works for retrieving those who are already addicts (as demonstrated by Teen Challenge), then it should be an even more powerful tool in preventing addiction in the first place.

My point in writing this <u>is not to promote religion; it is to promote truth,</u> to emphasize that parents, and the children of those parents, should be encouraged to pursue and answer the basic questions of life <u>for themselves</u>. Then they should be encouraged to present and defend those answers within the community at large. <u>In doing this, more people will discover what works in life, and what works in life will increasingly influence our communities.</u> My observations spanning three generations indicates that kids grow up and frequently throw off the values of their parents. However, after experiences in life have kicked their teeth out a few times, many who have "bolted from the barn" gravitate back to the values of their parents because the experiences of life force them to learn who they are and what works in life. What works, works; what doesn't work, just doesn't work, and the differences can be seen.

People who come from large and close-knit families are very aware that this happens in their family, but it is my belief that this happens to a much lesser extent when parents and kids are isolated to wallow in their personal problems without help and guidance from extended family and friends who love them and desire to help them. **Certainly one positive way to promote an extended family atmosphere is to promote communitywide, family-type activities and an atmosphere where public discourse on personal values and morals <u>is encouraged rather than discouraged</u>.** Of course, all participation in this type of community must be entirely voluntarily. **<u>But what works in life is very apparent in families that form, reproduce, and influence extended family and friends.</u>**

Perhaps public discussion of values and morals cannot happen in the school classroom, but certainly it can happen in extracurricular activities sponsored by local civic leaders including parents, clergy, teachers, and community planners. For that reason, it is my view that the community should promote the discussion of truth, values, morals, and the reasons these things are important to the individual and the community in an open forum as coordinated by civic leaders. We must learn to communicate these values that work openly in the community so that many people, including children, will participate in the discussion. **If it is true that we have been pursuing the wrong goal in overstudying drug abuse, then perhaps we have been guilty of harming America by silencing people who know how to build a family.** **Certainly history demonstrates how the idea of separation of church and state has had a negative impact on American culture.** Perhaps it is time to rethink our individual philosophical positions on Who am I? Where did I come from? Why am I here? Where is my journey through life taking me? What is the meaning and significance of life?

¶#89: The Third Obvious Solution

Clearly parents should control what their children engage in as entertainment, and the best way for parents to do this is to participate in that entertainment with their kids as much as possible. My experience with raising kids is that they cannot be relied upon to choose forms of entertainment that are healthy. Diverse forms of addictions actually work together to lead from one addiction to another. Research is showing that electronic games, drug abuse, and pornographic websites frequently work together to destroy a young life. NIDA is currently looking at the possibility of including electronic games and pornographic behavioral problems within the framework of addictions. Of course there is resistance to recognizing this correlation, but that does not prevent it from being true. Whatever works to foster isolationist behavior in teens and adults will probably encourage addictive behavior. In addition, it is very logical that this observation is true (see website *www.wooglabs.com/gamingaddiction.pdf*). *Readers are encouraged to visit this website.*

¶#90: Drug Abuse and Enforcement Authority

Drug abuse can be a difficult issue for enforcement authorities, because it addresses the issue of government restricting the rights of drug abusers, so that the rights of non-drug abusers to inhabit a drug-free society can be protected. Pertinent questions to drug enforcement are (1)

Does government exist to serve the people or to rule the people? (2) How is serving the people versus ruling the people to be implemented in the form of government?[34]

Some states are now debating what their legal position should be on the decriminalization or legalization of marijuana because enforcement of existing law is simply too expensive (e.g., law enforcement can't arrest 48.2 percent of high school seniors who have experimented with drugs or even 23.8 percent who do it once or more monthly; see Table 1). **The unvarnished truth is growing numbers of people want marijuana legalized, and the strategy to accomplish this has become loosely organized around a plan to make enforcement of marijuana laws so expensive and intrusive into the lives of so many families that the law can't be enforced.** Even though marijuana has long been termed a gateway drug to much harder drugs, political pressure on authorities to change the law is essentially being accomplished through civil disobedience. **Unless people who understand the issues <u>rally together</u>, those who want to change the law <u>are going to win the debate,</u> and they are going to use our kids and political correctness to do it.**

In addition, it is very evident that those who want to use marijuana as a mind-altering drug are using the recognized medicinal properties in marijuana as an excuse to decriminalize it or to unconditionally legalize it. This highlights the fact that our society has lost much of the form needed for evaluating what is right versus what is wrong. **The legalization of marijuana highlights the fact that in a civil society, each man <u>cannot</u> do what is right in his own eyes because <u>doing so limits the rights of others</u>.** This issue in fact highlights the idea that there historically was a philosophical form for making moral choices that gave birth to the legal structure of American society. For society to be strong and resilient, there must be structure; it is undeniable that when social structure breaks down, chaos takes over.

---

[34] This is essentially the same issue as separation of church and state. The First Amendment states:

> **Congress shall make no law respecting an establishment of religion, or prohibiting the free exercise thereof; or abridging the freedom of speech,** or of the press; or the right of the people peaceably to assemble, and to petition the Government for a redress of grievances.

The part of the First Amendment of interest in this footnote is known as the establishment clause and the freedom of speech clause. These statements are bolded and underlined in the quote above. Looking over how the idea of separation of church and state has developed through the years, it is very obvious that the courts have interpreted the statements in the First Amendment to effectively mean that "freedom *OF* religion" effectively means "freedom *FROM* religion." This is a complex legal issue, and it is not the purpose of this book to resolve it. However, it is the purpose of this book to promote ideas that strengthen families and reduce drug abuse within the law. Certainly there is nothing in the First Amendment that prevents communitywide discussion and even debate of values addressing how to build a successful family, including the influence of extended family and friends.

You Can Only Have Freedom within Form

Dr. Francis Schaeffer once said, "You can only have freedom within form." Is there a philosophical form that is conducive to producing freedom? Dr. Schaeffer thought there was, and he wrote several books examining the question of truth and how the presence of absolutes helps society. The thought-form that Schaeffer had in mind historically has been called the Judeo-Christian ethic. Without question, this thought-form has been the basis for the freedoms we have enjoyed in the United States for nearly 400 years (since the Pilgrims landed 1620). Certainly we have implemented that form imperfectly, but it has always been there to give us guidance. That form is now being challenged by the courts under the guise of separation of church and state. Effectively a few vocal people have used the courts to force what they perceive as their right to be free from any religious influence onto the great majority of Americans, who have been raised within the form produced by the Judeo-Christian ethic. **The ironic thing is that vocal people have been able to use the courts and the First Amendment to overpower traditional values even though it is very evident that their views are destroying the social order of the society that gave birth to their right known as freedom of religion.**

How does government stop the minority population of a free society from hurting itself (and the entire society) through its own willful choices? I have heard it said, "You can't legislate morality"; however, that is specifically what law attempts to do, as well as to prescribe punishment when found guilty of violating the law. This specific issue is currently being politically debated over the issue of eating an unhealthy diet and using tobacco products. If, in the form of paying for health care, taxpayers are required to pick up the cost of health care for citizens who willfully make unhealthy life choices; shouldn't those taxpayers have a voice in the choices that are possible for the citizens to make that influence their long-term health care costs? Certainly the issue of marijuana and drug abuse also falls into this arena. These questions immediately spill over into the issue of who is responsible for paying for my health care, me or the taxpayer through the government, and this question immediately leads to the question of how compassionate should a society be, and whom should the benefits of a public health care system in a compassionate society be defined to include?

This issue has been framed in the context of a nanny state versus our freedom to make informed choices about health care and a multitude of other choices that cost tax dollars.

These are very, very real questions, and the answers we make as a nation to these questions will have far reaching consequences. These questions are hard and probably will never be completely answered because they bleed into moral issues as well as financial issues. **Without question, <u>the issue of drug abuse and drug prevention also lies at the very heart of these questions, and the answers to these questions will be found as we answer the basic questions of life</u>.**

Freedom Requires Civic Responsibility

I have raised these very volatile questions to reassert that it is the responsibility of every person in a free society to ask the basic questions about life and then to personally pursue answering those questions. We cannot wait for someone else to answer these questions for us; indeed, we should not allow anyone to answer the questions for us; the personal consequences are too great. Individuals must begin to answer these questions for themselves, and this begins in the home under the tutelage of parents and the extended family and community. It is my view that local civic leaders, as explained above, can encourage this to happen. The answer to the basic questions in life will become the foundation of the meaning of life for the one who has answered them.

Family Values Based in Truth Will Bring Positive Change to American Society

So, we come to the obvious questions: <u>How can I raise my children to pursue a path that will bring fulfillment to them?</u> How will my children raise my grandchildren? My answer to this question is, if parents, civic leaders, and perhaps the educational system can instill a sense of community in the individual built upon the answers to the question of meaning; it seems obvious that this will produce extremely positive results for American society in a short time through the prevention of drug abuse alone. The question is, do we have the political will and the political resources to do this? There will be opposition.

Strengthening the family unit by answering the questions posed above may provide the most viable answer for all of the questions raised in this book for three reasons:

1. It is the family unit that is the basic social unit (building block) that is the foundation of a drug-free society. Developing reasons why marriage is for life, and why building life on a solid foundation of values which extend into morals, will produce the most

far reaching and measurable forces for stability in the family unit. It is this foundation that will prevent drug abuse in the larger society.

2. Building stronger families is the least expensive answer to the questions of drug abuse and health care. Drug abuse is the visible issue that initiates and perpetuates several very expensive social problems in governing American society. The issue of drug abuse is a symptom of ineffective parenting. If the situation of ineffective parenting can be dealt with, it will open the door to solving a number of social problems at their root, rather than continuing to deal with symptoms instead of the root problem.

3. If people will analyze the issue of drug abuse, I believe it will become evident that building stronger families is the least politically explosive answer to the question of drug abuse. There will be opposition, but what is happening now clearly is not working. If building strong families can reduce money spent in other areas, then perhaps the efforts will pay for themselves.

It is my belief that NIDA, in the interest of preventing drug abuse, should seriously study how to strengthen the family unit. However, if NIDA does not do this, it is still the responsibility of parents to teach their children how to build fulfilling lives. In addition, it is the responsibility of civic leaders in local government to help families deal with problems that are destroying them. **Strengthening families is not only a good thing to do, it is the right thing to do, simply because <u>strengthening the family structure is in the best interest of the people.</u>**

All education assumes that if someone knows how something will affect him, he will make better choices when addressing it. Certainly one function of education is teaching the student how to find and assimilate information that will help him. In today's fast-paced world, one must be a lifelong learner if he is to stay abreast of technology that will assist him in performing his job.

If it is true that we are more interested in technology and in learning to how to control fire than in raising our children, perhaps we should step back and reexamine how important our families are to us. My history of drug abuse and escape from the trap of addiction has encouraged me (and my cowriter) to develop this book. Our message is that life can be fulfilling and have long term meaning when built around a base of truth that our forefathers brought with them into this new world; our culture has turned from the values that made this country great. The most visible reason that my drug awareness training is successful among teens is because it reveals, in graphic terms, the consequences of making bad choices about drugs, and teens can identify with this. My emphasis in drug awareness training is that **drug abuse destroys the teens that do it, and in the process, drug abuse significantly harms the families of those teens.** In concluding Day #1 of my drug awareness presentation, I tell the kids:

> When you go home from school this afternoon, I want you to do something, and I really mean it; **when you go home from school this afternoon, I want you to walk up to your parents and put your arms around them and give them a hug and tell them <u>thanks for doing all the stuff they do for you;</u>** whether you want to admit it or not, they do. I don't know if you know it or not, but your parents are out there struggling right now. There may be homeless teenagers sitting in this room right now.

It is this message that grabs and holds the attention of young people and causes them to choose to turn away from drug abuse. This is a powerful message, and I believe it is this message given to teens that reduces drug abuse more proactively than all the teaching about what drugs do to your brain or who is at risk for drug abuse (as important as these things are). **The truth is important; truth allows us to build enduring family units, and truth allows us to prevent drug abuse, and truth will free us from drug abuse if we have fallen into this trap.**

Shouldn't we raise this issue to the next higher level and address the more effective parenting of kids as one viable approach to lessening drug abuse?

SECTION FOUR
<u>LETTERS TO MARTY</u>

¶#91: <u>Letters to Marty Are One of the Great Rewards for Presenting This Program</u>

The following ten letters were written by teens in the Clark County School District, which covers most of the public school system in Las Vegas, Nevada. Each letter was forwarded to me by the teacher of the class at the school where I presented drug awareness training. The names of the teens and the teachers have been blocked out to protect each writer's identity. As of the end of the 2010–2011 school year, I have received about 80,000 such letters, and over the ten years that I have presented this drug awareness program in the school district, I have spoken to approximately 150,000 teens. From this, it seems that about half of the teens who hear my presentation respond by writing me a letter about their life and my presentation. [35]

These letters address what is going on in their lives at the moment, including their experiences with drugs. As such, these letters are a window into their world. When we read these letters as adults, we must remember that they reveal the individual teen's understanding of life, drugs, and the effects of drugs on the user and on the people who care about the user. These letters present the teens' perceptions of their world, which may not agree with the adult's perception. I believe the teens who write these letters are trying to honestly present what they feel when they write. These letters are very uplifting; they are also frequently heartbreaking.

These letters illustrate voids in the lives of teens that are increasingly being filled by drugs. Based on my experience of personally getting drawn into chemical abuse, it is my belief that America's teens frequently are looking for answers to the questions of life when they experiment with drugs. In many instances, it seems the void in the teen's life is substantially due to a lack of parenting skills born out of the fact that many parents simply do not know their children and don't take steps to assist their children with the issues they are facing as they grow to maturity. Please read the following letters with the understanding that these teens have been very candid about how drugs and the circumstances of life have effected them.

---

[35] A book entitled "LETTERS TO MARTY" will be forthcoming in the next year. In this book approximately 500 letters similar the those presented below will be presented and discussed.

Letter #1: Page #1

14 YEAR OLD GIRL

April 30, 2007

Dear Marty Gruber,

BASIC H/S 04/26/27/07

I want to thank-you not only for coming to talk to my class but for saving my life. Before you came in I was an everyday potsmoker, every weekend alcohol drinker, every other day pill popper and I started getting into smoking crack & cocaine. Your presentation has helped me see what horrid poisons I've been putting in my body. I had an intervention. I was sitting at my "friends" house on 16 coricedin about to take a hit of primo marijuana when I felt in my pocket for a lighter & all I found was the poem you gave me "My name is Crystal meth". I passed the pipe & spent the next hour reading and re reading it. All I could think to myself was, "what am I doing with my life?" "I'm killing myself" "my future will be gone if I continue". I hate to have to admit that I'm going to start my adult life as a chemical freak. But I'm GOING to college. I'm HAVING a future. and I'm not going to give

Letter #1, Page #2

up on myself because I'll always know you have faith in me.

With drugs there is no self satisfaction & the happiness is gone in a matter of hours. I gave up volunteering at St. Rose Dominican hospital because of drugs. I gave up my friends who wouldn't get high with me not realizing they were the ones to hold onto longest. I lost interest in everything that once made me happy because I wanted to kill myself with drugs.

My whole personality changed. I was ditching my friends to go smoke crack giving up my sister's birthday present money for coke, blowing off homework to party, get drunk & get high. And I ditched a week straight of school to smoke weed. All of my enthusiasm has been taken from me & im not sure when or if it will return but I do know that im willing to wait, I'm ready to break the addiction

Letter #1, Page #3

cycle and try to get my life back in order and I want you to know it's all because of you.

you've given me the strength to recognize my mistakes, take accountability for them & attempt to fix them.

When I said you've saved my life I meant it.

Thank-you again Marty Gruber. I think you are my angel.

Love,

Letter #1: This letter is from a fourteen-year-old girl who was a regular drug user prior to hearing me speak in her class. She indicates that I helped her realize how drugs were affecting her and the influence of drugs in the lives of other users; she also indicates that my presentation helped her realize that her drug-using friends were a bad influence, and because of this, they were not acting like real friends. This letter also indicates that she now realizes that an education will enrich her life more than drugs. **It is letters like this that keep me going at seventy-five.**

Letter #2 is from a teenage girl who says she never considered doing drugs, but she is aware that several acquaintances who were doing drugs came to realize that the drugs they were doing were not safe to use. Teens do not intentionally set out to destroy their lives with drugs,

Letter #2

Dear Mr. Gruber,

I just wanted to say thank you so much for coming to Leavitt Middle School. You are an amazing person.

I wasn't even thinking about drugs in the first place, but the stories you were telling my class and I, made me realize, (even more) that drugs are horrible.

I know, just through that presentation, for the two days you were here, you changed so many kids, and me also.

Thank you so much Mr. Gruber. Keep doing what your doing, because there are many more kids that need to here your stories, and need to here what your family, friends, and especially you went through.

You have the power to change a person. Please believe me when I tell you that, because, you changed me.

Thank You

always & forever,

but as presented in "Questions About the Decision Making Process of Life," kids do not always have the personal experience needed to evaluate the safety of something they are willing to experiment with. Youthful ignorance is part of what enables the drug predator to lure unsuspecting kids into experimenting with drugs. Much of the impact of my drug awareness presentations lies in the fact that I speak from personal experience rather from the academic study of drugs. I am living proof that using drugs illegally will damage your life, and I can tell teens what the active pursuit of chemical addiction will eventually produce if taken to the logical result (i.e., a poor quality of life and then jail, physical incapacitation, or death). I am not speaking about something I have read about; I have been there, and I speak with confidence about the road into chemical addiction and the pain it brings into the lives of those who take it. I have been there to the point of attempted suicide.

Letter #3

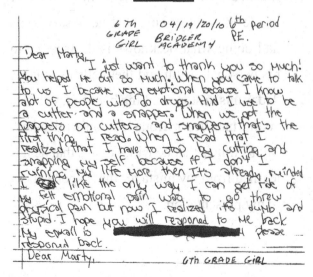

6Th GRADE GIRL   04/19/20/10 6th period BRIDGER ACADEMY PE.

Dear Marty, I just want to thank you so much! You helped me out so much. When you came to talk to us I became very emotional because I know alot of people who do drugs. And I use to be a cutter and a snapper. When we got the papers on cutters and snappers that's the first thing I read. When I read that I realized that I have to stop by cutting and snapping myself because if I don't I ruining my life more then It's already ruined. I felt like the only way I can get rid of my felt emotional pain was to go threw physical pain but now I realized it's dumb and stupid. I hope you will respond to me back. My email is _____ please respond back.

Dear Marty,   6Th GRADE GIRL

Letter #3 illustrates that this teen has realized the ultimate destination the drug freak is choosing. This girl was a cutter and snapper and had friends who did drugs, and she was concerned. She read the info from NIDA that I handed out, and it helped her make an important decision to change her life—that was to quit cutting and snapping and doing drugs.

Letter #4

BOY   BRIDGER ACADEMY
6TH GRADE   04/19/20/10
April 21, 2010

Dear Marty,
My name is ████ I am in 6th grade and almost 12 years old and attend Jim Bridger Middle School. What you have taught me the two days that you came to my school was tremendously helpful. Yes, in fifth grade I had a D.A.R.E officer teach my class about drugs and alcohol, but between you and my D.A.R.E officer, there's a big difference. You in two days have taught me the real and detailed truth about these bad substances, substances that kill its victim mentally through its way of being addictive and then for real killing its victim silently. You have taught me some true horrors about drugs and I do thank you so much for teaching me the real truth. I learned some new things about drugs and alcohol that I never really knew. One new thing I learned was that alcohol will kill your brain cells, and once that happens, they're never replaced! Another thing I never knew about was something I learned from the folded paper about steroids I picked up. I didn't know that steroids did so many things to you like stop bone growth, heart attack, strokes, and give you cancer in bones and your liver. WoW! That's a lot! You had purposes to the lesson you taught us. The most important one is most likely for us to use the info. we learned. With the information I learned from you I can tell anyone who approaches me with the intent for me to take drugs what such horrible and evil things these devilish drugs do to you, and then those approachers will loose. Trust me I've never had anyone tell me that much about drugs in two days, and that is why I can trust you with all of my trust.
Sincerely ████
Boy

Letter #4 is from a sixth grade boy that had previous DARE training; with the additional training this year, the tumblers of his mind fell into place. This letter illustrates how personal experience versus academic training helps drug awareness presenters connect with kids. This teen took the handouts and read them; he was interested in what drugs will do to his body; was he considering steroids for personal use? His final two sentences are very revealing. This is what some people would call an "ah-ha" moment, when truth comes crashing into one's awareness.

Letter #5

BRIDGER ACADEMY
04/19/20/10 6TH GRADE
BOY

Dear Marty,
Thanks for coming to Jim Bridger Middle School. I really appreciate it. I am drug free. I know you don't get paid for this so I'm going to repay you with this letter. My dad smokes. He is trying to quit but he can't. I'm helping him quit. If If I ever see someone doing drugs I will stop them. I learned from your mistakes. Thanks for showing us that video about what drugs do to you. I will never end up like that. I am glad you came. Congratulations for being drug free. Happy early Birthday. I hope you stay drug free like me. I will always stay in school and say no to drugs
From
Boy sixth Grader
from Jim Bridger.

Letter #5 is from a sixth grade boy. What this young man writes illustrates that he realizes that "free" education is not free, a timely lesson and one that will serve him well later in life. It is interesting that he observes his dad doing what he knows is destructive to his personal health and then tells us that his dad wants to stop smoking but can't; will this young man learn from his dad's mistakes? My feeling is that he will; he says that he has learned from my mistakes that I spoke about in my presentation.

Letter #6:

BASIC H/S,   4-30-07

Marty,   04/26/27/07

Thank you for coming to our school and telling us about life. Also thank you for teaching us about drugs and how bad the can ruin your life. After you told us about your life and dealing with drugs I never want to do them or even try. Now I know who my real friends are. Thank you so much.

Always,

Letter #6: If all letters I received were like this one, I would be a very happy man. Chemical abuse would not be destroying the lives of millions of young people each year, and I could retire from my second full-time job. Sadly, drugs are a problem, and millions of young people are becoming addicts each year. However, studies show that warning programs work (see http://www.drugabuse.gov/scienceofaddiction/strategy.html).

Letter #7 was also a good letter to receive. This young man did the right thing; he went to his parents and asked for help and received the help he needed to become drug free and stay

Letter #7

04/19/20/10

Dear Marty, Boy 6th BRIDGER ACADEMY
GRADE

Thank you for coming to Jim Bridger school. I learned a lot from you. Your teachings saved my life from drugs. Its been a while since I don't do drugs. One month ago I stoped from using marijuana. At first it is very hard to stop because you are used it, getting you high. How I stopped is when I went into my parents bedroom and told them I had been doing drugs. They helped me by talking to me about the dangers and causes drugs have. That when I realized I was doing bad things to my body. A question I want to ask you is; How can I stop myself from going back and doing drugs?

My email is:

from your friend,

EMAILED
4/28/10   Male

drug free. He then asked a question that every person involved in reducing drug abuse would like to have the answer to: How can I stop myself from going back and doing drugs? This thought is partially addressed under "Teen Challenge Success in Drug Abuse Treatment as Verified by the National Institute on Drug Abuse—Significant Research That Everyone Should Know." Teen Challenge clearly demonstrates that faith is a helpful component in turning away from chemical abuse and then staying drug free. This has also been clearly demonstrated by twelve-step programs where the role of a Higher Power is emphasized. In addition, the effect of this component has been recognized by the National Institute on Drug Abuse (see http://www.acadc.org/page/page/2495014.htm).

<u>Letter #8</u> came from a fourteen-year-girl who is crying out for help in making the tough decisions of life. "Tweak" is street lingo for methamphetamines, one of the hardest white powder drugs to quit. This girl cites the classic path into white powder drugs: cigarettes to marijuana to methamphetamine. This teen seems to love her family, but they also seem uninvolved in her pain of growing up. As adults we sometimes forget just how painful going through the transition from adolescent to adult can be, especially in the fast-paced modern world where our kids are dealing with adult decisions from before puberty, and many times they are making the transition into adulthood in the almost complete absence of adult guidance. This teen says she doesn't know why she did tweak; she loves her mother, her stepdad, and her younger sisters, but it seems the danger of drug usage that she heard in my presentation was new information for her. This is why this program is so important; it is estimated that for every dollar spent on drug awareness training, seven to eleven dollars are saved in dealing with drug abuse. But this just speaks of the dollars; more important are the broken lives that spending money on drug awareness saves (see http://www.drugabuse.gov/tib/prevention.html).

<u>Letter #8; Page #1</u>

04/12/13/07

Hello marty! My name is
_____. I was the girl in 1st
period, with the black skull sweat
shirt on. I just wanted to say thank
you so much for helping me figure
out what I was going to do
about so many problems I was
having. Last year, I was also
in 8th grade. I got held back
because I was ditching almost
everyday and smoking cigerettes,
weed, and yes, I did do tweak
once or twice, but I had the
carrage to stop only after 3months,
and im proud of myself for that.
I dont even understand why I
did that stuff, maybe to be cool, or
something, because my whole life
was wonderful! I love my mother
so dearly, and my stepdad is always
there for me, and I have 2 little sisters
that I have to be a big sister
too. I absolutely did not want to go
down that road. sometimes I thought.
Back

<u>Letter #8; Page #2</u>

I need a cigerette..... or some weed.
But after I talked to you, every
single day I tell myself.... I
dont need that junk! What does
it do? nothing. Kill you. listen
to the people that love you,
thats all you need. so I thank
you, from the bottom of my
heart for turning me away
from a dead end life. My friend
was doing tweak, and last weekend
I told her mother, she hates me
now, but its just something I
had to do. I'd rather her hate
me, then be dead. You gave
me the courage to tell her
mother. You'll will forever be in
my heart, marty. I will never
forget you. Thank you.

Your friend,

Letter #9: Page #1

LiED M/S 05/15/16/08

May 19, 2008

Dear Marty Gruber,
    Thank you so much for coming to this school. It was really an eye opening experience. It made me realize that if I don't stop what I'm doing now, I could die. I am currently in 8th grade and 14 years of age. I have been smoking cigarettes since 4th grade. I have been smoking marijuana since March 29th of this year. I have smoked hooah since 7th grade, I have played the choking game to many times to count. I have also been cutting myself since the end of 5th grade, and tried suicide 3 times. I have been drinking alcohol over half my life, and popping prescription pills for about 2 months. I want you to know that you have truly saved my life. The first day of your presentation, I was going to attempt my 4th suicide, but your presentation stopped me. It made me stop and realize, that when I leave this cruel world, I wanted to be clean. It made me realize how my life could be so much worse. Mr. Gruber, when I looked you in the eyes, I saw so much pain, All I could do is cry. You have saved my life. I have been clean since your first presentation. I still get

Letter #9: Page #2

second hand smoke everyday, but that's not something I have a choice on. I really appreciate everything you have said and done. You are really my hero. And I look up to you ammensily. I am going to stay sober. Meeting you was an amazing and life changing experience. You have opened my eyes.
                        Thank you.

Letter #9 is one of the most upsetting letters that I can print. This fourteen-year-old needs a loving but firm hand of guidance but is apparently not getting it. He tells me he has repeatedly been doing drugs and other things that will kill him, and that he has been drinking alcohol since he was seven. Now he realizes where his choices were taking him (i.e., to the grave; the implication is that he did not realize that drugs were contributing to his suicidal tendencies). He was going to attempt suicide for the fourth time the day of my presentation, but he heard the message of hope and chose not to. This young man does not think of death as the end of existence; he seems to view death as going to another place, but he wanted to be clean when he left this "cruel world." He also states that he realizes that life could be worse, but what could be worse than being driven to attempt suicide multiple times? I believe this is an illustration of the emotional roller coaster that teens can be on; it also illustrates why they need input from a caring adult that can provide a model for them to follow and guide them into seeking answers to their questions about life.

Letter #10 is from a girl who sees herself as a failure in life and as a problem for her family to provide for. Letters like this bring sorrow to my heart because I know the pain this child feels in believing she is not wanted by her family (perhaps she feels this from her mom or grandmother). She writes that if she was not alive, **"everyone would be happier so they would not have to pay or use there money on me."** She writes as if she believes her value as a person comes only from pleasing those around her and how hard she tries to be what she believes others expect her to be, but that she cannot be what she thinks is expected. Because this child cannot be what is expected of her, she believes she is a failure. Where is this child to find hope that will enable her to find her way to a healthy life? This child is crying out for advice from a caring adult; what can anyone tell her that will bring healing to her innermost being? If this child does not find help, she is a candidate for abusing drugs that will temporarily lift her burden through a temporary chemical euphoria but will lead her to a destroyed life.

Table 1 presents convincing statistics that chemical abuse is on the rise. I believe that the letters I receive suggest that the reason drug abuse is on the rise is that parents are not fulfilling their obligations to their children by demonstrating a fulfilling life to them and then leading them into that fulfilling life. At the end of 2010, 48.2 percent of high school seniors report that they had used illegal substance sometime in their lifetime, 38.3 percent had used illegal substance in the last year, and 23.8 percent had used illegal substance in the last month. Table 1 also presents the increased usage from the eighth grade through the twelfth grade

Letter #10

Dear Marty Gruber

Thank you for coming to one school, I remember last year too you came to bob miller. Will my real mom smokes every day in the house I true my best to get over the smell. My gramma smokes too, I would take one or tue for my self to tole it. Now I no how they feel. I some times think of my self as a failer. I cut my self a couple of times because if I would kill my self every one would be happyer. So they wouldn't have to pay or use there mouny on me, they placed me in the spicel ED class's, I can't read or speal right. I can't hear good ether, I true my best every day to true to be like everyone. But I can't, when I true my best I alluays fail. Will I don't cut my self any more but, I still want too but I can't right now everything is going down hill. I went to the dotor and sied that anti bodys are attacing my heart. I'm a little scarred right now. I true to act strong for everyone but I can't hold back anymore I need advice. what should I do I'm scared to death that I mite not know my self.

from 2007 through 2010. It also breaks illegal substance abuse down for most of the popular drugs. This table seems to suggest that drug awareness training is a wise investment of time and resources by the public school system, and information presented by Teen Challenge suggests that it may be a wise undertaking to investigate how faith-based drug awareness can be achieved in substantially reducing drug abuse.

The above ten letters are just a small sampling of the 80,000 letters I have received. I believe these letters illustrate why it is important for part of a drug awareness presentation to point to a source of answers that are authoritative and show that they work where the rubber meets the road in life. These letters suggest that kids are looking for something that works for them in real life.

Many of the letters that I receive are letter of appreciation expressed by the teens that have heard my presentations. But as illustrated in the above ten letters, they present a mixture of information about the world of teens and the pressures and confusion they experience in life. I believe this mixture demonstrates that the information presented in Table 1 is accurate, although I have not attempted to tabulate the letters I have received.

This is a picture of the letters I received during the second half the 2009–2010 school year. From the total weight of all the letters received, I calculate that I have received about 80,000 letters from the 150,000 students I have spoken to over the ten years I have been doing this program. Thus, I get letters from a little more than half of the students who hear my presentations. These letters are collected by teachers, who forward them to me. I usually receive these letters about two weeks after the presentation.

Dear Educators,

August 28, 2011

My name is Marty Gruber, I am a volunteer drug awareness presenter in Clark County School District. School year 2010–2011 will be my eleventh year presenting drug awareness to high school and middle school students. I have presented to over one hundred and fifty thousand high school and middle school students in the Clark County School District. This program is a two-day program and is still free. The program is my contribution to the young people of Clark County. I would like to present drug awareness to your students.

This program targets six groups of young people. The first group is the pre-teen or young teenager who has made the commitment not to do drugs. This program reaffirms their commitment and cements forever in their minds **not** **to do drugs**.

The second group of young people targeted by this program are teenagers who have never done drugs but would like to try them. Either they are trying to get enough nerve to try drugs, or are under a lot of peer pressure to do drugs. This program puts many of them back into the **non-drug user status** **forever**.

The third group are young people who are experimenting with drugs. I tell them like it is; I hold nothing back. Judging from the mail I receive from students, **this program** **has changed** **a lot of young minds about drugs.**

The fourth group are the hard core drug users who are in a state of denial about their addiction to drugs. I encourage them to seek help for their addiction. I provide different avenues for them to get help before it is too late. I also give them some insight about what is in store for them **if they continue on their** **chosen path** **in life**.

The fifth and sixth groups are the potential school dropouts and teens that may become involved with the law. I encourage these young people to **stay in school** and **stay out of** **trouble**.

I could tell you of the numerous young people this program has prevented from starting on drugs. I could also tell you of the teens this program has led to stop doing drugs and, for many, reaffirmed decisions not to do drugs. However, perhaps it is best to let Clark County School District students tell you what they think of this program in their own words. Please read the attached letters from young people this program has helped.

If you are interested in this program, please contact me at the telephone number or e-mail address listed below.

Sincerely,

Marty Gruber
Volunteer Drug Awareness Presenter

A MESSAGE FROM MARTY

I think one of the worst things that can happen to a person is to get hooked on drugs. Drugs take away everything in life that is decent and good. Addicts lose their family, friends, home, career, freedom—and their health.

More teens who get hooked on drugs are kicked out of their home than people think. Addicts pay a hefty price to feel good on drugs.

Don't join the "feel good society," don't become one of them; make good choices in life. Peer pressure does not go away, so you must learn to deal with it and make good choices. Don't give in to peer pressure. **FRIENDS DON'T HOOK FRIENDS ON DRUGS!**

Fifty percent of any addiction is denial, and it goes like this: "Who, me? I don't have a problem with drugs. I can quit any time I want to." This is denial because it is not true. In fact, by the time a person makes a statement like this, they are already hooked on drugs.

Drugs become number one in an addict's life; family, friends, school—all take a back seat to feeling good with drugs.

Drugs make you ugly, both on the inside and on the outside. Addicts will become a thief and a liar. Addicts will steal from their friends and family to get money to buy drugs.

Drugs are like a cancer that is spread from one "friend" to another. Drugs will take you down dark alleys to bad people and bad drug deals. Drugs will lead you into the grave at an early age.

You would be surprised at how many letters I get from teens who have lost friends and family to drugs and alcohol.

Listen to the people in this world who care about you.

Listen to Marty. **I CARE ABOUT YOU!**

FOR A LOT OF TEENS, ONE TIME IS FOREVER!

Marty Gruber
Volunteer Drug Awareness Presenter

PRESCRIPTION DRUGS
COUGH MEDICATION, AND STEROIDS

1. Drugs prescribed by a doctor are usually safe as long as they are taken in the amount prescribed by the doctor.

2. Uppers like Dexedrine, Ritalin, and Adderall can cause sleeplessness, twitching, fast and irregular heart beats, severe weight loss, high blood pressure, and panic attacks.

3. It is dangerous to mix downers like Xanax and Valium. The combination slows down the body so much that you can become unconscious and stop breathing.

4. Mixing uppers and downers changes the basic way your body and brain work together. The central nervous system is the control center for everything you do, and this includes things that the brain automatically regulates such as breathing and blood pressure, and these functions will be severely affected.

5. Never leave a drink of any kind unattended at a party. Someone can slip a drug into your drink without you knowing it. The result may be fatal. People frequently get their drinks spiked at parties.

6. Steroids can make boys look like girls and girls look like boys. Some boys develop female breasts and start to lose their hair, and over time they become bald. Boys with enlarged breasts may require surgery to reduce their breast size. Girls who take steroids may become masculine. They may begin to grow facial hair, their voice may get deep, and their breasts may shrink. These effects may also be permanent. Steroids can also cause heart damage.

7. Oxycontin can kill you after only one dose; you may just stop breathing. This drug is extremely addicting and kills many people.

8. Vicodin, Oxycontin, and Ecstasy, taken in high doses, change your brain chemistry forever. Ecstasy can kill you on the first dose.

9. Cough syrup taken in high doses can cause hallucinations and make you violent and act irrationally. You may look freaked out and spend lot of time throwing up. High doses can also make you lose control of your body to the extent that people can do anything they desire to you, and you can't stop them.

10. Opium-based pain relievers are the most addicting drugs ever made. Once you are hooked, you are hooked for life.

11. Be smart. Make good choices in your life. Listen to the people in your world who care about you. Life is short; it's too short to be chemical freak.

12. Help your friends get off drugs. You may just save a life.

Marty Gruber
Volunteer Drug Awareness Presenter

STEP UP

YOU HAVE THE POWER TO HELP A FRIEND OR FAMILY MEMBER WHO HAS A DRUG OR ALCOHOL PROBLEM

A GUIDE FOR TEENS

DON'T WALK AWAY

So you think your friend or brother or sister has a problem with drugs or alcohol? Maybe he seems like a different person since starting to get high or starting to drink. Maybe she's been letting you down because she's been doing drugs. Maybe you are seeing patterns in his drug or alcohol use and he seems to need drugs or alcohol before he goes out to school or a party. Or maybe some of the things he does when he's high or drunk are just plain scary. Whatever it is, the important thing is that you've noticed that your friend may be heading for trouble.

You can help your friend now, before something really bad happens. Your friend will probably insist that his drug use or drinking is not a big deal. This is very common among people with drug or alcohol problems. Don't let your friend's denial keep you from talking with him. If he continues to use drugs or alcohol, he could use bad judgment or make a bad decision and face consequences like getting caught or arrested, losing his driver's license, getting suspended, or more seriously, getting involved in a drug- or alcohol-related car crash, overdosing, or becoming addicted.

NO WAY TO KNOW WHAT WILL HAPPEN

If a friend smokes marijuana or uses other drugs or alcohol, there is no way to predict how she will act or what will happen when she is high or drunk. All drugs, including marijuana, can be harmful or addictive. There is no magic number of drug experiences it takes to get addicted. But drug and alcohol use can lead to abuse, and continued use can lead to addiction.

Common sense tells us that helping a friend address a drug or alcohol problem early can keep it from getting out of control and doing serious harm. This is why it is important to **STEP UP** and talk with your friend sooner rather than later; you never know what consequences lie ahead if he or she continues to do drugs or drink.

HOW TO START A CONVERSATION

If you decide to sit down with your friend and talk to him about his drug use or drinking problem, you may not know what to say. You may wonder how she will respond. Will he get defensive? Will she deny she has a problem? Will he get mad at you and tell you to mind your own business? It's likely that she will. People with drug or alcohol problems usually defend their use or make excuses for it. It is hard for people to admit to themselves that they have a drug or alcohol problem.

- Start by telling your friend how much she means to you and that you are worried about her.
- Give examples of how his use of drugs or alcohol has caused problems or affects you or others.
- Let her know that you want to help and tell her what you will do for her.
- Discuss this issue with your friend when he is not high.
- If you are not comfortable having this conversation with your friend by yourself, get some other friends to help you; there is safety and support in numbers. Be careful not to gang up on your friend.
- Try talking in confidence to an adult that you trust before talking to your friend. There are many people that can help you figure out the best approach: a trusted family member, teacher, coach, school councilor, student assistance professional, family doctor, school nurse, or faith leader.
- If you are not comfortable talking with your friend face-to-face, try writing a note or e-mail to him.

Finally, remember that talking to your friend is only the first step. It may take several conversations before he understands how serious you are about his drug use or drinking. Don't give up if she doesn't stop after the first conversation. Your friend may need additional help to face his drinking problem, like talking to a councilor or getting treatment. Tell her that you will help her get the help she needs, and then follow through.

For examples of how to address your friends' drug use and drinking, and to hear from kids who have been in your situation, go to www.freevibe.com.

IT'S NOT YOUR FAULT

Helping a friend with a drug or alcohol problem can be a very difficult experience for you as well as your friend. You may feel a great deal of pressure to stop your friend from doing drugs or drinking. Or you may get discouraged if your efforts to convince your friend to stop doing drugs or drinking don't work. But it is important to know that your friend's drug or alcohol use is not your fault. Remember that it is ultimately up to him to make the change; you can't do that for him. Sometimes, as hard as you may try to get your friend to quit or seek help, you just can't seem to make it happen. If you find yourself in this situation, you should do one of the following:

- Seek support from other friends or trusted adults; your friend is not the only one who needs help in this situation.
- Limit the time you spend with your drug- or alcohol-using friend. Remember, your friend's use may be putting you at risk.
- Start thinking about yourself; get out and participate in activities that you enjoy to take your mind off of the situation.

THE POWER OF FRIENDSHIP

Working up the courage to confront a friend about his drug use or drinking is very difficult. In fact, it may be one of the hardest things you'll ever do. But part of being a good friend is recognizing when your friend needs help, even if it wasn't requested. After all, you'd help your friend out and give him advice on other stuff—like family, dating, or school—so why wouldn't you talk to him about drugs?

Sometimes just bringing up the subject with your friend is a wake-up call that is sorely needed. Did you know that 68 percent of teens say they would turn to a friend or brother or sister about a serious problem related to drug abuse? This means that when you talk to your friend, your friend will listen, even if you have tried drugs or alcohol yourself.

Don't underestimate your own power to influence your friend and explain to him how you see his drug use getting out of hand. Sure, it may have been his choice to start using drugs in the first place, and you may be afraid that your friend will get mad at you and tell you that his choices are none of your business. But if you really think that your friend needs help, you have a responsibility to him—and to your friendship—to **STEP UP** and say something.

By not talking to your friend about your concerns, you are sending him the silent message that his drug or alcohol problem is not big deal. Remember, if you can save one person's life in your lifetime, you have done something great.

For more information, or to talk to a specialist who can refer your friend to help, call (800) 788-2800 or go to www.health.org.

If you are concerned about your own drug or alcohol use, go to www.checkyourself.org.

For more information about underage drinking and peer pressure problems, go to www. thecoolspot.gov.

For science-based facts about how drugs affect the brain and body, go to www.teens.drugabuse. gov.

SIGNS AND SYMPTOMS[36]

Does your friend have a drug or drinking problem? If your friend does one of the following, chances are there is a problem:

- She is using regularly and has to use drugs or alcohol to have a good time or to cope with everyday life.
- He starts hanging out with new friends who do drugs with him or who can score drugs for him.
- She shows up at school drunk or high or has skipped class to use.
- He broke plans with you or showed up late because he was getting drunk or high.
- She shows little interest or drops out altogether from activities she once enjoyed, like sports or music.
- He uses drugs or drinks when he is alone.
- She has driven a car while high or drunk, or has ridden with someone who was high or drunk.
- He borrows money from you to buy drugs or alcohol, or asks you to hold his drugs for him.
- You feel you must baby sit her when she is high or drunk to keep her from doing things she might regret, like having sex or getting into a fight with her parents.
- He is having difficulty with family relationships and letting his family and friends down.
- You feel you are being used by someone who was your best friend at one time.

FOR A LOT OF TEENS, ONE TIME IS FOREVER

Marty Gruber

Volunteer Drug Awareness Presenter

---

[36] Portions of this document were taken from an out of print Substance Abuse and Mental Health Services Administration (SAMHSA) document. This document is in the public domain and may be used without permission.

SECONDHAND SMOKE

In America, it is estimated that secondhand smoke kills at least 55,000 people every year.

Some estimates go much higher than that. When a child or teenager is subject to secondhand smoke, it does a lot of damage to their developing respiratory system. Secondhand smoke causes bronchitis, asthma, lung cancer, breast cancer, and heart disease. When your child is subject to secondhand smoke, it sets the stage for things to come in the future. It is possible they may experience poor health for the rest of their lives because of the effects of secondhand smoke.

Recent research on secondhand smoke has confirmed that it causes breast cancer in females. It is not in doubt, it's not maybe, it's a done deal. Forty thousand women die in America every year from breast cancer. Depending on how long your female child has been subjected to secondhand smoke, the odds may go as high as 90 percent she will develop breast cancer at some time in her life.

Smoking cigarettes is the worst health hazard the world has ever known. **More people die in America every year from smoking cigarettes than have died in all the wars America has fought COMBINED.** Lung cancer is a very horrible way to leave this world. Stop smoking cigarettes, you will be glad you did.

If your child has given you this information bulletin, he or she is asking you to stop smoking around them. They love you very much and want to have a loving relationship with you, but they need your help to grow up and become healthy and productive adults.

Would you please stop smoking around them?

Marty Gruber
Volunteer Drug Awareness Presenter

THE PRACTICE OF CUTTING OR SNAPPING

When a person cuts, they are either crying out for help or punishing themselves for things that are not their fault. When you abuse yourself by cutting or snapping, you're saying, "I don't like myself very much." You're replacing love and closeness with pain. You would really like to have people closer to you, but the act of cutting is so grotesque it pushes people away from you, it does not draw them closer.

Most cutters are girls, but boys cut too. Like drugs, cutting is another dead end street to nowhere. Cutting is as addictive as drugs. When you cut or snap yourself, your body releases heroin-like chemicals called endorphins to combat pain. Just like drugs, you get hooked on the feelings your own chemicals give you.

If you are snapping yourself, it is as addictive as cutting. Snapping can lead to cutting. I've had cutters tell me they quit cutting and went to snapping. I've had snappers tell me they quit snapping and went to cutting. Did you ever stop to think that you could bleed to death by cutting or get a very serious infection or disease? You can also be scarred for life.

If you have a cutting or snapping problem, ask for help. Talk to your teacher or school counselor about your problem. Don't try and go it alone. I care about you!

Books: (1) *Bodily Harm* by Karen Conterio and Wendy Lader. (2) *A Bright Red Scream* by Marlee Strong. Website: Teen Hope Line: www.teenhopeline.com.

Marty Gruber
Volunteer Drug Awareness Presenter

THE HOOKAH MYTH

What is hookah? Is it safe to smoke?

Hookah is a very strong tobacco. It is imported from other countries like India. The strength of hookah is masked by adding different flavors. The amount of impurities in hookah is staggering: four thousand trace chemicals are found in hookah. This is a gateway drug for sure.

Hookah is smoked from a water pipe. This in itself can cause a lot of problems for the smoker. When you share a pipe with other people, you can transmit a number of communicable diseases, including tuberculosis, hepatitis, herpes, and a lot of other diseases.

Because of the volume of smoke you take into your lungs, forty-five minutes of smoking hookah is equal to smoking a pack of cigarettes. Hookah contains significantly high levels of arsenic, lead, and nickel.

- ❖ Hookah has one hundred times more tar than cigarettes.
- ❖ The nicotine content of hookah is four times that of cigarettes.
- ❖ The carbon monoxide content of hookah smoke is eleven times that of cigarettes.
- ❖ Smoking hookah can lead you into smoking cigarettes, because by smoking hookah you can become addicted to the very addictive drug called nicotine.

Don't listen to uninformed people; hookah is not safe to smoke. Get the facts before you make bad choices in your life. If you would like to know more facts about hookah, go to www.google.com and enter "hookah" in the search window. Or go to http://www.mayoclinic.com/health/hookah/AN01265 to find information on hookah from the Mayo Clinic.

Hookah is just another trap for young people to fall into. It is another path that will lead you to self-destruction with drugs. Remember, "**For a lot of teens, one time is forever**."

Marty Gruber
Volunteer Drug Awareness Presenter

THE CHOKING GAME

The choking game is a very deadly game. When you engage in certain activity to feel good, and at the same time choke yourself to the point of passing out, what you are doing is starving your brain of oxygen. When you do this, two bad things can happen:

1. You go too far and die.
2. You go too far but don't die, but you become brain damaged and lay in a bed for the rest of your life while someone spoon feeds you and changes your dirty diaper.

When you choke yourself, you are demonstrating to yourself and the rest of the world how little you care about yourself, and how little you care about the people around you who do care about you.

If you are playing the choking game, **STOP NOW!**

If you know someone who is playing the choking game, try and get them to stop doing what they are doing to themselves. Remember, "**For a lot of teens, one time is forever**."

Marty Gruber
Volunteer Drug Awareness Presenter

THE MARIJUANA MYTH

"Hey man, want to get high? Don't be chicken, everybody is doing it. Weed is all natural and makes you feel good."

Does this sound familiar? Well, don't believe it; marijuana is not the innocent drug some people will tell you it is. I smoked weed for twelve years, all three of my sons smoked weed, and a lot of their friends smoked it also. Over and over again, I watched teens start drinking alcohol then start smoking cigarettes or marijuana. This is what we call drug progression.

Marijuana is a gateway drug to the white powder drugs. One of the reasons this happens is through association with people who do more than marijuana and through association with drug dealers.

The other way is through human nature, and it goes something like this: Weed makes me feel good, I wonder how I would feel if I laced my weed with coke or meth or heroin? Basically what happens is that you join the "feel good society." Feeling good becomes the number one thing in your life. Friends, family, your education don't matter anymore. You reject your friends and replace them with drug buddies.

Marijuana will lead you down the garden path to self-destruction and make you feel good all the way to jail or the grave.

It is your choice, and I hope you make the right choice and **DO NOT** do drugs. Drug addiction is a dead end street to nowhere. Druggies go nowhere in this world. Listen to the people in your life who care about you.

The other point I would like to make is this: not everybody who tries drugs becomes addicted to drugs, but far too many do; don't you become one of them. Peer pressure does not go away, so you must learn to deal with it. People who offer you drugs are not your friends; in fact, they don't even like you. Friends don't try to hook friends on drugs. **TELL THEM TO GET LOST!**

Does marijuana have medical uses? Yes it does, but the risks far outweigh the benefits. I get letters from kids all the time telling me they used to be good in sports until they started smoking weed. Now they can't breathe anymore.

Keep it cool out there, and if you stay in school, stay drug free, and stay out of trouble, you will do fine in this very tough world we have created for ourselves, and it's getting tougher every day.

FOR A LOT OF TEENS, ONE TIME IS FOREVER!

Marty Gruber
Volunteer Drug Awareness Presenter

TEEN HELP TELEPHONE LIST

Alanon/Alateen: 602-615-9494.
Free twelve-step groups for addicts and family members of addicts—alcohol.

Bridge Counseling: 602-474-6450; 1120 Almond Tree Lane; Las Vegas, NV.
Mental heath counseling. Sliding fee.

National Treatment Reference Service: 800-662-4357.

Las Vegas Recovery Center: 602-515-1373; free.

Mental Health Services: 602-486-6100; West Charleston Blvd; Las Vegas, NV.
Sliding fee.

Alcohol-Drug Treatment: 800-454-8955.

Montevista Hospital: 602-364-1111.

Outreach Counseling: 602-877-0133.
Youth counseling service; sliding fee.

Westcare: 602-385-3332; 5659 Duncle Drive; Las Vegas, NV.
Detox; residential and outpatient; crisis intervention; emergency shelter; sliding fee.

Westcare: Call 602-385-2020.
Youth residential facility.

Narcotics Anonymous Hotline: 602-369-3362.

Alcoholics Anonymous: 602-598-1888.

Child Protective Services Hotline: 602-399-0081.

Rape Crisis Hotline: 602-366-1640.

National Suicide Hotline: 800-273-8355.

Teen Challenge International/NorWestCal Nevada: 408-583-2200.

MY NAME IS METH

I destroy your homes, I tear families apart,
    Take your children, and that's just the start.

I'm more costly than diamonds, more precious than gold,
    The sorrow I bring is a sight to behold.

If you need me, remember I'm easily found.
    I live all around you in schools and in town.

I live with the rich, I live with the poor,
    I live down the street, and maybe next door.

I'm made in a lab, but not like you think,
    I can be made right under the kitchen sink.

In your child's closet and even the woods.
    Does this scare you? Certainly it should.

I have many names, but there's one you know best,
    I'm sure you've heard of me, my name is crystal meth.

My power is so awesome, try me you'll see,
    But if you do, you may never break free.

Just try me once and I might lct you go,
    But try me twice and I'll own your mind, body, and soul.

When I possess you, you'll steal and you'll lie, you'll do what
    You have to—just to get high.

The crimes you'll commit for my narcotic charms
    Will be worth the pleasure you feel in your lungs, nose, and arms.

You'll lie to your mother, you'll steal from your dad,
    When you see their tears you should feel sad.

But you'll forget your morals and how you were raised,
    I'll be your conscience, I'll teach you my ways.

I take kids from parents, and parents from kids.
    I take people from their Higher Power, and separate friends.

I'll take everything—your looks and your pride,
    I'll be with you always—right by your side.

You'll give me everything—your family, your home,
    Your friends, your money, then you'll be alone.

I'll take and take, till you have nothing more to give,
    When I'm finished with you, you'll be lucky to live.

If you try me be warned, this is no game,
    If given the chance I'll drive you insane.

I'll ravish your body, I'll control your mind.
    I'll own you completely, your soul will be mine.

The nightmares I'll give you while lying in bed,
    The voices you'll hear from inside of your head.

The sweats, the shakes, and the visions you'll see,
    I want you to know these are all gifts from me.

But when it's too late and you'll know in your heart,
    That you are mine and we are never to part.

You'll regret that you tried me, they always do,
    But you came to me, not I to you.

You knew this would happen, many times you were told,
    But you challenged my power, and chose to be bold.

You could have said no, and just walked away,
    If you could live that day over, now what would you say?

I'll be your master, you'll be my slave
    I'll even go with you when you go to the grave.

Now that you've met me, what will you do?
    Will you try me or not? It's all up to you.

I can bring you more misery than words can tell.
    Come take my hand, let me lead you to crystal meth hell.

Author Unknown

HOW TO HELP SOMEONE STOP SMOKING CIGARETTES

Many people start smoking when they are teenagers. The younger a person is when they begin smoking and the longer they have smoked, the harder it is for them to quit. A smoker becomes addicted to nicotine, a very powerful drug. A cigarette smoker is a drug addict. The only difference between a cigarette smoker and a cocaine addict is that smoking is legal and cocaine is not.

Cigarette smokers, like other addicts, are in a state of denial about their addiction. Seventy five percent of smokers say they want to quit, but only an average of about 8 percent of smokers each year are able to quit. If you are currently a smoker and want to quit, this means that you have your work cut out for you; the rate of success is very small.

Learn all you can about smoking. Take "Tips for Teens: The Truth About Tobacco" (http://store.samhsa.gov/pages/searchResult/Tips+for+teens) and make your own presentation on smoking. If you are trying to help someone quit smoking, it is very important that you tell them how much you care for them. Let them know that you are concerned about their health and the health of other people who must inhale secondhand smoke. Take home the handout on secondhand smoke and read it to them, or let them read it.

There are good products on the market to help people stop smoking. Nicotine patches and pills work well for some people. Others people may need a doctor's care to help them accomplish their goal. Keep in mind that for some people, it goes beyond difficult to stop smoking; they are drug addicts, and for a drug addict, it is not just a simple choice to quit their addiction, because their bodies require nicotine to function normally; for smokers, their bodies have established a new normal, requiring nicotine.

It does little good to harp on the subject day in and day out. They will just tune you out, and it becomes a lost cause. It took me two years to quit smoking, even though I wanted to quit. I started smoking when I was eleven years old and smoked for forty-two years. It was hard, but it was worth it to quit. Don't give up on them. If your efforts didn't work the first time, wait a while and try again.

If you are living in a secondhand smoke environment at home, the choice to smoke made by someone else has become your health problem as well; these smokers are forcing you to breathe their secondhand smoke.

The most frequent complaint I hear from teenagers is their problem of being exposed to secondhand smoke; their living environment requires that they inhale secondhand smoke, and they know their health is being damaged by it. At the very least, see if you can get the smoker to go outside and smoke.

The up side of quitting is the money saved over one year, which amounts to hundreds of dollars. **GOOD LUCK!**

NOTE: If you feel the above is not much help, you may be right. There is no easy answer to getting someone to quit smoking; all you can do is try to help them.

Marty Gruber
VOLUNTEER PRESENTER/DRUG AWARENESS

I WENT TO A PARTY, MOM

I went to a party, Mom … and remembered what you said …
You told me not to drink … so I had Sprite instead.

I felt proud of myself … the way you said I would …
That I didn't drink and drive … though some friends said I should.

I made a healthy choice … and your advice to me was right …
The party finally ended … and the kids drove into the night.

I got into my car … to get home in one piece …
I never knew it was coming, Mom … something I expected least.

Now I'm lying on the pavement … and I hear the policeman say …
"The kid that caused this wreck was drunk" … his voice seems far away.

My own blood all around me … as I try hard not to cry …
I hear the paramedic say … "This girl is going to die."

I'm sure the guy had no idea … while he was flying high …
Because he chose to drink and drive … now I would have to die.

So why do people do it, Mom? … Knowing that it ruins lives …
And now the pain is cutting me … like a thousand stabbing knives.

My breath is getting shorter, Mom … I'm really getting scared …
These are my final moments … and I'm so unprepared.

Tell sister not to be afraid … tell Daddy to be brave …
And when I leave this world … Put "Mommy's and Daddy's Girl" … on my grave.

I wish that you could hold me, Mom … as I lay here about to die …
I love you … I love you, Mom … but now it is good-bye.

Someone should have taught him that it's wrong to drink and drive …
Maybe if his parents had … I would be still alive.

Author Unknown

ATTACHMENTS 1–14

DRUG INFORMATION PUBLISHED BY
THE NATIONAL INSTITUTE ON DRUG ABUSE
ATTACHMENT #1

NATIONAL INSTITUTE ON DRUG ABUSE (NIDA)
ALCOHOL

**This complete document may be found at NIDA's website:
http://www.nida.nih.gov/drugpages/alcohol.html
where MUCH information is accessible with a click of the mouse**

Brief Description

Ethyl alcohol, or ethanol, is an intoxicating ingredient found in beer, wine, and liquor. Alcohol is produced by the fermentation of yeast, sugars, and starches. It is a central nervous system depressant that is rapidly absorbed from the stomach and small intestine into the bloodstream. A standard drink equals 0.6 ounces of pure ethanol, or 12 ounces of beer; 8 ounces of malt liquor; 5 ounces of wine; or 1.5 ounces (a "shot") of 80-proof distilled spirits or liquor (e.g., gin, rum, vodka, or whiskey). NIDA does not conduct research on alcohol; for more information, please visit the National Institute on Alcohol Abuse and Alcoholism (NIAAA) and the Centers for Disease Control (CDC).

Effects

Alcohol affects every organ in the drinker's body and can damage a developing fetus. Intoxication can impair brain function and motor skills; heavy use can increase risk of certain cancers, stroke, and liver disease. Alcoholism or alcohol dependence is a diagnosable disease characterized by a strong craving for alcohol, and/or continued use despite harm or personal injury. Alcohol abuse, which can lead to alcoholism, is a pattern of drinking that results in harm to one's health, interpersonal relationships, or ability to work.

Statistics and Trends

In 2009, 51.9% of Americans age 12 and older had used alcohol at least once in the 30 days prior to being surveyed; 23.7% had binged (5+ drinks within 2 hours); and 6.8% drank heavily (5+ drinks on 5+ occasions). In the 12-17 age range, 14.7% had consumed at least one drink in the 30 days prior to being surveyed; 8.8% had binged; and 2.1% drank heavily. *Source:*

National Survey on Drug Use and Health (Substance Abuse and Mental Health Administration Website). The NIDA-funded 2010 Monitoring the Future Study showed that 13.8% of 8th graders, 28.9% of 10th graders, and 41.2% of 12th graders had consumed at least one drink in the 30 days prior to being surveyed, and 5.0% of 8th graders, 14.7% of 10th graders, and 26.8% of 12th graders had been drunk. *Source: Monitoring the Future (University of Michigan Website)*

For more information, read the following:

National Institute on Alcohol Abuse and Alcoholism (NIAAA)

Rethinking Drinking: Alcohol and your health

The Cool Spot: for kids 11-13.

College Drinking: Changing the Culture

NATIONAL INSTITUTE ON DRUG ABUSE (NIDA) CLUB DRUGS

This complete document may be found at NIDA's website: http://www.nida.nih.gov/drugpages/clubdrugs.html where MUCH information is accessible with a click of the mouse

Brief Description

Club drugs tend to be used by teenagers and young adults at bars, nightclubs, concerts, and parties. Club drugs include GHB, Rohypnol®, ketamine, and others. [MDMA (Ecstasy), Methamphetamine, and LSD (Acid), are considered club drugs and are covered in their individual drug summaries.]

Street Names

special K, vitamin K, jet (ketamine); G, liquid ecstasy, soap (GHB); roofies (Rohypnol®); *More at Street Terms (Office of National Drug Control Policy Website)*

Effects

Club drugs have varying effects. Ketamine distorts perception and produces feelings of detachment from the environment and self, while GHB and Rohypnol are sedating. GHB abuse can cause coma and seizures. High doses of ketamine can cause delirium and amnesia. Rohypnol® can incapacitate users and cause amnesia, and especially when mixed with alcohol, can be lethal.

Statistics and Trends

The NIDA-funded 2010 Monitoring the Future Study showed that 0.5% of 8th graders, 0.6% of 10th graders, and 1.5% of 12th graders had abused Rohypnol®; 0.6% of 8th graders, 0.6% of 10th graders, and 1.4% of 12th graders had abused GHB; and 1.0% of 8th graders, 1.1% of 10th graders, and 1.6% of 12th graders had abused ketamine at least once in the year prior to their being surveyed. *Source: Monitoring the Future (University of Michigan Website)*

NATIONAL INSTITUTE ON DRUG ABUSE (NIDA) COCAINE

**This complete document may be found at NIDA's website:
http://www.nida.nih.gov/drugpages/cocaine.html
where MUCH information is accessible with a click of the mouse**

Brief Description

Cocaine is a powerfully addictive central nervous system stimulant that is snorted, injected, or smoked. Crack is cocaine hydrochloride powder that has been processed to form a rock crystal that is then usually smoked.

Street Names

Coke, snow, flake, blow; *More at Street Terms (Office of National Drug Control Policy Website)*

Effects

Cocaine usually makes the user feel euphoric and energetic, but also increases body temperature, blood pressure, and heart rate. Users risk heart attacks, respiratory failure, strokes, seizures, abdominal pain, and nausea. In rare cases, sudden death can occur on the first use of cocaine or unexpectedly afterwards.

Statistics and Trends

In 2009, 4.8 million Americans age 12 and older had abused cocaine in any form and 1.0 million had abused crack at least once in the year prior to being surveyed. *Source: National Survey on Drug Use and Health (Substance Abuse and Mental Health Administration Website).* The NIDA-funded 2010 Monitoring the Future Study showed that 1.6% of 8th graders, 2.2% of 10th graders, and 2.9% of 12th graders had abused cocaine in any form and 1.0% of 8th graders, 1.0% of 10th graders, and 1.4% of 12th graders had abused crack at least once in the year prior to being surveyed. *Source: Monitoring the Future (University of Michigan Website).*

NATIONAL INSTITUTE ON DRUG ABUSE (NIDA)
HEROIN

**This complete document may be found at NIDA's website:
http://www.nida.nih.gov/drugpages/heroin.html
where MUCH information is accessible with a click of the mouse**

Brief Description

Heroin is an addictive drug that is processed from morphine and usually appears as a white or brown powder or as a black, sticky substance. It is injected, snorted, or smoked.

Street Names

Smack, H, ska, junk; *More at Street Terms (Office of National Drug Control Policy Website)*

Effects

Short-term effects of heroin include a surge of euphoria and clouded thinking followed by alternately wakeful and drowsy states. Heroin depresses breathing, thus, overdose can be fatal. Users who inject the drug risk infectious diseases such as HIV/AIDS and hepatitis.

Statistics and Trends

In 2009, 605,000 Americans age 12 and older had abused heroin at least once in the year prior to being surveyed. *Source: National Survey on Drug Use and Health (Substance Abuse and Mental Health Administration Website).* The NIDA-funded 2010 Monitoring the Future Study showed that 0.8% of 8th graders, 0.8% of 10th graders, and 0.9% of 12th graders had abused heroin at least once in the year prior to being surveyed. *Source: Monitoring the Future (University of Michigan Website)*

NATIONAL INSTITUTE ON DRUG ABUSE (NIDA)
HIV/AIDS AND DRUG ABUSE

This complete document may be found at NIDA's website:
http://www.nida.nih.gov/drugpages/hiv.html
where MUCH information is accessible with a click of the mouse

MESSAGE FROM THE NIDA DIRECTOR ON

HIV/AIDS AND DRUG ABUSE In the United States, approximately 1 million people currently live with HIV, and 56,000 new cases occur each year, an incidence rate that has held steady for the past 10 years. Internationally, the pandemic has been devastating, with an estimated 33 million current infections and about 2 million deaths every year.

From the time it began, the HIV/AIDS epidemic has been closely linked with drug abuse and addiction; indeed, drug abuse treatment is HIV prevention, in that it reduces the behaviors that put people at risk. In this country, several groups are especially vulnerable, including African Americans, drug users, and people in prison or otherwise involved in the criminal justice system, where both HIV and drug use disorders are overrepresented. Internationally, in regions like Central Asia and Eastern Europe, the disease is raging, driven largely by injection drug use. Improved access both to highly active antiretroviral therapy (HAART) and to proven drug abuse treatments, such as buprenorphine and methadone, stand to have a major health impact, particularly when populations at highest risk are targeted.

To that end, participants at the 2010 AIDS Conference held in Vienna, Austria, in July 2010 and attended by more than 20,000 people from all over the world called for transforming the public health by increasing access to drug abuse treatment (to reduce HIV risk) and expanding coverage of HAART therapy. Innovative NIDA researchers are rising to these formidable challenges by demonstrating the effectiveness of drug abuse treatment—including medications for treating opioid addiction—and promoting their adoption globally. NIDA is also supporting research to develop and test strategies to expand HAART coverage, shown to reduce viral load and incidence at the population level. Known as "Seek, Test, Treat, and Retain," this initiative seeks out individuals who have not recently been tested, initiates HAART therapy for those who test positive, and monitors their progress over time.

To commemorate World AIDS Day 2010, interviews with several of NIDA's top scientists are posted here, along with recent NIDA-supported research findings on HIV, drug abuse, and their intersection. As in previous years, we will also display a portion of the AIDS quilt in the lobby of our Neuroscience Center in Bethesda, Maryland, to remember those who have died and to remind our staff and visitors of the importance of research aimed at tackling HIV disease and its devastating consequences.

Sincerely,

Nora D. Volkow, M.D.
Director

NATIONAL INSTITUTE ON DRUG ABUSE (NIDA)
INHALANTS

**This complete document may be found at NIDA's website:
http://www.nida.nih.gov/drugpages/inhalants.html
where MUCH information is accessible with a click of the mouse**

Brief Description

Inhalants are breathable chemical vapors that users intentionally inhale because of the chemicals' mind-altering effects. The substances inhaled are often common household products that contain volatile solvents, aerosols, or gases.

Street Names

Whippets, poppers, snappers; *More at Street Terms (Office of National Drug Control Policy Website)*

Effects

Most inhalants produce a rapid high that resembles alcohol intoxication. If sufficient amounts are inhaled, nearly all solvents and gases produce a loss of sensation, and even unconsciousness. Irreversible effects can be hearing loss, limb spasms, central nervous system or brain damage, or bone marrow damage. Sniffing high concentrations of inhalants may result in death from heart failure or suffocation (inhalants displace oxygen in the lungs).

Statistics and Trends

In 2009, 2.1 million Americans age 12 and older had abused inhalants. Source: *National Survey on Drug Use and Health* (Substance Abuse and Mental Health Administration Website). The NIDA-funded 2010 Monitoring the Future Study showed that 8.1% of 8th graders, 5.7% of 10th graders, and 3.6% of 12th graders had abused inhalants at least once in the year prior to being surveyed. Source: *Monitoring the Future* (University of Michigan Website)

NATIONAL INSTITUTE ON DRUG ABUSE (NIDA)
LSD (ACID)

This complete document may be found at NIDA's website:
http://www.nida.nih.gov/drugpages/acidlsd.html
where MUCH information is accessible with a click of the mouse

Brief Description

LSD can distort perceptions of reality and produce hallucinations; the effects can be frightening and cause panic. It is sold as tablets, capsules, liquid, or on absorbent paper.

Street Names

Acid, blotter, dots; *More at Street Terms (Office of National Drug Control Policy Website)*

Effects

LSD produces unpredictable psychological effects, with "trips" lasting about 12 hours. With large enough doses, users experience delusions and hallucinations. Physical effects include increased body temperature, heart rate, and blood pressure; sleeplessness; and loss of appetite.

Statistics and Trends

In 2009, 779,000 Americans age 12 and older had abused LSD at least once in the year prior to being surveyed. Source: *National Survey on Drug Use and Health* (Substance Abuse and Mental Health Administration Website). The NIDA-funded 2010 Monitoring the Future Study showed that 1.2% of 8th graders, 1.9% of 10th graders, and 2.6% of 12th graders had abused LSD at least once in the year prior to being surveyed. Source: *Monitoring the Future* (University of Michigan Website)

NATIONAL INSTITUTE ON DRUG ABUSE (NIDA)
MARIJUANA

**This complete document may be found at NIDA's website:
http://www.nida.nih.gov/drugpages/marijuana.html
where MUCH information is accessible with a click of the mouse**

Brief Description

Marijuana is the most commonly used illegal drug in the U.S. It is made up of dried parts of the Cannabis sativa hemp plant.

Street Names

Pot, ganga, weed, grass, 420; *More at Street Terms (Office of National Drug Control Policy Website)*

Effects

Short-term effects of marijuana use include euphoria, distorted perceptions, memory impairment, and difficulty thinking and solving problems.

Statistics and Trends

In 2009, 28.5 million Americans age 12 and older had abused marijuana at least once in the year prior to being surveyed. Source: *National Survey on Drug Use and Health* (Substance Abuse and Mental Health Administration Website). The NIDA-funded 2010 Monitoring the Future Study showed that 13.7% of 8th graders, 27.5% of 10th graders, and 34.8% of 12th graders had abused marijuana at least once in the year prior to being surveyed. Source: *Monitoring the Future* (University of Michigan Website)

NATIONAL INSTITUTE ON DRUG ABUSE (NIDA) METHAMPHETAMINE

This complete document may be found at NIDA's website: http://www.nida.nih.gov/drugpages/methamphetamine.html where MUCH information is accessible with a click of the mouse

Brief Description

Methamphetamine is a very addictive stimulant that is closely related to amphetamine. It is long lasting and toxic to dopamine nerve terminals in the central nervous system. It is a white, odorless, bitter-tasting powder taken orally or by snorting or injecting, or a rock "crystal" that is heated and smoked.

Street Names

Speed, meth, chalk, ice, crystal, glass; *More at Street Terms (Office of National Drug Control Policy Website)*

Effects

Methamphetamine increases wakefulness and physical activity, produces rapid heart rate, irregular heartbeat, and increased blood pressure and body temperature. Long-term use can lead to mood disturbances, violent behavior, anxiety, confusion, insomnia, and severe dental problems. All users, but particularly those who inject the drug, risk infectious diseases such as HIV/AIDS and hepatitis.

Statistics and Trends

In 2009, 1.2 million Americans age 12 and older had abused methamphetamine at least once in the year prior to being surveyed. Source: *National Survey on Drug Use and Health* (Substance Abuse and Mental Health Administration Website). The NIDA-funded 2010 Monitoring the Future Study showed that 1.2% of 8th graders, 1.6% of 10th graders, and 1.0% of 12th graders had abused methamphetamine at least once in the year prior to being surveyed. Source: *Monitoring the Future* (University of Michigan Website)

NATIONAL INSTITUTE ON DRUG ABUSE (NIDA)
MDMA (ECSTASY)

This complete document may be found at NIDA's website:
http://www.nida.nih.gov/drugpages/mdma.html
where MUCH information is accessible with a click of the mouse

Brief Description

MDMA is a synthetic drug that has stimulant and psychoactive properties. It is taken orally as a capsule or tablet.

Street Names

XTC, X, Adam, hug, beans, love drug; *More at Street Terms (Office of National Drug Control Policy Website)*

Effects

Short-term effects include feelings of mental stimulation, emotional warmth, enhanced sensory perception, and increased physical energy. Adverse health effects can include nausea, chills, sweating, teeth clenching, muscle cramping, and blurred vision. MDMA can interfere with the body's ability to regulate temperature; on rare occasions, this can be lethal.

Statistics and Trends

In 2009, 2.8 million Americans age 12 and older had abused MDMA at least once in the year prior to being surveyed. Source: *National Survey on Drug Use and Health* (Substance Abuse and Mental Health Administration Website). The NIDA-funded 2010 Monitoring the Future Study showed that 2.4% of 8th graders, 4.7% of 10th graders, and 4.5% of 12th graders had abused MDMA at least once in the year prior to being surveyed. Source: *Monitoring the Future* (University of Michigan Website)

NATIONAL INSTITUTE ON DRUG ABUSE (NIDA) PCP/PHENCYCLIDINE

**This complete document may be found at NIDA's website:
http://www.nida.nih.gov/DrugPages/PCP.html
where MUCH information is accessible with a click of the mouse**

Brief Description

PCP is a synthetic drug sold as tablets, capsules, or white or colored powder. It can be snorted, smoked, or eaten. Developed in the 1950s as an IV anesthetic, PCP was never approved for human use because of problems during clinical studies, including intensely negative psychological effects.

Street Names

Angel dust, ozone, wack, rocket fuel; *More at Street Terms (Office of National Drug Control Policy Website)*

Effects

PCP is a "dissociative" drug, distorting perceptions of sight and sound and producing feelings of detachment. Users can experience several unpleasant psychological effects, with symptoms mimicking schizophrenia (delusions, hallucinations, disordered thinking, extreme anxiety).

Statistics and Trends

In 2009, 122,000 Americans age 12 and older had abused PCP at least once in the year prior to being surveyed. *Source: National Survey on Drug Use and Health (Substance Abuse and Mental Health Administration Website).* The NIDA-funded 2010 "Monitoring the Future" study showed that 1.0% of 12th graders had abused PCP at least once in the year prior to being surveyed. *Source: Monitoring the Future (University of Michigan Website)*

NATIONAL INSTITUTE ON DRUG ABUSE (NIDA) <u>PRESCRIPTION MEDICATIONS</u>

**This complete document may be found at NIDA's website:
http://www.nida.nih.gov/drugpages/prescription.html
where MUCH information is accessible with a click of the mouse**

Brief Description

Prescription drug abuse means taking a prescription medication that is not prescribed for you, or taking it for reasons or in dosages other than as prescribed. Abuse of prescription drugs can produce serious health effects, including addiction. Commonly abused classes of prescription medications include opioids (for pain), central nervous system depressants (for anxiety and sleep disorders), and stimulants (for ADHD and narcolepsy). Opioids include hydrocodone (Vicodin®), oxycodone (OxyContin®), propoxyphene (Darvon®), hydromorphone (Dilaudid®), meperidine (Demerol®), and diphenoxylate (Lomotil®). Central nervous system depressants include barbiturates such as pentobarbital sodium (Nembutal®), and benzodiazepines such as diazepam (Valium®) and alprazolam (Xanax®). Stimulants include dextroamphetamine (Dexedrine®), methylphenidate (Ritalin® and Concerta®), and amphetamines (Adderall®).

Street Names

oxy, cotton, blue, 40, 80 (OxyContin®); *More at Street Terms (Office of National Drug Control Policy Website)*

Effects

Long-term use of opioids or central nervous system depressants can lead to physical dependence and addiction. Opioids can produce drowsiness, constipation and, depending on amount taken, can depress breathing. Central nervous system depressants slow down brain function; if combined with other medications that cause drowsiness or with alcohol, heart rate and respiration can slow down dangerously. Taken repeatedly or in high doses, stimulants can cause anxiety, paranoia, dangerously high body temperatures, irregular heartbeat, or seizures.

Statistics and Trends

In 2009, 16 million Americans age 12 and older had taken a prescription pain reliever, tranquilizer, stimulant, or sedative for nonmedical purposes at least once in the year prior to being surveyed. *Source: National Survey on Drug Use and Health (Substance Abuse and Mental Health Administration Website).* The NIDA-funded 2010 "Monitoring the Future" study showed that 2.7% of 8th graders, 7.7% of 10th graders, and 8.0% of 12th graders had abused Vicodin and 2.1% of 8th graders, 4.6% of 10th graders, and 5.1% of 12th graders had abused Oxycontin for nonmedical purposes at least once in the year prior to being surveyed. *Source: Monitoring the Future (University of Michigan Website).*

NATIONAL INSTITUTE ON DRUG ABUSE (NIDA) STEROIDS (ANABOLIC)

This complete document may be found at NIDA's website:
http://www.nida.nih.gov/drugpages/steroids.html
where MUCH information is accessible with a click of the mouse

Brief Description

Most anabolic steroids are synthetic substances similar to the male sex hormone testosterone. They are taken orally or are injected. Some people, especially athletes, abuse anabolic steroids to build muscle and enhance performance. Abuse of anabolic steroids can lead to serious health problems, some of which are irreversible.

Street Names

Juice, gym candy, pumpers, stackers; *More at Street Terms (Office of National Drug Control Policy Website)*

Effects

Major effects of steroid abuse can include liver damage; jaundice; fluid retention; high blood pressure; increases in "bad" cholesterol. Also, males risk shrinking of the testicles, baldness, breast development, and infertility. Females risk growth of facial hair, menstrual changes, male-pattern baldness, and deepened voice. Teens risk permanently stunted height, accelerated puberty changes, and severe acne. All users, but particularly those who inject the drug, risk infectious diseases such as HIV/AIDS and hepatitis.

Statistics and Trends

The NIDA-funded 2010 "Monitoring the Future" study showed that 0.5% of 8th graders, 1.0% of 10th graders, and 1.5% of 12th graders had abused anabolic steroids at least once in the year prior to being surveyed. *Source: Monitoring the Future (University of Michigan Website).*

NATIONAL INSTITUTE ON DRUG ABUSE (NIDA) TOBACCO/NICOTINE

**This complete document may be found at NIDA's website:
http://www.nida.nih.gov/drugpages/nicotine.html
where MUCH information is accessible with a click of the mouse**

Brief Description

Through the use of tobacco, nicotine is one of the most heavily used addictive drugs and the leading preventable cause of disease, disability, and death in the U.S. Cigarette smoking accounts for 90% of lung cancer cases in the U.S., and almost 50,000 deaths per year can be attributed to secondhand smoke. Cigarettes and chew tobacco are illegal substances in most U.S. states for those under 18; a handful of states have raised the age to 19.

Effects

Nicotine is highly addictive. The tar in cigarettes increases a smoker's risk of lung cancer, emphysema, and bronchial disorders. The carbon monoxide in smoke increases the chance of cardiovascular diseases. Pregnant smokers have a higher risk of miscarriage or low birthweight babies. Secondhand smoke causes lung cancer in adults and greatly increases the risk of respiratory illnesses in children.

Statistics and Trends

In 2009, nearly 70 million Americans age 12 and older had used a tobacco product at least once in the month prior to being surveyed. *Source: National Survey on Drug Use and Health (Substance Abuse and Mental Health Administration Website).* The NIDA-funded 2010 "Monitoring the Future" study showed that 7.1% of 8th graders, 13.6% of 10th graders, and 19.2% of 12th graders had used cigarettes and 4.1% of 8th graders, 7.5% of 10th graders, and 8.5% of 12th graders had used smokeless tobacco at least once in the month prior to being surveyed. And while rates of smoking have been declining since the mid-nineties, those declines have been slowing in the last two years. *Source: Monitoring the Future (University of Michigan Website)*